THE CAMBRIDGE COMPANION TO MODERNIST WOMEN WRITERS

Women played a central role in literary modernism, theorizing, debating, writing, and publishing the critical and imaginative work that resulted in a new literary culture during the early twentieth century. This volume provides a thorough overview of the main genres, the important issues, and the key figures in women's writing during the years 1890–1945. The essays treat the work of Woolf, Stein, Cather, Barnes, H. D., Hurston, and many others in detail; they also explore women's salons, little magazines, activism, photography, film criticism, and spirituality. Written especially for this *Companion*, these lively essays introduce students and scholars to the vibrant field of women's modernism.

A complete list of books in the series is at the back of this book.

THE CAMBRIDGE
COMPANION TO
MODERNIST WOMEN
WRITERS

EDITED BY
MAREN TOVA LINETT
Purdue University, Indiana

CAMBRIDGE
UNIVERSITY PRESS

CAMBRIDGE UNIVERSITY PRESS
Cambridge, New York, Melbourne, Madrid, Cape Town, Singapore,
São Paulo, Delhi, Dubai, Tokyo, Mexico City

Cambridge University Press
The Edinburgh Building, Cambridge CB2 8RU, UK

Published in the United States of America by Cambridge University Press, New York

www.cambridge.org
Information on this title: www.cambridge.org/9780521515054

First published 2010

Printed in the United Kingdom at the University Press, Cambridge

A catalogue record for this publication is available from the British Library

Library of Congress Cataloguing in Publication data
The Cambridge companion to modernist women writers / edited by Maren
Tova Linett.
p. cm. – (Cambridge companions to literature)
Includes bibliographical references.
ISBN 978-0-521-51505-4 – ISBN 978-0-521-73570-4 (pbk.)   1. Modernism
(Literature)   2. Literature – Women authors – History and criticism.   3. Literature,
Modern – 20th century – History and criticism.   4. Women and literature – 20th century –
History and criticism.   I. Linett, Maren Tova.
PN56.M54C365   2010
809′.912082–dc22
2010026357

ISBN 978-0-521-51505-4 Hardback
ISBN 978-0-521-73570-4 Paperback

CONTENTS

NOTES ON CONTRIBUTORS

THADIOUS M. DAVIS is Geraldine R. Segal Professor of American Social Thought and Professor of English at the University of Pennsylvania and the author of *Games of Property: Law, Race, Gender, and Faulkner's* Go Down, Moses.

LAURA DOYLE is Professor of English at the University of Massachusetts-Amherst. She is author of *Bordering on the Body: The Racial Matrix of Modern Fiction and Culture* (1994, Perkins Prize Award) and *Freedom's Empire: Race and the Rise of the Novel in Atlantic Modernity, 1640–1940* (2008), and she is editor of two collections, *Bodies of Resistance: New Phenomenologies of Politics, Agency, and Culture* (2001) and, with Laura Winkiel, *Geomodernisms: Race, Modernism, Modernity* (2004). Her current project, supported by an ACLS Fellowship, is a study of the transcultural dynamics and histories that have given rise to diverse modernisms in world literature.

PENNY FARFAN is Professor of Drama at the University of Calgary. Her book *Women, Modernism, and Performance* was published by Cambridge University Press in 2004, and she is the co-editor of a special issue of *South Central Review* on "Staging Modernism" (2008), which includes her article "Man as Beast: Nijinsky's Faun." She is currently completing a project on queer modernist performance and co-editing *Theatre Journal*.

SUZETTE A. HENKE is Thruston B. Morton Sr. Professor of English at the University of Louisville in Louisville, KY, USA. She is author of *James Joyce and the Politics of Desire* and has published widely in the field of modern literature. A revised edition of her book *Shattered Subjects: Trauma and Testimony in Women's Life-Writing* was published in 2000, and she has co-edited, with David Eberly, a collection of essays on *Virginia Woolf and Trauma* (2007). Professor Henke is currently working on a study entitled *Modernist Trauma: Gender and Abjection in Woolf, Joyce, and Lawrence*.

MIRANDA HICKMAN is an Associate Professor of English at McGill University. She is the author of *The Geometry of Modernism* (2006); she has also published on Ezra

Pound's deluxe editions, H. D. and the body, and the legacy of Raymond Chandler in contemporary culture. Forthcoming work includes articles on the minor works of James Joyce, H. D. and the canon, and Ezra Pound and Vorticism. She is currently completing an annotated edition of Ezra Pound's letters to publisher Stanley Nott (forthcoming, 2011) and co-editing a volume of essays entitled *Rereading the New Criticism*.

MAGGIE HUMM is a Professor of Cultural Studies, University of East London, UK. She has been a Distinguished Visiting Scholar and Professor at many universities including Massachusetts, San Diego State, Stanford, Rutgers, Queen's Belfast, and Karachi. Her publications include *Snapshots of Bloomsbury: The Private Lives of Virginia Woolf and Vanessa Bell* (2006) and the *Edinburgh Companion to Virginia Woolf and the Arts* (2010).

HEATHER INGMAN lectures in the School of English, Trinity College, Dublin. She has published extensively on women's writing, particularly inter-war women's writing and Irish women's fiction. Her study *Twentieth-Century Fiction by Irish Women: Nation and Gender* was published in 2007, and she is the author of *A History of the Irish Story* (Cambridge University Press, 2009).

MAREN TOVA LINETT is Associate Professor of English at Purdue University. She is the author of *Modernism, Feminism, and Jewishness* (Cambridge University Press, 2007) and the editor of *Virginia Woolf: An MFS Reader* (2009). She has edited a special issue of *Modern Fiction Studies* entitled "Modernism's Jews / Jewish Modernisms," and has published articles on Dorothy Richardson, Virginia Woolf, Jean Rhys, and James Joyce.

JAYNE MAREK is Professor of English at Franklin College, where she teaches English and world literatures, film studies, and creative and expository writing. Her articles include studies of Amy Lowell, Katherine Mansfield, Marianne Moore, British Imagism, and Ernest Boyer's *Scholarship Reconsidered*. She compiled a comprehensive index to *Poetry* magazine (1997) and is completing a book about women editors and the Harlem Renaissance. Her earlier book, *Women Editing Modernism: "Little" Magazines and Literary History*, appeared in 1995.

SOWON S. PARK is college lecturer in English at Oxford University. She has co-edited a six-volume anthology, *Women's Suffrage Literature* (2007), and is the author of a number of studies on twentieth-century literature, published in journals that include *The Review of English Studies*, *MLQ*, and *English Literature in Transition*.

JEAN RADFORD, formerly of Goldsmith's College, University of London, is a freelance writer/researcher, author of books on Norman Mailer and Dorothy Richardson and of various articles on women and modernism, including "Impersonality and the Damned Egotistical Self: Dorothy Richardson's *Pilgrimage*," in *Impersonality and Emotion in Twentieth-Century British Literature*, ed. Christine Reynier and

Jean-Michel Ganteau (2005), "Modernist Melancholy: Edith Sitwell's Black Sun," in *At Home and Abroad in the Empire*, ed. Robin Hackett (2009), and "A Question of Justice: Hilary Mantel's Experiment in Love," in *Autonomy and Commitment in Contemporary British Literature* (2009). She is currently researching a book on modernism and ethics.

BONNIE KIME SCOTT is Professor and Chair of Women's Studies at San Diego State University. Much of her work concerns modernism and gender, starting with *Joyce and Feminism*, and including the critical anthologies *The Gender of Modernism* and *Gender in Modernism: New Geographies, Complex Intersections* and the two-volume study, *Refiguring Modernism*, which focused on Virginia Woolf, Rebecca West, and Djuna Barnes. She is finishing a new book, *Virginia Woolf and Modernist Uses of Nature*.

PATRICIA JULIANA SMITH is associate professor of English at Hofstra University. She is the author of *Lesbian Panic: Homoeroticism in Modern British Women's Fiction* (1997), editor of *The Queer Sixties* (1999), and co-editor of *En Travesti: Women, Gender Subversion, Opera* (1995) and *Catholic Figures, Queer Narratives* (2007). She has published numerous essays on twentieth-century British literature, queer theory, and popular culture.

ACKNOWLEDGEMENTS

I would like first to thank the contributors to this volume both for their hard work on their excellent essays and their cooperation during the editing process. For their sage advice when I was first conceptualizing this *Companion* I thank Sara Blair, Laura Doyle, Amy Feinstein, Venetria Patton, and especially Suzanne Raitt. Three anonymous readers of the first proposal for Cambridge University Press gave enthusiastic, detailed, and wonderfully constructive suggestions. Deena Linett, Peter Linett, John Whittier-Ferguson, Jennifer Martson William, and Dominic Naughton gave valuable feedback when I was drafting the introduction. I much appreciate Ray Ryan's wise guidance as the proposal gradually developed into a finished product. The editorial and production staff at Cambridge University Press are uniformly professional and helpful and I would particularly like to thank Maartje Scheltens, Joanna Garbutt, Thomas O'Reilly, and Caroline Howlett. I am grateful to Rebecca Nicholson-Weir for help in preparing the manuscript and for creating the index.

CHRONOLOGY

1895   Alice Dunbar-Nelson, *Violets and Other Tales*

       Wilhelm Roentgen discovers x-rays

       Invention of the wireless

       Invention of the motion picture

1896   United States Supreme Court upholds "separate but equal" in *Plessy v. Ferguson*

       National Association of Colored Women formed in the United States

       First commercial motion picture exhibition given in New York using Thomas Edison's Kinetoscope

1897   National Union of Women's Suffrage Societies founded by Millicent Garrett Fawcett

1898   Marie and Pierre Curie discover radium and polonium

1899   Charlotte Perkins Gilman's *The Yellow Wallpaper* published in book form

       Anglo-Boer War begins

1900   International Ladies' Garment Workers Union founded

       Sigmund Freud, *The Interpretation of Dreams*

       Pauline Hopkins, *Contending Forces: A Romance Illustrative of Negro Life North and South*

1901   Queen Victoria dies; Edward VII succeeds

       President William McKinley killed; Theodore Roosevelt succeeds

1902   Augusta Gregory, *Kathleen Ni Houlihan*

William James, *Varieties of Religious Experience*

First structure built in the United States specifically to show movies, Tally's Electric Theater, opens in Los Angeles

Anglo-Boer War ends

1903 Jane Harrison, *Prolegomena to the Study of Greek Religion*

Edwin S. Porter, *The Great Train Robbery*

Marie Curie, Pierre Curie, and Henri Becquerel awarded the Nobel Prize in Physics for research on radiation

Wright brothers' first successful flight

Women's Social and Political Union (WSPU) founded by Emmeline, Christabel, and Sylvia Pankhurst

1904 Abbey Theatre opens in Dublin

1905 Albert Einstein publishes "On the Electrodynamics of Moving Bodies"

Edith Wharton, *The House of Mirth*

First militant suffrage incident at Free Trade Hall, Manchester

Aliens Act introduces immigration controls and registration in Britain

Russian Revolution

1906 Liberals win landslide victory in Britain

1907 Edith Wharton, *The Fruit of the Tree*

Augusta Gregory, *The Rising of the Moon*

Elizabeth Robins, *Votes for Women* (play)

Votes for Women (newspaper) founded, edited by Emmeline and Frederick Pethick-Lawrence

Henri Bergson, *Creative Evolution*

WSPU splits, Women's Freedom League founded in Britain

Cubist Exhibition in Paris

1908 Henry Ford produces first Model T Ford

Women Writers Suffrage League (WWSL) founded

National Association for the Advancement of Colored People (NAACP) founded

1909 Christopher St. John, *A Defence of the Fighting Spirit*

Gertrude Stein, *Three Lives*

F. T. Marinetti, "The Founding and Manifesto of Futurism"

Suffragette Marion Wallace Dunlop begins first hunger strike in July; in September, forcible feeding begins in British prisons

Roosevelt is succeeded by William Howard Taft

1910 Cicely Hamilton, *Pageant of Great Women*

Augusta Gregory, *Grania*

Crisis founded by W. E. B. Du Bois

First postimpressionist exhibition, organized by Roger Fry

F. T. Marinetti, "Futurist Speech to the English"

Mann Act prohibits the transportation of women across state lines for "immoral purposes" in United States

Edward VII dies; George V succeeds

1911 Charlotte Perkins Gilman, *The Man-Made World: Or, Our Androcentric Culture*

Edith Wharton, *Ethan Frome*

Cicely Hamilton, *Jack and Jill and a Friend*

Christopher St. John, *The First Actress*

Teresa Billington-Grieg, *The Militant Suffrage Movement*

Marie Curie awarded a second Nobel Prize in Chemistry for her discovery of radium and polonium

Dora Marsden founds and edits *The Freewoman*, under the patronage of Harriet Shaw Weaver

1912 Willa Cather, *Alexander's Bridge*

Mary Antin, *The Promised Land*

Edith Wharton, *The Reef*

Jane Harrison, *Themis: A Study of Greek Religion*

May Sinclair's *Feminism* published as a pamphlet by the Women's Suffrage League

Poetry magazine founded in Chicago by Harriet Monroe

Second postimpressionist exhibition, organized by Roger Fry

Titanic sinks, more than 1,500 people die

1913 Willa Cather, *O Pioneers!*

Edith Wharton, *The Custom of the Country*

Jane Harrison, *Ancient Art and Ritual*

Armory Show in New York, includes paintings by Van Gogh, Gauguin, Monet, Manet, Matisse, Kandinsky, and others

The Freewoman becomes *The New Freewoman*

Suffragist demonstrations in London

Taft is succeeded by Woodrow Wilson

1914 Gertrude Stein, *Tender Buttons*

Mina Loy, "Aphorisms on Futurism" and "Feminist Manifesto"

Evelyn Underhill, *Practical Mysticism*

Suffragist Mary Richardson slashes the Rokeby Venus

The New Freewoman becomes *The Egoist*; Harriet Shaw Weaver becomes editor

Margaret Anderson founds *The Little Review*; Jane Heap joins as co-editor

First World War begins, August 4

1915 Dorothy Richardson, *Pointed Roofs*, the 1st novel-chapter of *Pilgrimage*

Virginia Woolf, *The Voyage Out*

Djuna Barnes, *The Book of Repulsive Women*

Willa Cather, *The Song of the Lark*

Charlotte Perkins Gilman's *Herland* published as a serial in the *Forerunner*

Amy Lowell, ed., *Some Imagist Poets* (3 vols., 1915–17)

1916   Dorothy Richardson, *Backwater*, the 2nd novel-chapter of *Pilgrimage*

H. D., *Sea Garden*

Amy Lowell, *Men, Women, and Ghosts*

Susan Glaspell, *Trifles*

Albert Einstein, *General Theory of Relativity*

Easter Rising in Dublin

Alice Paul founds the National Woman's Party in the United States

Great Migration begins: 1.3 million African Americans move from the south to the north, midwest, and west

1917   Dorothy Richardson, *Honeycomb*, the 3rd novel-chapter of *Pilgrimage*

Edna St. Vincent Millay, *Renascence and Other Poems*

Edith Wharton, *Summer*

May Sinclair, *Tree of Heaven*

Mina Loy's "Songs to Joannes" published in *Others* magazine

May Sinclair, *A Defence of Idealism*

Leonard and Virginia Woolf found the Hogarth Press

Russian Revolution

United States enters the war

1918   Willa Cather, *My Ántonia*

Georgia Douglas Johnson, *The Heart of a Woman and Other Poems*

Rebecca West, *The Return of the Soldier*

Marie Stopes, *Married Love*

Tristan Tzara, "Dada Manifesto"

May Sinclair introduces the term "stream of consciousness" to literary studies in her review of Richardson's *Pilgrimage*

Women over 30 receive the right to vote in Great Britain (Representation of the People Act)

Constance Markiewicz is first woman to be elected to British parliament but does not take her seat

First World War ends with Armistice, November 11

1919   Dorothy Richardson, *The Tunnel*, the 4th novel-chapter of *Pilgrimage*

May Sinclair, *Mary Olivier*

Virginia Woolf, *Kew Gardens* and *Night and Day*

Amy Lowell, *Pictures of the Floating World*

Nancy Astor becomes first woman Member of Parliament

League of Nations founded

1920   Dorothy Richardson, *Interim*, the 5th novel-chapter of *Pilgrimage*

Edith Wharton, *The Age of Innocence*

Katherine Mansfield, *Bliss and Other Stories*

Anzia Yezierska, *Hungry Hearts*

Sigmund Freud, *Beyond the Pleasure Principle*

Jessie Weston, *From Ritual to Romance*

Augusta Gregory, *Visions and Beliefs in the West of Ireland*

Edna St. Vincent Millay, *Aria da Capo*

Prohibition begins in the United States

Women receive the right to vote in the United States (Nineteenth Amendment)

1921   Dorothy Richardson, *Deadlock*, the 6th novel-chapter of *Pilgrimage*

Virginia Woolf, *Monday or Tuesday*

Marianne Moore, *Poems*

Emergency Quota Act restricts immigration to the United States

Margaret Sanger founds the American Birth Control League

Wilson is succeeded by Warren G. Harding

1922 Virginia Woolf, *Jacob's Room*

Willa Cather, *One of Ours*

Rebecca West, *The Judge*

Georgia Douglas Johnson, *Bronze*

Creation of the Irish Free State

Report of the British War Office Committee of Enquiry into "shell shock"

British Broadcasting Company (BBC) founded

Mussolini becomes Italian Prime Minister

1923 Dorothy Richardson, *Revolving Lights*, the 7th novel-chapter of *Pilgrimage*

Djuna Barnes, *A Book*

Willa Cather, *A Lost Lady*

Elizabeth Bowen, *Encounters*

May Sinclair, *Uncanny Stories*

Anzia Yezierska, *Salome of the Tenements*

Mina Loy, *Lunar Baedeker* and first part of *Anglo-Mongrels and the Rose*

Harding dies; Calvin Coolidge succeeds

1924 Marianne Moore, *Observations*

Edith Wharton, *Old New York*

Jessie Redmon Fauset, *There Is Confusion*

May Sinclair, *Arnold Waterlow*

Jane Harrison, *Mythology*

André Breton, *Manifesto of Surrealism*

British Empire exhibition in London

First Labour government in Britain

1925 Dorothy Richardson, *The Trap*, the 8th novel-chapter of *Pilgrimage*

Virginia Woolf, *Mrs. Dalloway* and *The Common Reader*

Gertrude Stein, *The Making of Americans*

Willa Cather, *The Professor's House*

Anzia Yezierska, *Bread Givers*

Evelyn Underhill, *Mystics of the Church*

Mary Butts, *Ashe of Rings*

Mina Loy, "Mongrel Rose," final part of *Anglo-Mongrels and the Rose*

Josephine Baker debuts in *La Revue nègre* in Paris

Scopes "Monkey" Trial in the United States

1926 Willa Cather, *My Mortal Enemy*

Zora Neale Hurston, *Sweat*

Georgia Douglas Johnson, *Blue-Blood*

H. D., *Palimpsest*

Sylvia Townsend Warner, *Lolly Willowes*

Vita Sackville-West, *Passenger to Teheran*

General Strike in Britain

1927 Dorothy Richardson, *Oberland*, the 9th novel-chapter of *Pilgrimage*

Virginia Woolf, *To the Lighthouse*

Elizabeth Bowen, *The Hotel*

Willa Cather, *Death Comes for the Archbishop*

Gertrude Stein, *Four Saints in Three Acts*

Jean Rhys, *The Left Bank and Other Stories*

Georgia Douglas Johnson, *Plumes*

Sylvia Townsend Warner, *Mr. Fortune's Maggot*

Vita Sackville-West, *The Land*

First successful sound film, *The Jazz Singer*

First issue of avant-garde film journal *Close Up*

1928   Virginia Woolf, *Orlando*

Djuna Barnes, *Ladies Almanack* and *Ryder*

Zora Neale Hurston, *How It Feels to Be Colored Me*

Nella Larsen, *Quicksand*

Radclyffe Hall, *The Well of Loneliness*

Rebecca West, *The Strange Necessity*

Sophie Treadwell, *Machinal*

Georgia Douglas Johnson, *An Autumn Love Cycle*

Mary Butts, *Armed with Madness*

Arthur Eddington, *The Nature of the Physical World*

Voting age for British women lowered to 21

1929   Virginia Woolf, *A Room of One's Own*

Nella Larsen, *Passing*

Jean Rhys, *Quartet*

Rebecca West, *Harriet Hume*

Elizabeth Bowen, *The Last September*

Georgia Douglas Johnson, *Safe*

Natalie Barney, *Adventures of the Mind*

Jessie Redmon Fauset, *Plum Bun*

Bryher, *Film Problems of Soviet Russia*

Great Depression begins with stock market crash on October 29, "Black Tuesday"

Coolidge is succeeded by Herbert Hoover

1930   Vita Sackville-West, *The Edwardians*

1931   Dorothy Richardson, *Dawn's Left Hand*, the 10th novel-chapter of *Pilgrimage*

Virginia Woolf, *The Waves*

Willa Cather, *Shadows on the Rock*

Elizabeth Bowen, *Friends and Relations*

H. D., *Red Roses for Bronze*

Jean Rhys, *After Leaving Mr. Mackenzie*

Jessie Redmon Fauset, *The Chinaberry Tree*

Vita Sackville-West, *All Passion Spent*

1932   Elizabeth Bowen, *To the North*

Mary Butts, *The Death of Felicity Taverner*

Amelia Earhart becomes first woman to make a solo transatlantic flight

Oswald Mosley founds the British Union of Fascists

1933   Virginia Woolf, *Flush*

Gertrude Stein, *The Autobiography of Alice B. Toklas*

Vera Brittain, *Testament of Youth*

Jessie Redmon Fauset, *Comedy: American Style*

Antonia White, *Frost in May*

Hoover is succeeded by Franklin D. Roosevelt

Adolf Hitler becomes Chancellor in Germany

1934   Zora Neale Hurston, *Jonah's Gourd Vine* and "Characteristics of Negro Expression"

Jean Rhys, *Voyage in the Dark*

Elizabeth Bowen, *The Cat Jumps and Other Stories*

Edna St. Vincent Millay, *Wine from These Grapes*

Kate O'Brien, *The Ante-Room*

Nancy Cunard, *Negro: An Anthology*

Mary Butts, *Last Stories*

Zora Neale Hurston, *Tell My Horse: Voodoo and Life in Haiti and Jamaica*

Gwen Pharis Ringwood, *Still Stands the House*

Sylvia Townsend Warner, *After the Death of Don Juan*

Elizabeth Bowen, *The Death of the Heart*

1939   Zora Neale Hurston, *Moses, Man of the Mountain*

Jean Rhys, *Good Morning, Midnight*

Spanish Civil War ends

Second World War begins, September

1940   Virginia Woolf, *Roger Fry: A Biography*

Gertrude Stein, *Paris France*

Willa Cather, *Sapphira and the Slave Girl*

Vera Brittain, *Testament of Friendship*

Germany launches sustained bombing campaign on England, known as the Blitz

1941   Virginia Woolf dies, March 28

Virginia Woolf, *Between the Acts*

Gertrude Stein, *Ida: A Novel*

Marianne Moore, *What Are Years*

Elizabeth Bowen, *Look at All Those Roses*

Kate O'Brien, *The Land of Spices*

Rebecca West, *Black Lamb and Grey Falcon*

Japan bombs Pearl Harbor; United States enters war

1942   Zora Neale Hurston, *Dust Tracks on a Road*

1943   Vita Sackville-West, *The Eagle and the Dove*

1944   H. D., *The Walls Do Not Fall* and *What Do I Love?*

Marianne Moore, *Nevertheless*

1945   Gertrude Stein, *Wars I Have Seen*

H. D., *Tribute to the Angels*

Elizabeth Bowen, *The Demon Lover and Other Stories*

Roosevelt is succeeded by Harry S. Truman

Germany surrenders in May

United States drops atomic bombs on Nagasaki and Hiroshima; Japan surrenders in August: Second World War ends

MAREN TOVA LINETT

Modernist women's literature: an introduction

"New fields are opening and new laborers are working in them," proclaimed Charlotte Perkins Gilman in 1911.[1] In the early years of the twentieth century, practitioners of the arts saw a world of expanding possibilities. Gilman's metaphor, simultaneously nostalgic for rural authenticity and energized by modern productivity, captures a moment of self-conscious transition during which writers and artists sought to break with tradition and open "new fields" of artistic endeavor. Indeed Gilman (1860–1935) and her younger British contemporary Virginia Woolf (1882–1941) each wrote about the new ways fiction could represent life. Gilman wrote that "[t]he art of fiction is being re-born in these days. Life is discovered to be longer, wider, deeper, richer, than these monotonous players of one tune would have us believe."[2] Woolf said much the same thing, if in more poetic language, when she wrote that "[l]ife is not a series of gig-lamps symmetrically arranged; life is a luminous halo, a semi-transparent envelope surrounding us from the beginning of consciousness to the end . . . We are not pleading merely for courage and sincerity; we are suggesting that the proper stuff of fiction is a little other than custom would have us believe it."[3]

The stress both writers placed on what others would "have us believe" shows a shared resistance to convention, an impatience with the *modus operandi* of workmanlike writers – attitudes that mark the modernist period. The American poet Wallace Stevens similarly described a process of shifting the "proper stuff" of literary art in "Of Modern Poetry": "The poem of the mind in the act of finding / What will suffice. It has not always had / To find: the scene was set; it repeated what / Was in the script."[4] T. S. Eliot and Ezra Pound too demanded newness in literature. Eliot wrote that for a new work of art "to conform merely would be for the new work not really to conform at all; it would not be new, and would therefore not be a work of art."[5] And Pound famously advocated that artists "make it new."[6] Women modernists joined their male counterparts in working toward this goal.

But beyond the predictable inertia of convention, Woolf and Gilman saw an additional hindrance to their quest to "make it new." What Woolf later called "sex-consciousness" was interfering with modernism's experiment; gender was inhibiting art. And so both writers advocated transcending sex, achieving an androgyny that would allow one's art to flow "unimpeded." Gilman wrote, "The true artist transcends his sex, or her sex. If this is not the case, the art suffers."[7] Woolf agreed: "it is fatal for anyone who writes to think of their sex. It is fatal to be a man or woman pure and simple; one must be woman-manly or man-womanly ... And fatal is no figure of speech; for anything written with that conscious bias is doomed to death. It ceases to be fertilized."[8]

Modernist literature, then, had to be daring, to break with convention and show life as its falling atoms were experienced rather than as it was conventionally recorded. It had to be androgynous, so that consciousness of sex did not weigh down the work of art. Gilman and Woolf further agreed that modernism needed to execute its daring not only in terms of form but also in terms of content: it had to write about women in new ways, particularly by placing the deserved significance upon relationships among women. Gilman noted that "[t]he humanizing of woman of itself opens ... distinctly fresh fields of fiction. [For example,] the inter-relation of women with women – a thing we could never write about before because we never had it before: except in harems and convents."[9] And Woolf described a contemporary novel that focused on the relations between two women working in a laboratory: "For if Chloe likes Olivia and Mary Carmichael knows how to express it she will light a torch in that vast chamber where nobody has yet been."[10] Relationships among women were only one chamber newly lit; women's lives generally – their relationships to their work, to their rural or urban landscapes, to philosophy, to religion, to politics – needed imaginative expression.

British novelist Dorothy Richardson (1873–1957) joined her contemporaries in pointing out how challenging it was to portray women's lives. In an essay called "Women and the Future," she wrote, "how difficult it is, even for the least prejudiced, to *think* the feminine past, to escape the images that throng the mind from the centuries of masculine expressiveness on the eternal theme: expressiveness that has so rarely reached beyond the portrayal of woman, whether Madonna, Diana, or Helen, in her moments of relationship to the world as it is known to men."[11] If anything unites the women authors of the modernist period, it is this desire to reach beyond such masculine portrayals of women.

One particularly masculine image of a woman, Diego Velázquez's painting *The Toilet of Venus* (c. 1650) became a symbol of women's resistance to patriarchal norms when (as Sowon Park describes in her chapter of this

Companion on activism) it was slashed by the suffragist Mary Richardson in 1914. Richardson damaged the painting to protest the rearrest of fellow suffragist Emmeline Pankhurst. In the painting, known as the *Rokeby Venus*, Venus reclines on a luxuriously draped settee, nude, with her back to us; she gazes at her face in a mirror held by Cupid. Lynda Nead notes that the choice of this particular painting, which was brought to England by the Duke of Wellington in 1806, and a hundred years later purchased by the National Art Collections Fund for the National Gallery, seems inevitable: "'The Rokeby Venus,' hailed as a paragon of female beauty, an exemplar of the female nude, a national treasure and worth a fortune – surely this combination of values and meanings distinguished it from other works in the Gallery, including other female nudes."[12] Richardson's strike was a direct attack on the patri- archal and nationalistic ideals embodied in the painting and its history. But the painting is also of a woman considering her reflection – that is, reflecting upon her own image. That the mirror is held by Cupid indicates that in the image Venus sees, she is defined according to the heterosexual romance plot: she sees herself in relation "to the world as it is known to men." Moreover, the fact that Cupid is Venus' son suggests that her image is important insofar as it is reflected back to her by her male offspring. She has served as a vessel to carry the son, and takes her meaning from his existence and from his view of her. And so Richardson's attack on the painting was also a protest against woman's view of herself in Cupid's mirror. Her act enjoins women to see themselves differently, neither as objectified players in the romance plot nor as mothers of sons merely. Modernist writers were tackling this very problem: how women might find ways to view themselves outside the parameters of patriarchy. The damage to the *Rokeby Venus* can serve as an appropriate starting point, then, not only for militant suffragism, but for modernist women's reinvention of what it meant to be, or to become, a woman.

The striking parallels in the commentary of such dissimilar writers as Woolf and Gilman, and implicitly in such acts as Mary Richardson's destruc- tion of the painting, suggest a thread of shared concerns and goals encircling the diverse field of transatlantic women's modernism. *The Cambridge Companion to Modernist Women Writers* aims to introduce readers to this body of work by considering both its common efforts to labor in the "fresh fields" of Gilman's ideal and its great variety of methods for so doing. Until feminist criticism was institutionalized in the 1980s, modernist women writers – when they were taught or written about at all – were viewed as lesser, feminine counterparts of male modernists such as Pound, Eliot, James Joyce, and Joseph Conrad. In understandable reaction to women's margin- alization and assimilation, feminist criticism in the 1980s and 1990s over- emphasized two related aspects of modernist women's writing: its difference from male modernist writing and its comparably laudable political stances. More recent criticism has begun to recognize the common historical, literary, and political contexts surrounding both male and female modernist work, study the complex relationship between women writers and reactionary politics, and credit women writers with formative roles in inventing literary modernism. This *Companion* contributes to such a nuanced account by seeking to understand women's modernism in its own terms. It does not excessively compare women's modernism to men's, but neither does it shy away from acknowledging areas in which women's modernism does speak back to, or simply speak to, modernism practiced by men.

One of the most important influences on women's lives during this period was of course the First World War. In *The Great War and Women's Consciousness*, Claire Tylee writes:

> Although it is not clear quite what effect the First World War had on British women's consciousness and the movement for women's rights in Britain, it is clear that this is a matter of supreme importance to the history of women, and thus to the proper understanding of British society. It would not be absurd to argue that the creation of women's citizenship in 1918 (and its extension in 1928) was at least as important a determinant of modern consciousness as the Battle of the Somme. What is curious is that many women who lived through that period saw the War itself as overriding their interest in women's suffrage. With the War came the opportunity for them to achieve what they had struggled for: entry to what had been seen before as male centres of power.[13]

Such opportunity may have contributed to the decision by leaders of women's suffrage organizations in Britain and the United States to suspend their campaigns of militancy when the war began. Tylee describes the atmosphere of excitement that coexisted with anxiety about the war: "If we look at journalism and diaries of the period, we can see that the war represented an opportunity for 'adventure' for many women. They used it to escape domestic restrictions, to get 'out of the cage.'"[14] The war made it possible for many middle- and upper-class women who longed for adventure to find it; they could join Voluntary Aid Detachments and nurse wounded soldiers or drive ambulances. And it made it possible for many working women to move into better-paying jobs. Approximately 200,000 women moved from domestic labor into the munitions industry, for example, for shorter (though still long!) hours and better pay.[15]

Gail Braybon describes the situation for women's employment after people accepted that women were going to take the place of men who were away at the front:

> the rush of women into engineering and explosives began in the autumn of 1915 and by 1916 there was actually a shortage of female labour in the textile and

clothing trades, as women moved into more lucrative munitions work. This rapid expansion in munitions continued in 1916 and 1917, and women also increasingly replaced men in private, non-munitions industries, like grain milling, sugar refining, brewing, building, surface mining, and shipyards.[16]

Although this expansion began slowly, during the war more than 1.5 million English women joined the ranks of paid workers, and were able, as the above passage shows, to perform a variety of kinds of work which before the war would not have been available to them.

The press on both sides of the Atlantic was full of stories about women workers that, in spite of their inaccuracies, created an aura of excitement and change around conceptions of women's status. In an essay entitled "Women and the War," Braybon notes that English newspapers regularly discussed women's newfound self-confidence, questioned whether women would reject domestic duties after the war, and speculated that women's suffrage would be granted in response to women's wartime service.[17] There is some evidence that the changes brought to women by the war were far-ranging and largely positive. Having done useful wartime work often permanently changed women's evaluations of their own powers, even if that work was temporary. In her book-length study, Braybon quotes labor historian Mary Macarthur writing in 1918: "Of all the changes worked by the war none has been greater than the change in the status and position of women: and yet it is not so much that woman herself has changed, as that man's conception of her has changed."[18]

In her discussions of the 1920s, however, Braybon shows that in fact men's attitudes toward women's status did not change in the dramatic ways it was supposed. "[M]any commentators, then and now, have been cynical about the praise heaped on women by the press and the wartime propaganda machine, pointing out that women were still paid less than men, that their working conditions were often appalling, that there remained many areas of work from which they were excluded completely, and that it proved impossible for women to hold onto their wartime jobs when peace returned."[19] Tylee makes a similar point, noting that "within ten years after the War [engineering and transport] jobs were predominantly male again."[20] The 1920s, as it turned out, saw a backlash against women working. Were they to take jobs from wounded former soldiers? Ought they not return to the home and bear children to replace the young men lost in the war, to shore up the nation's health and pride?

Although the war did change many women's lives for the better, at least by giving them confidence in their newfound abilities, in some ways it reinforced ideas about men's and women's separate spheres. Tylee argues that:

the War emphasized an essential difference between men and women. Women were not combatants. [...] Even independent, adventurous women like Cicely Hamilton and Rose Macaulay expressed a humiliated sense of their own inferiority at being non-combatant burdens on the male part of the population. While the War permitted women to do all sorts of things which had been regarded as strictly masculine before the War, it required of men a more extreme form of masculine activity which was prohibited even to men in peacetime: not merely physical violence, but savage murder in battle. The war re-asserted gender distinctions that women had been contesting: women were frail and had to be defended by strong protectors, who were prepared to kill or die on their behalf.[21]

In this sense the war could be said to have impeded, rather than furthered, the women's movement. The sense of humiliation evident in Hamilton and Macaulay is a key aspect of women's responses to war, one that has been overlooked until recently. According to Suzanne Raitt, "[f]or many women, especially older women who had no children to look after, and were beyond the age where they could be recruited for war service, the war heightened their feelings of uselessness."[22] Raitt explores the British novelist, suffragist, and critic May Sinclair's humiliation at being extraneous, arguing that Sinclair's case demonstrates that "femininity is repeatedly experienced and represented as shame at times of social and cultural crisis."[23] So, although many women felt liberated by the war, many also felt superfluous; and many felt both of these in succession. In her chapter in this volume, Patricia Juliana Smith describes a short story by Radclyffe Hall in which an ambulance driver watches from a Calais quay while her vehicle is towed onto a ship bound for England after the war, taking with it her short-lived sense of purpose. This story encapsulates the social and emotional roller-coaster the war created for many women who were brought "out of the cage" into public life, but a few years later asked to step politely back in.

The upheaval created by the war was one important factor in the larger atmosphere of change that marked the modernist period. Scholars have also looked to changes in philosophy, psychology, science, technology, and mass culture to explain the emphasis on innovation, the idea that the postwar years in particular made a radical break from the previous century's stodginess and conservative mentality. And there were developments within given arts that seemed to emerge independently of technological change. In his important study *The Culture of Time and Space*, Stephen Kern explains the complex causality of the changes in the way people experienced time and space:

Some cultural developments were directly inspired by new technology. James Joyce was fascinated by the cinema, and in *Ulysses* he attempted to recreate in words the montage techniques used by early filmmakers ... Many conceptions of time and space, however, were altered independently of technology, in response to pressures within various genres and disciplines. Paul Cézanne revolutionized the treatment of space in art as he concentrated on the eternal form of *Mont Sainte-Victoire* and the arrangement of bottles and apples in his still lifes ... The thematic similarity between developments inspired by technology and those independent of it suggests that a cultural revolution of the broadest scope was taking place, one that involved essential structures of human experience and basic forms of human expression.[24]

Such an atmosphere of cultural revolution can be seen in a 1918 review of Dorothy Richardson's *Pilgrimage* (1915–1967) by May Sinclair. In this review, Sinclair discusses Richardson's experimental narrative technique in the context of larger philosophic questions. She begins by questioning the categories into which criticism places literary art:

> I do not know whether this article is or is not going to be a criticism, for so soon as I begin to think what I shall say I find myself criticizing criticism, wondering what is the matter with it ... Only a live criticism can deal appropriately with a live art. And it seems to me that the first step towards life is to throw off the philosophic cant of the nineteenth century. I don't mean that there is no philosophy of Art, or that if there has been there is to be no more of it; I mean that it is absurd to go on talking about realism and idealism, or objective and subjective art, as if the philosophies were sticking where they stood in the eighties.[25]

Sinclair – following J. B. Beresford's assessment – describes Richardson's method as a "plunge" into reality, a plunge so deep that it undermines the distinction between objective and subjective narration. "For this and this alone is the way things happen. What we used to call the 'objective' method is a method of after-thought, of spectacular reflection." A narrative method that seems objective and realistic, Sinclair points out, is really a construct, a convention through which we can describe "reality" retrospectively. That Richardson's method of portraying "the way things happen" is also a construct, Sinclair does not admit. Her desire to make criticism come alive by throwing off the shackles of nineteenth-century philosophy is a characteristically modernist move; like the literary works about which she is writing, her essay adopts a radical tone, insists that it is taking part in a definitive break with past literature, criticism, and philosophy. The word "live" was a signal term for modernist writers, many of whom viewed literary works of the recent past as mummified, with (to use Richardson's words from another context) "no depth of life in them, mere husks."[26]

Sinclair's review also brings to light some important facets of modernist literary invention. First, it makes clear the inherent link between specific formal experiments – for example with limiting point of view – and a blurring of literary categories which made it impossible to decide whether a work should be labeled realism or idealism. That is, it highlights the extent to which, like Cézanne's almost inadvertent revolutionizing of space in painting, modernism's generic inventiveness was a function of technical decisions on a much narrower level. Second, Sinclair's review shows how this experimentation was bound up with contemporary philosophical concerns about, as Andrew Ramsay puts it in *To the Lighthouse*, "subject and object and the nature of reality." The extreme first-person point of view Richardson uses in *Pilgrimage* is patently subjective, but Sinclair reads the result as more objective than the allegedly objective, prior realism. Indeed, Richardson describes her writing as a "feminine equivalent" to the "current masculine realism," implying that she aims at some form of objectivity. The collapse of the formerly stable distinction between objectivity and subjectivity in literature echoed a similar destabilization in contemporary philosophy, which was in turn reinforced by discoveries in the physical sciences popularized by scientists such as Arthur Eddington and James Jeans. Eddington's widely read *The Nature of the Physical World* (1928), for example, brought the meaning of reality into question by explaining Einstein's theory of relativity and considering the implications for everyday life of the fact that material objects are composed of atoms and can be penetrated by x-rays.[27]

Early twentieth-century writers were informed about these developments through the work of popular scientists, through newspapers, and often through lectures sponsored by universities or intellectual societies in London or New York. In Dorothy Richardson's *Deadlock* (1921), one of the "novel-chapters" that make up *Pilgrimage*, Miriam Henderson attends a university extension lecture by the Cambridge philosopher J. M. E. McTaggart. McTaggart was a real-life Hegel scholar who presented a series of lectures from 1899 to 1914 that were later published as *Introduction to the Study of Philosophy*; Richardson was working from a printed syllabus when she wrote this section of the novel.[28] In the lecture Miriam attends, McTaggart questions the ability of pre-Einsteinian science, which he describes as concerning itself only with surfaces, to account for the mysterious character of matter. Miriam learns that there is no single, stable explanation for the complexity of the universe; she is "relieved to find that science is only half true" when it comes to "the study of the ultimate nature of reality."[29] Gertrude Stein may mean something similar when she remarks that "The nineteenth century believed in science but the twentieth century does not."[30] Science, that is, no longer seemed scientific, if by "scientific" one meant observable, empirical, objective certainty.

A lecture similarly representative of the intellectual fare of the time was entitled "Bergson's Theory of Knowledge and Einstein's Theory of Relativity," delivered by Professor Wildon Carr at the Lyceum Club of London in November 1924. Carr treats Bergson and Einstein as initiators of "the extraordinary revolution in the fundamental conceptions of philosophy and science which marks the first quarter of this twentieth century." Their theories together "show two aspects of the change, the one its subjective, the other its objective aspect." After contextualizing Bergson's work as a reaction against the positivism of nineteenth-century science, Carr summarizes Bergson's theory of the human intellect: "It does not reveal things as they are, but it frames the actions which serve us in our life activity. It frames the changing, stream of existence, making it assume the staid forms of spatial things. It geometrizes space and it spatializes time."[31] Turning to Einstein, Carr points out that according to Einstein's theory of relativity, "[e]very observer of nature measuring phenomena takes a frame of reference and whatever frame he chooses it must be for him a system at rest. Thus just as we saw in Bergson's theory when we considered the subjective factor, or mind, or intellect, so in Einstein's theory when we consider the objective factor, the world, or universe, we have nothing absolute to refer to." He concludes that objectivity has given way, in modern times, to a pervasive subjectivity. "Einstein has brought us back to the concept of nature as a system, and Bergson has given us the concept of our intellect as itself a product of creative evolution. On each side, mind and nature, the idea of the absolute – absolute knowledge of absolute reality – has given place to the principle of relativity."[32] Relativity, that is, had many implications: it cast doubt upon the solidity of matter in the universe, but also upon distinctions that had bolstered philosophical and literary inquiry.

Freudian psychology was of course another vital force undermining the idea of objectivity and impelling modernist probings into the mysterious. Freud's ideas made their way quickly to the English-speaking world, with several professional societies being founded in England and the United States in the early years of the twentieth century.[33] In the 1920s, Freud's collected works were translated by Alix and James Strachey and published by the Woolfs' Hogarth Press. In her psychoanalytic study of Woolf, Elizabeth Abel describes the cultural impact of psychoanalysis, citing Bronislaw Malinowski's comment that "psycho-analysis has had within the last ten years [1917–27] a truly meteoric rise in popular favor. It has exercised a growing influence over contemporary literature, science, and art."[34] And Abel also quotes the poet Bryher, who claimed, "You could not have escaped Freud in the literary world of the early twenties. Freud! All literary London discovered Freud about 1920."[35] Freud's ideas dovetailed with those of Einstein and Bergson in that all questioned empirical ways of knowing. If, as psychoanalysis made clear, human beings could not be sure of their own motives, if the unconscious, that which could neither be seen nor felt directly, was the real animator of our behavior, this was yet another blow to the idea of objective, knowable reality. When May Sinclair complained about the absurdity of the opposition between "realism and idealism, or objective and subjective art," then, she participated in the growing and overdetermined skepticism about these crumbling distinctions.

The third aspect of modernist writing Sinclair's review highlights is the question of realism in works of this period. Sinclair implicitly asks us to look beyond the appearance of realism in women's literature that is not on its face experimental. Consider Nella Larsen's *Passing* (1929), for example. It is written in a relatively straightforward style, apparently realistic. But the narration is far from objective. Readers very soon discover that the narrative's focalizer, Irene Redfield, though she does not narrate in the first person, gives us a skewed account of events. Subtler and more engaging than Ford Madox Ford's *The Good Soldier* (1915), *Passing* raises similar issues of reliability, and, more profoundly, questions the degree to which "reality" is objective. Larsen's text can be described as the inverse of Richardson's *Pilgrimage*: Larsen approaching subjectivity via objective narration, and Richardson approaching objectivity via subjective narration. Both can be read as testaments to the changing scientific and philosophical ideas of the early twentieth century.

Whether or not their work is evidently and formally experimental, all of the writers considered in this volume break new ground by approaching modernity from women's perspectives, as diverse as those perspectives turn out to be. As Douglas Mao and Rebecca Walkowitz note in the introduction to their collection *Bad Modernisms*, the "new modernist studies" "reconsiders the definitions, locations, and producers of 'modernism.'"[36] The main thrust of this reconsideration has been toward expansion: as their volume demonstrates, there is much more to modernism than was apparent when analysis of "the men of 1914" with occasional mention of Virginia Woolf dominated courses and conferences about modernist literature.

The expansion of the "new modernist studies" has taken place along axes of location and time. In keeping with the geographical expansion, this collection reaches toward a transnational account of modernist literary production in English. Although the majority of the writers examined are English or American, contributors also analyze works by Canadian, Irish, Indian, African, and Caribbean authors. The volume also participates in the parallel temporal expansion of modernist studies. Each chapter ranges historically according to its topic: some begin with events in the late nineteenth century, others situate themselves in the years between the wars, and some extend past the Second World War, especially when examining texts from postcolonial nations. Women's literature, as it emerges in this volume, has many well-known names and locations, but also many less familiar players and locales that are nevertheless crucial to understanding women's participation in the burst of creativity that later became known as modernism.

The first three chapters of the collection consider the major genres through which writers declared themselves modern: the novel, poetry, and drama. Bonnie Kime Scott's chapter on the novel explores the ways formal experiment, interest in psychology, and feminist commitments come together in the work of the major women novelists of the period. Scott helpfully breaks the first forty years of the twentieth century into smaller periods, noting major thematic and formal trends. Through the decades from 1900 to 1940, she argues, women writers remade the novel, eschewing what they saw as the superficiality of realism, and delving deeper to "accommodat[e] fantasy, the unconscious, and madness."

Miranda Hickman turns our attention to poetry, reading Mina Loy, H. D., Marianne Moore, and Canadian poet P. K. Page through their negotiations with theories and movements more commonly associated with their male contemporaries. Considering Loy's engagement with Futurism and F. T. Marinetti, H. D.'s involvement with Imagism and Pound, Moore's association with the theory of poetic impersonality and Eliot, and Page's links to Imagism and Eliot, Hickman traces the reverberations of these connections in the ways we have read the women poets' work. She moves the debates about their engagement with their contemporaries beyond questions of complicity, reading the connections productively for the light they shed on the varieties of feminism and aesthetic approaches of the women poets.

Penny Farfan's chapter completes the first section of the *Companion* by exploring the contributions of playwrights and performers to the modernist scene. Farfan surveys a broad range of dramatic performances, from Djuna Barnes's voluntary submission to force-feeding for an article on the hunger-striking suffragists to plays produced by suffragists, by the Provincetown Players in the United States, by the Pioneer Players in London, and by the Abbey Theatre in Dublin. She describes salons where playwrights of the Harlem Renaissance gathered, Josephine Baker's controversial performances, Gertrude Stein's experimental dramas, and Isadora Duncan's ballets. In these disparate kinds of performance, Farfan argues, the female "performing body" served as a "liminal zone between aesthetic practice and everyday life."

Next in the volume is Jayne Marek's introduction to the spaces of women's creativity: the salons, little magazines, and presses that enabled women's literary production. From Marek's account we learn about the lively and intellectually productive gatherings around women such as Natalie Barney, Ottoline Morrell, Gertrude Stein, Mabel Dodge Luhan, and Georgia Douglas Johnson. As Marek points out, salon culture freed writers, visual artists, and dancers from the preconceptions of their trades (including preconceptions about women artists) and gave them the opportunity to exchange experimental ideas. Marek also describes the enormous impact of women's publishing in little magazines such as *Poetry*, *The Little Review*, *The Egoist*, *Crisis*, and others, as well as in presses run by women. Without women's patronage, personal encouragement, and innovative publishing ventures, much of the body of canonical and emerging modernist work by both women and men would not have found an audience.

After this the *Companion* turns to salient thematic and contextual aspects of women's modernism, though not without demonstrating that these have formal and performative repercussions: gender, race, postcoloniality, visual culture, trauma, activism, and finally religion and the occult. In Patricia Juliana Smith's chapter on "Gender in Women's Modernism" Smith explains the concept of the "New Woman" and contextualizes that figure in terms of contemporary sexology. She discusses varying conceptions of lesbianism, homosexuality, and inversion, showing how the First World War changed women's practical opportunities as well as the ways sex and gender were understood. Turning to writers such as Stein, Willa Cather, Hall, Vera Brittain, Winifred Holtby, and Woolf, Smith traces the roles the New Woman and the lesbian play in their texts. The chapter shows that shifting understandings of the ways gender, sex, and sexuality interrelated had a substantial impact on modernist writing.

The next two chapters look at the ways race is inscribed in literature by authors of African descent and authors of European descent. Although the terms "black" and "white" are obviously mere social constructs and vague to the point of inaccuracy, we do feel it productive to divide representations of what is seen as the self (blackness in writers who identify as black) from representations of what is seen as the other (blackness, Jewishness, Irishness in writers who identify as white, nominally Christian, Anglo-Irish) and treat them in separate chapters. Thadious Davis therefore analyzes literature by African American women of the period, noting how Woolf's desire for a "room of one's own" is constricted in the case of black women writers to desire for mere "elbow room." Quoting Georgia Douglas Johnson, who longed for "a clearing space, elbow room in which to think and write," Davis traces the ways space and place, freedom and security structure the works of authors such as Johnson, Anne Spencer, Jessie Fauset, Larsen, and Zora Neale Hurston. In their poetry, fiction, critical writings, and documentary films, these authors portray the entrapment experienced by black female bodies but at the same time locate black women firmly within the spaces of representation, making manifest their complex subjectivities.

Jean Radford for her part explores the ways minority ethnicities serve authors from dominant groups – Woolf, Richardson, Mary Butts, Sylvia

Townsend Warner, Djuna Barnes, Cather, and Nancy Cunard – as well as how ethnicity works in the writings of authors who themselves were precariously positioned between categories of nation, race, or ethnicity: Stein, Loy, Elizabeth Bowen, and Jean Rhys. Radford finds that religious, racial, or ethnic "difference" often functions as a catalyst for change within the fictions and conjures "the repressed or the uncanny." Her readings reveal some of the ways that literary texts "exceed, undermine, or complicate the explicit commitments of their authors."

Moving the volume from race to similarly complex notions of national identity, Laura Doyle traces the intersections between modernism and postcoloniality in women's writing of the twentieth century. Arguing that "Anglo-European and postcolonial writers emerge together from a violent history and a post/colonial consciousness that pressed on all of their worlds," Doyle describes the responses of modernist and postcolonial writers to such history. Using what Doyle calls "horizon reversals," women writers from Woolf and Rhys to Michelle Cliff, Ama Ata Aidoo, Arundhati Roy, and Phyllis Shand Allfrey employ innovative narrative techniques that create "geomodernism": a modernism aware of real-world violence, responding to historical crisis through fragmented perspectives and looping temporalities.

Maggie Humm examines the ways the visual impacted modern life and modernist literature. Noting that the generation that included Virginia Woolf and her sister Vanessa Bell was the first to be "active photographers and cinema-goers from childhood," Humm considers the impact visual culture had on the lives and writing of several major modernists. Reading women writers' film criticism in journals such as *Close Up*, she analyzes their creation of gendered spectators. And remarking their persistent involvement with visual culture – film, painting, design, and photography – she demonstrates how visuality becomes a site for modernist women to approach the struggle between public and private, "the formally expressive and the everyday moment."

In her chapter on political activism, Sowon Park makes a case for the interdependence of politics and aesthetics during the women's movement of the late nineteenth century. Park describes the ways militant suffragists used aesthetic maneuvers to juxtapose femininity with violence, creating an estrangement effect similar to what we find in Brecht and the Russian formalists. She then provides an overview of the immense written output of the suffrage movement in newspapers, pamphlets, and plays. Throughout, she questions the distinction current in feminist studies between subversive experimental writings and humdrum realism: in Park's account, certain kinds of feminist realism become significant sites of subversion.

The final chapter, on religion and the occult in women's modernism, argues for the importance of spirituality in the work and aesthetic theories of women modernists. Here Heather Ingman shows how organized religion, mysticism, images of the female divine, myth, and the occult influenced modernist women's writing. Noting the aesthetic component of religious experience for the writers she discusses, Ingman demonstrates that their mystical experiences "underpinned their careers as artists." H. D., Butts, Sinclair, Woolf, and others found ways to intervene in and revise spiritual systems, crafting practices or beliefs that met their needs for feminine empowerment and artistic vision.

Together the chapters in this *Companion* demonstrate the major role played by women writers in producing modernism: conceptualizing, debating, writing, and publishing the critical and imaginative work that resulted in the tilling of "fresh fields" in literary culture. By highlighting gender in their theorizations of modernism, and yet often working to transcend it in their imaginative works, women modernists painted a new picture of modern womanhood. They analyzed older ideals of reproductive femininity, as in Woolf's portrait of Mrs. Ramsay, and offered new models of productive womanhood, as in Cather's portrait of Thea Kronborg. They looked with clear eyes at the options available to women and implicitly demanded more. And yet for most of the writers studied here, their commitment was only secondarily to gender equality: it was first to artistic integrity. But as their imaginative and critical writings suggest, they could not envision an expansive, truthful art without expansive, true portraits of women's consciousness, and so they revolutionized literary art.

NOTES

1. Charlotte Perkins Gilman, *The Man-Made World, or Our Androcentric Culture* (New York: Charlton Company, 1911), p. 103.
2. *Ibid.*, p. 104.
3. Virginia Woolf, *The Common Reader, First Series* (London: The Hogarth Press, 1951), p. 189.
4. Wallace Stevens, *The Palm at the End of the Mind: Selected Poems and a Play*, ed. Holly Stevens (New York: Vintage Books, 1972), p. 174.
5. T. S. Eliot, *Selected Prose of T. S. Eliot*, ed. Frank Kermode (New York: Harcourt Brace Jovanovich, 1975), p. 39.
6. Ezra Pound, *Make It New: Essays* (Irvine, CA: Reprint Services Corporation, 1988).
7. Gilman, *Man-Made World*, p. 79.
8. Virginia Woolf, *A Room of One's Own* (New York: Harcourt Brace and Company, 1981), p. 105.
9. Gilman, *Man-Made World*, p. 105.
10. Woolf, *Room*, p. 83.
11. Dorothy Richardson, "Women and the Future" (1924), in *The Gender of Modernism*, ed. Bonnie Kime Scott (Bloomington: Indiana University Press, 1990), p. 411.

12. Lynda Nead, *The Female Nude: Art, Obscenity and Sexuality* (New York: Routledge, 1992), pp. 36–7. See also Suzanne MacLeod, "Civil Disobedience and Political Agitation: The Art Museum as a Site of Protest in the Early Twentieth Century," *Museum and Society* 5.1 (2006), 44–57.

13. Claire M. Tylee, *The Great War and Women's Consciousness: Images of Militarism and Womanhood in Women's Writings, 1914–63* (Iowa City: University of Iowa Press, 1990), p. 14.

14. *Ibid.*, pp. 253–4.

15. Gail Braybon, *Women Workers in the First World War: The British Experience* (Totowa, NJ: Barnes and Noble, 1981), p. 48.

16. *Ibid.*, pp. 45–56.

17. Gail Braybon, "Women and the War," in *The First World War in British History*, ed. Stephen Constantine, Maurice W. Kirby, and Mary B. Rose (London: Edward Arnold, 1995), p. 141.

18. Braybon, *Women Workers*, p. 157.

19. Braybon, "Women and the War," p. 143.

20. Tylee, *Great War*, p. 250.

21. *Ibid.*, pp. 253–4.

22. Suzanne Raitt, "'Contagious Ecstasy': May Sinclair's War Journals," in *Women's Fiction and the Great War*, ed. Suzanne Raitt and Trudi Tate (Oxford: Clarendon Press, 1997), p. 65.

23. *Ibid.*, p. 66.

24. Stephen Kern, *The Culture of Time and Space, 1880–1918* (Cambridge, MA: Harvard University Press, 1983), p. 6.

25. May Sinclair, "The Novels of Dorothy Richardson," in *The Gender of Modernism: A Critical Anthology*, ed. Bonnie Kime Scott (Bloomington: Indiana University Press, 1990), p. 442.

26. Dorothy Richardson, *Pilgrimage* (London: J. M. Dent & Sons, 1967), vol. IV, p. 427.

27. Michael Bell situates questions of objective and subjective reality in late nineteenth- and early twentieth-century philosophy and science in his fine essay, "The Metaphysics of Modernism," in *The Cambridge Companion to Modernism*, ed. Michael Levenson (Cambridge: Cambridge University Press, 1999). Holly Henry discusses the influence of Eddington and Jeans on Woolf in her study, *Virginia Woolf and the Discourse of Science: The Aesthetics of Astronomy* (Cambridge: Cambridge University Press, 2003).

28. George H. Thompson, *Notes on* Pilgrimage: *Dorothy Richardson Annotated* (Greensboro, NC: ELT Press, 1999), p. 161.

29. Dorothy Richardson, *Pilgrimage*, vol. III (New York: Alfred A. Knopf, 1967), p. 162. McTaggart uses this phrase when he defines "Metaphysic" as "[t]he systematic study of the ultimate nature of Reality." See John M. E. McTaggart, *Philosophical Studies* (London: Edward Arnold and Co., 1934), p. 183.

30. Gertrude Stein, *Wars I Have Seen* (New York: Random House, 1945), p. 56.

31. Wildon Carr, "Bergson's Theory of Knowledge and Einstein's Theory of Relativity," *The Philosopher* 2 (1924); *The Philosopher: Interactive Electronic Incarnation of the Journal of the Philosophical Society of England*, www.the-philosopher.co.uk/bergson.htm, March 12, 2006, viewed on March 2, 2009.

32. *Ibid.*

33. The British Psychological Society was founded in 1901; the British Psycho-Analytical Society, more heavily Freudian, in 1924; in the United States, the Psychopathological Association was founded in 1910, the New York Psychoanalytic Society in 1911, and the American Psychoanalytic Association in 1914.

34. Quoted in Elizabeth Abel, *Virginia Woolf and the Fictions of Psychoanalysis* (Chicago: University of Chicago Press, 1989), p. 16.

35. Quoted in *ibid.*, pp. 16–17.

36. Douglas Mao and Rebecca Walkowitz, eds., *Bad Modernisms* (Durham, NC: Duke University Press, 2006), p. 1.

I

BONNIE KIME SCOTT

Transforming the novel

As critics and creative writers, modernist women actively transformed the novel to reflect their unique perceptions of everyday life. These included experiences of modernity, with its urban, technological, and cross-cultural developments; colonialism, with empires in decline; national, racial, and ethnic differences; and biased systems of gender and sexuality. While the ideals and exemplars of male modernism received imbalanced critical attention well into the 1980s, women were very much involved in the making of various modernist genres, including the novel, and they engaged in their own formal and thematic experimentation. Women had remarkable networks, facilitating one another's work through literary circles, publishing and editing endeavors, and the writing of criticism and reviews. Their work tested boundaries, reaching varied audiences, blending genres to create poetic novels and fictionalized essays, and accommodating fantasy, the unconscious, and madness into modernist writing.

A change in consciousness: 1900–19

May Sinclair (1863–1946) is probably best known today for assigning the "stream of consciousness" style to another woman novelist, Dorothy Richardson. Describing the thought process of the central character in Richardson's *Pilgrimage*, Sinclair finds that "the moments of Miriam's consciousness pass one by one, or overlapping; moments tense with vibration, moments drawn out fine, almost to the snapping-point."[1] In Richardson's depiction of a tragic event, Sinclair finds a method that "seizes reality alive. The intense rapidity of the seizure defies you to distinguish between what is objective and what is subjective" (446). Like many modernists, Sinclair was a reader of Freud and Jung, and psychology emerges in her writing. The "psychological method," which she attributed to James Joyce as well as Richardson, allows narrative movement from outside spectator to internal consciousness. Readers are limited to the subject's blind spots, but with significant gain in intensity.[2] Sinclair was an ally of Ezra Pound and, in deriding the "mush" of sentimental poetry, echoes one of his masculine formulas. Yet H. D. (Hilda Doolittle) was her favorite Imagist. Imagists move away from what Sinclair considers worn-out symbolic and decorative forms. "The Image is not a substitute: it does not stand for anything but itself . . . The Image, I take it, is Form. But it is not pure form. It is form *and* substance" and it can be expressive of mood.[3]

Sinclair's own novels partake of the nineteenth century and are akin to later "middlebrow" writing, but they have modernist attributes. She records shifting gender expectations and focuses on a mother's relation to her children. Frances Harrison, seated beneath the iconic ash tree in *Tree of Heaven* (1917), is at the center of family life, much like Mrs. Ramsay in Woolf's *To the Lighthouse* (1927). The mothers in this novel and *Mary Olivier* (1919) privilege their sons. Frances's own privilege as a married woman in her fine home in Hampstead contrasts with her widowed mother and unmarried sisters, housed on the margin in a modest cottage. Frances's children are drawn away from her into the "vortex" of modernity and the sacrifice of war. The Freudian term "herd instinct," applied to suffragism (a movement that attracts the daughter) and Vorticism (which attracts one son), may bring these twentieth-century endeavors into question, but Sinclair herself joined these same movements. At novel's end, two sons have perished in the First World War and the third is setting off to war, with parental encouragement. Sinclair thus joins other modernist women in questioning nationalist, militant values that start at home.

Mary Olivier: A Life, which focuses intensely on the mother/daughter dyad, is of great psychological interest. We enter Mary's consciousness from the time she is in the cradle, fingering a green knob like a little Imagist. She has a nightmare of a deformed man, and is comforted by touching her mother's breast. Attracted to reading philosophy, and attractive for her precocious intelligence to a series of older men, Mary is denied and/or evades the marriage plot. She serves her mother (as did Sinclair) until death, but resists her religious training. Mary has moments of intense, even erotic happiness, elicited by natural settings or music – events comparable to modernist epiphany. She processes colliding, accumulating memories of dark family history – a sequestered aunt suspected of nymphomania, and the death of her alcoholic father. That Mary does not repeat family patterns may owe something to fears implanted by eugenic theory, which had an important presence in modernist thinking. She has liberation of a sort, but it is costly in terms of human attachment.

Dorothy Richardson (1873–1957) used the phrase "a feminine equivalent of the current masculine realism" to describe *Pilgrimage*, which is comprised of thirteen segments, all but one published between 1915 and 1938.[4] Unlike

Balzac's or Arnold Bennett's realism, hers focused upon "contemplated reality," a perception that, as she explained, had many faces, each disqualified as another face grew out of it. Concerning gender, Richardson theorizes a variety of types of woman, including the "man-trained woman" whom men like H. G. Wells imagine "following modestly behind the vanguard of males at work upon the business of reducing chaos to order."[5] The "womanly woman" has a "complete, self-centered consciousness" and thinks "flowingly, with her feelings" across times. She is "indifferent to the fashions of men" (413). This figure shows what we would consider today essentialist limitations. But the womanly woman's most important gift, "imaginative sympathy" (414), is a capacity Richardson would like to see in the council of nations. Diane Gillespie credits Richardson with achieving an "outspokenly feminine version of modernism" while remaining connected with other experimental modernists.[6]

Throughout *Pilgrimage*, Miriam Henderson is a gifted, sympathetic contemplator of reality. Her observations exceed a simple "stream of consciousness" form. Woolf attributed to her "the psychological sentence of the feminine gender."[7] Woolf appreciated not only the variety of impressions recorded, but the way "they flicker through Miriam's mind, waking incongruously other thoughts, and plaiting incessantly the many-coloured and innumerable threads of life" (191). Miriam's reaction to her mother's suicide, noted for intensity by Sinclair, is also evocative of post-traumatic stress disorder, showing dysphoria, flashbacks, and estrangement.[8] Julia Kristeva's theory of the feminine semiotic – a state identified with maternal flow that precedes the masculine symbolic order – does apply well to Richardson's experiments with consciousness.

Although plot and action recede in Richardson's novels, Miriam's intellectual encounters approach concerns of modernity, particularly after she moves into the urban world so prominent in modernist texts. Seven volumes of *Pilgrimage* are set in London, where Miriam encounters diverse classes and ethnicities. She reacts to recent works of literature and science, noting particularly the politics of gender and sexuality. Her relationships with men permit her to discover their foibles. Hypo Wilson (identified with H. G. Wells in her own life) introduces her to the equivalent of the Fabian Society and ideas of eugenics; he makes the anti-modernist recommendation that she write documentary realism. But she finds childish needs rather than sexual prowess in him. Miriam meets the tide of Eastern European immigration through another lover, Michael Shatov, a Russian Jew studying in London. Jean Radford remarks on their divergent readings of Tolstoy's *Anna Karenina* in the aptly named volume, *Deadlock*. The lovers also diverge in their reading of women. Miriam develops sympathy and identification with prostitutes, who can be picked up by men like Shatov at the same coffee shop she patronizes.[9] Miriam has a mutually declared love relationship with Amabel, which moves toward a love triangle with Michael, and eventually her renunciation of both, when she encourages them to marry. As Sinclair does in *Mary Olivier*, Richardson is "writing beyond the ending" of the traditional novel, which typically ends with the marriage or death of the heroine.[10]

The strikingly different formal experiments of Gertrude Stein (1874–1946) began earlier than those we have been considering, but attracted fewer successors. Still, like Richardson, she shared the goal of representing successive moments of lived experience. Though Stein initially thought of herself as a novelist, typical definitions of that genre do not represent what she left out in terms of action and character, or put in, by way of temporality, syntax, and repetition. She was just as innovative in works she called plays or poems, offering forms that could be imported into modernist novels. In *Tender Buttons* (1914), she represents domestic objects and experiments using relatively few nouns, and achieving a "lively words" style, which is often sensual in effect.[11] Many sections of *Tender Buttons* resemble a painter's still life, en route to the cubism of her friend, Pablo Picasso.

Three Lives (begun 1905, published 1909) is among the most accessible of her fictional writings. Its longest story, "Melanctha: Each One as She May," is derived from *Q.E.D.*, an earlier autobiographical account of Stein's first serious lesbian relationship. Stein's central character is Melanctha Herbert, an African American woman who is observed by a bland, naïve narrator. Repetitive, defining words approximate Melanctha's shifting feelings and behavior. We follow her waxing and waning relationships with a series of women and men, beginning and ending with Rose Campbell. Melanctha wanders as she pleases among working men. She becomes "quiet" and at ease with Dr. Jeff Campbell as he tends her dying mother, but the relationship is inconclusive and he, like other men, flees their intimacy. Intelligent and complex in her desire, Melanctha is left feeling "blue," to the point of considering suicide. Instead, she fades away of consumption. That she was wandering "on the edge of wisdom" makes hers an enduring dilemma.[12] One can question generalizations made about blacks in this work, and how familiar Stein was with black language. Stein chose repeatedly to represent race, perhaps as a code for lesbian sexuality.

The Making of Americans, a family history of the Herslands and the Redferns (begun 1903, completed 1911–13) is Stein's longest "novel," at over 1,000 pages. By offering rhythmic shifting repetition of simple words, it carries her "insistent style" to an extreme.[13] Stein sought to understand the being of her characters as they range through relationships, stages of growth, and disillusionment with society. Like other modernists, she found the depiction of character an important challenge, not fully addressed by realism.

The nature of Stein's experiments comes clearer through her lectures, which bear her typical syntactical, repetitive, and accretive traits. "Composition as Explanation" was presented at Oxford and Cambridge and then published by the Hogarth Press, at the instigation of Virginia and Leonard Woolf, in 1926. The Woolfs had earlier rejected *The Making of Americans*, Virginia feeling that Stein's "dodge is to repeat the same word 1000 times over in different connections, until you feel the force of it."[14] Like Woolf in her essay "Modern Fiction," Stein thought of the distinct identity of different generations and sought to characterize her own period. She notes of "Melanctha": "I created then a prolonged present naturally. I knew nothing of a continuous present but it came naturally to me to make one, it was simple it was clear to me."[15] *The Making of Americans* achieved that continuous present. Stein was depicted largely as an eccentric by renowned critic Edmund Wilson, and dismissed for an obsession with time by Wyndham Lewis, one of the male makers of modernism. Yet she brings the process of becoming into fiction in memorable ways.

Transformative feminist modernism: the 1920s

Virginia Woolf (1882–1941) has become a focal figure for modernist/feminist transformation of the novel, which came into its own around 1928.[16] *The Voyage Out* (published 1915) took nearly a decade to write, perhaps because Woolf was addressing her own demons relating to marriage and sexuality.[17] Experimentation starts with immersion in the consciousness of Woolf's central female character, Rachel Vinrace. An inexperienced young woman visiting South America among other British travelers, Rachel has a series of encounters that are burdened by sexual and imperial politics. Following a kiss seized by the statesman Richard Dalloway, she has a nightmare involving a deformed man encountered in a damp tunnel, which extends into lasting trauma. During a tour down a jungle river ending at a native village, she is drawn reluctantly and inarticulately into an engagement with Terence Hewet, who aspires to his own experimental novel on the subject of silence. Their love plot is triangulated by Helen Ambrose, Rachel's aunt, when the women tumble in pampas grass. The native encounter resonates with various modernist encounters with racial others, most notably Joseph Conrad's *Heart of Darkness*. Both the churning waters of the jungle and Rachel's terminal illness, with its hallucinations of submersion and horrific human figures, can be seen as an exploration of the maternal and the unconscious.[18]

Among those who appreciated *The Voyage Out* was Katherine Mansfield (1888–1923), whose short story techniques were the envy of Woolf. Mansfield and Woolf held animated discussions about their writing. They were working on stories that bear comparison – Woolf's "Kew Gardens" and Mansfield's "The Prelude." It is significant that the Woolfs accepted "The Prelude" as the second publication of the Hogarth Press (founded 1917). Its plot is uncomplicated – a family group settles in a house outside of town. Technically, it focuses on intense moments of perception, moving from one character to the next as they approach their new environment, explore their fears and fantasies, and react to one another. As in *The Voyage Out*, nightmares betray sexual anxieties, especially for the mother, Linda Burnell, who is weary of childbearing. An immense, aged aloe tree with thorny leaves lends psychological meaning as pairs of observers pass it by. Mansfield is attentive to gender dynamics – the demanding, self-congratulatory masculinity of Stanley Burnell, the domestic labor cheerfully rendered by Linda's elderly mother and more tyrannically by her sister, Beryl. Feeling cut off from life, Beryl courts her slim body image in the mirror, fantasizing male interest. Kezia, the most adventurous of the family's three little girls, has intense, layered perceptions as she finds forgotten objects in the house, explores garden paths, nestles close to her grandmother in bed, and witnesses the bloody slaughter of a duck by the manservant. Varied, precise, and layered in meaning, this work set a standard for modernism.

Mansfield's book reviewing took up numerous women novelists, including Sinclair, Stein, and Richardson. She appreciated Sinclair's *Mary Olivier*, but was more critical of Stein and Richardson. Vita Sackville-West and Rose Macaulay, who are generally treated as middlebrow, and hence on the peripheries of modernism, also received her attention. Her verdict on Woolf's second novel, *Night and Day* (1919), shocked its author; Mansfield felt she had failed to meet the expectations of an "age of experiment." The work also lacked the "scars" expected after the outbreak of the First World War, history that did have a significant impact on later Woolf and modernism in general.[19]

As she moved into the 1920s, Woolf, like Sinclair, Richardson, Stein, and Mansfield, not only exemplified transformations of the novel in her own fiction, but also offered accessible critical analysis of the modernizing of the novel. In "Modern Fiction" (1925), she identified qualities that have become standard in defining the modernist novel. Woolf finds that H. G. Wells, Arnold Bennett, and John Galsworthy no longer serve the contemporary mind. Life and spirit evade their "materialist" approach of amassing solid details in tight constructions. Moderns no longer find the "proper stuff of fiction" in expected places like plot, comedy, "tragedy, love interest or catastrophe."[20] She looks instead at "an ordinary mind on an ordinary day" as it "receives a myriad impressions" that shape themselves into "the life of Monday or Tuesday" (160). The writer must find and convey "the moment of importance" (160). S/he must also be free to seek out neglected areas of interest, including "the dark places of psychology" (162). In this essay, Woolf probes the work of Joyce and Chekov, disclosing qualms over Joyce's self-centering and "indecency" (161). In "Mr. Bennett and Mrs. Brown" (1923) Woolf again questions the adequacy of Bennett's methods, arguing that "on or about December, 1910, human character changed."[21] Focusing more on gender, she makes women central to her argument – starting with the cook emerging from the basement into the drawing room, and culminating with Mrs. Brown, an old woman observed on a train. Modernist efforts to represent Mrs. Brown have, to date, been "spasmodic, obscure and fragmentary," but are coming closer to "life itself" (119).

In *A Room of One's Own* (1929), Woolf responds to a request that she speak on "women and fiction" with an inquiry that moves from Elizabethan to contemporary times. Originally a lecture for undergraduate women at Newnham and Girton Colleges of Cambridge University (October 1928), the work blends fiction with the genres of lecture and essay, following the narrator's stream of daily impressions. By accepting a number of names for the narrator (Mary Beaton, Mary Seton, Mary Carmichael), she both identifies historical beings and seeks to avoid the egotism she had criticized in Joyce and Richardson.

To discuss the contemporary novel, Woolf invents Mary Carmichael and samples her imaginary novel, *Life's Adventure*. Mary is not necessarily an experimental modernist. She might be tempted to become "the less interesting branch of the species – the naturalist-novelist, and not the contemplative."[22] Yet her writing takes on remarkable aspects of style and subject. She does not move her sentences from one melody to the next with the ease of Jane Austen; her "terseness, this short-windedness, might mean that she was afraid of being called 'sentimental'" (79–80). Or it might mean that, having "broken the sentence," she is "tampering with the expected sequence" (80).[23] By writing "Chloe liked Olivia. They shared a laboratory together," Mary holds great promise, for if she can express this "she will light a torch in that vast chamber where nobody has yet been" (83). These lines suggest, not just the untraditional idea of women's liking one another, but lesbian sexuality, long in the dark. 1928 saw the obscenity trial of Radclyffe Hall's openly lesbian novel *The Well of Loneliness*, a challenge to freedom of expression that was answered by numerous writers, including both Woolfs, Rebecca West, and E. M. Forster.

The description of Mary Carmichael also fits a "middlebrow" audience, so this may indicate some breaking down of the hierarchies and boundaries patrolled by many makers of modernism. Vernon Lee and Rebecca West are two contemporary novelists mentioned in *A Room of One's Own*. Though capable of transforming the novel, neither writer is securely located as modernist. West's boundary crashing is recorded by a male critic who is offended by her remark that men are "snobs" (35), most likely occurring in West's collection of criticism, *The Strange Necessity* (1928). In her title essay, West presents a fictionalized commentator whose authoritative reactions to Joyce's *Ulysses* emerge through a stream of consciousness, as she simultaneously appreciates her walk through Paris. Through positive book reviews and other writings, West boosted the reputations of selected modernists, including D. H. Lawrence and Woolf.

Woolf's four novels of the 1920s – *Jacob's Room* (1922), *Mrs. Dalloway* (1925), *To the Lighthouse* (1927), and *Orlando* (1928) – as well as *The Waves* (1931), each offer new areas of experimentation. The accent does indeed fall differently from the traditional novel, as suggested in "Modern Fiction." Character is captured fleetingly, in a variety of perspectives, as suggested in "Mr. Bennett and Mrs. Brown." We come to know Jacob Flanders of *Jacob's Room* largely through the perspectives of other characters (especially women) who observe him. Woolf explained a new approach for *Mrs. Dalloway* through the development of a "tunnelling process": "I dig out beautiful caves behind my characters: I think that gives me what I want: humanity, humour, depth. The idea is that the caves shall connect and each comes to daylight at the present moment."[24] The process shows a rich investment in contexts and interdependence of perspectives, memories, and characters that "connect." Woolf also finds importance in extraordinary moments – what she would later term "moments of being."[25] These come to numerous characters, including Mrs. Dalloway, Peter Walsh, and Septimus Smith, as they walk through London on a single day. This capacity is further explored in *To the Lighthouse*, as Woolf ponders the watery depths of the mind of the young girl Cam, and follows the artistic process of Lily Briscoe, trying to bring together her experience of the Ramsay family on canvas. *Orlando* is unique in its experimentation with character, as the central character lives from the Elizabethan to the present age, changing sex in the eighteenth century. He/she maintains throughout a somewhat melancholy disposition, and the longing to be a poet. Orlando's tormented biographer emerges as a disembodied character by sharing the challenges of representing such a story. This lends self-reflexivity to Woolf's methodology. Despite its experimental aspects *Orlando* became Woolf's first best-seller, connecting her to a wider audience than many modernists enjoyed.

Genre blending was also becoming a staple for Woolf, with the central portion of *To the Lighthouse* providing a model for the increasing lyricism of *The Waves*, particularly in italicized inter-chapters that trace the course of a single day, centered in nature. In what is probably her consummate and most difficult modernist work, Woolf expands to a cast of six complementary characters (three male, three female), whose qualities are depicted through soliloquies. Here they evoke self-defining images and express preoccupations, at nine progressive stages of life. The soliloquies, too, connect in theme and image. The characters collaborate further in idolizing a seventh character, Percival. He, like Jacob, dies in youth, in his case from an undignified fall from a horse while serving the nation out in the empire. That a beautiful but brutal, privileged male is so central an ideal encourages cultural critique – increasingly the subject of 1930s modernism, as we shall see in the final section of this chapter.

From 1922 onward Woolf repeatedly took up the First World War and parallel traumas. At the end of *Jacob's Room*, Betty Flanders holds her son's empty shoes, left behind after he dies in the war. We share the flashbacks and hallucinatory experience of a shell-shocked veteran, Septimus Smith in *Mrs. Dalloway*. Her acceptance of Septimus's eventual suicide suggests that, despite differences in class and gender, Mrs. Dalloway harbors parallel trauma, as well as suppressed same-sex love. In the central, poetic section of *To the Lighthouse*, metaphors of war abound in the description of a decaying house, and we find the deaths of Andrew in war, Mrs. Ramsay of a brief illness, and Prue in childbirth – all printed in square brackets, as if to suggest cosmic indifference. It seems significant that Orlando's sex change comes in the midst of a violent uprising among native factions in Constantinople.

Another aspect of Woolf's experimental writing is her inclusion of lesbian sexuality. *Orlando* was conceived as a tribute to a woman Woolf loved, Vita Sackville-West, whose family home and history were its inspiration. Its exploration of women's same-sex love is muted. It is suggested, for example, in a scene where the cross-dressed heroine visits with prostitutes, and where a woman who was a man can be aroused by her former sex. This enabled Woolf to evade the same censors who were prosecuting Radclyffe Hall's *The Well of Loneliness*.

Also successful in the evasion of the sexuality police was Djuna Barnes (1892–1982), whose comic depiction of Natalie Barney's lesbian salon in *Ladies Almanack* (1928), distributed by friends in Paris, was beneath the censors' radar. At the time, Barnes lived in Paris with silverpoint artist Thelma Wood in a troubled lesbian relationship that would inspire her best-known novel, *Nightwood* (1936), to which we return in the final section. An admirer of Joyce and Eliot, whose work she reviewed, Barnes blended many genres, including the art of illustration, poetry, participatory journalism, plays, and short stories, as well as novels. *The Book of Repulsive Women* (1915), a pamphlet published while she was living in Greenwich Village, included sketches, poetry, and stories. This and short stories collected as *A Book* (1923) set the precedent for writing on the margins of society, including immigrant cultures and the *demimonde*. American folktale traditions connect her with the writing of African American novelist and anthropologist, Zora Neale Hurston. Barnes took delight in antique books and literary forms, whether fifteenth-century drawings or Chaucerian language, which gave her license for bawdiness. Her texts and illustrations probe the genitalia and engage in erotic imagery. Barnes's aphorisms and esoteric language yield multiple understandings. An incest survivor, Barnes engaged traumas of sexuality as well as war. Her family history lies behind the novel *Ryder* (1928). The work presents the phallocentric bigamist Wendell Ryder, and demonstrates the cost of his sexual and artistic exploits, particularly to female members of the family. Not without complaint, they are kept busy with childbirth and stitchery. The publisher of *Ryder* removed some of Barnes's illustrations, fearing censorship.

Rebecca West (1892–1983) incorporated modernist techniques in her criticism and novels through the 1920s, turning later to more traditional styles. *The Return of the Soldier* (1918) qualifies as a psychological novel, while it engages in cultural critique relating to class and warfare. Its central figure is a soldier suffering from amnesia after the First World War. Unable to remember his culturally correct wife or the cousin who loves him, he passionately reconnects with his first love, a working-class woman who was an inappropriate marital choice. The loss of a child is something the two have in common, and at the advice of a physician, she restores his memory by tendering a possession of his dead son. His recovery permits the return of the soldier, perhaps for sacrifice in the war.

The Judge (1922) is a monumental book, as much an inheritor of the Brontës as an example of modernism. The first of two interlocking plots concerns a young Scottish suffragist, Ellen Melville, and her long-suffering mother, as Ellen enters her first experience of love. Richard Yaverland is a virile young man with an imperial past, presently an explosives manufacturer. The book reverts a generation earlier to Marion Yaverland, who conceives Richard in a love affair with a neighboring squire. The beauties of West's female characters are under repeated assault from various forms of masculine violence, in her view. The novel's points of intensity feature internal monologue. *The Judge* is particularly concerned with maternal energies and economies, evocative of Kristeva's semiotic, and connected (like the psychological elements of *The Return of the Soldier*) to Freud.

Harriet Hume (1928), West's last modernist novel, moves into fantasy, offering a series of interviews between ill-fated lovers.[26] Harriet has magical feminine power. She is a mind-reader, an accomplished pianist, and a resourceful decorator, able to assign fanciful stories to eighteenth-century architectural details. Harriet repeatedly foils the destructive cycles of the ambitious political career man, Arnold Condorex, in the course of six meetings that begin in youth and move beyond their deaths. The work becomes an allegory of the gender binaries increasingly challenged by the women of modernism.

Recognition of some women authors active in the 1920s was delayed because their experiments were not sufficiently encouraged at the time. Until the 1980s, H. D. was primarily recognized for her early poetry touted by Ezra Pound, and not for long sequence poems that re-vision mythology, memoirs of Lawrence and Freud, and autobiographical fiction. Her novels, the story sequence *Palimpsest*, and especially *Bid Me to Live* (first published 1960) have a significant place in the novel as studied today. They have psychological value as healing texts, exploring feminine consciousness, bisexuality, pregnancy loss, and the impact of the First World War on the home front.[27] H. D.'s "Notes on Thought and Vision" defies genre designation. First published in 1982, though conceived in the early 1920s, this stream of consciousness reconnects womb with mind in an erotic poetics that qualifies as feminine writing. Though the men she consulted discouraged publishing these texts, her intimate supporters, including Sinclair and her long-term companion Bryher, saw their importance.

Jean Rhys's *Wide Sargasso Sea*, an experimental retake of Charlotte Brontë's *Jane Eyre* representing the point of view of Rochester's first wife, brought Rhys back to the attention of the literary world when it was first published in 1966. This drew attention to her much earlier experimental modernism, found in *The Left Bank and Other Stories* (1927), which explores women as commodified subjects of the gaze, offering fragmentary views of urban modernity and the marginal lives of struggling chorus girls. By 1934, with *Voyage in the Dark*, Jean Rhys had begun to probe her childhood in Dominica, experimenting with representations of racial difference, and to represent the mind under extraordinary physical circumstances, including the experience of a botched abortion.

Moving with crises of history: the 1930s

The tenor of the 1930s turned modernism toward impending international politics, and dark subject matter. *Nightwood*, Djuna Barnes's most celebrated modernist work, is fascinating for its exploration of cultural others, and the levels of psychological trauma it plumbs. But its gravity is also typical of later modernism. One of its storylines is autobiographical, treating the decline of the lesbian relationship of Nora Flood and Robin Vote. Robin wanders away from the Paris flat she and Nora had furnished to represent their love, its decor featuring church and circus relics. Largely in silence, Robin explores chapels on both sides of the Atlantic, marriage to Felix Volkbein (resulting in a child she does not want), an acquisitive, wealthy matron's salon, and the boundaries between animal and human. Felix, like his father, has assumed the false title of "Baron" and the historical burdens of the Jews. He enjoys "sham salons" in numerous European capitals and the company of circus folk, whose imaginary identities match his own.[28] A major character, emphasized in T. S. Eliot's editing of the text, is a homosexual, cross-dressing, unlicensed doctor, Matthew O'Connor, whose lengthy dialogues address characters ranging from Tiny O'Toole (his penis) to Nora. He shares the aphoristic language characteristic of much of Barnes's work. Clad in a granny night-gown, O'Connor serves as Nora's psychoanalyst. Though set mainly in the 1920s, this work belongs to the increasingly threatening 1930s contexts of rising fascism, presenting characters that soon would be targets for Hitler's destruction.

Amid its impressive experimental effects, noted above, Woolf's *The Waves* elicits questions about empire and takes issue with fascism.[29] Alongside her fiction, Woolf wrote the most outspoken essay of her career, *Three Guineas* (1938), offering a feminist tract against war and fascism, linking the latter to patriarchy at home. Indeed, in the village setting of her final novel *Between the Acts*, where a pageant reinterpreting English history is held outside a manor house, the threat of the Second World War has begun to settle on some of those present. Fascism also comes home, however, as hinted in the hyper-masculine behavior of Giles Oliver, who represents grown son, husband, and father within the central family. Between the acts, Giles stamps out the homosexual inversion suggested in a snake choking on a toad. The final scene looks to a post-human future that will provide the next act.

Woolf's proposal of an "outsiders' society" in *Three Guineas* responds to inequities in women's education and their place in the nation. It could be considered a model for the growing culture of women writers, with distinct reading audiences and goals apart from modernism.[30] Miss LaTrobe, the creator of a historical pageant in *Between the Acts*, is a decided outsider to the community – a lesbian of uncertain European origin. She concocts her art from "scraps, orts and fragments," and forces her audience to look at themselves, as well as their history.[31]

Modernist transformations continued to be felt by writers concerned with a wider audience and writing after 1941, the year when both Woolf and Joyce died. Rebecca West worked on more conventional fictions in the 1950s, but produced an amazing study of Yugoslavia under impending fascism, *Black Lamb and Grey Falcon* (1941). Anglo-Irish writer Elizabeth Bowen (1899–1973) was a late, valued acquaintance of Woolf, though less assuredly a feminist. In resonance with modernism, Bowen expressed an interest in representing the "immediate moment."[32] In the cases of Lois Farquar and Portia Quayne, the young girls of *The Last September* (1929) and *The Death of the Heart* (1938), this called for scrupulously limited, halting perceptions, as Bowen recollected having in her own youth. Like numerous other writers either branded "middlebrow" or surviving well past the heyday of modernism, Bowen is generally considered less transformative of the novel. Andrew Bennett and Nicholas Royle, however, claim that her "novels present dissolutions at the level of personal identity, patriarchy, social conventions and language" that make her more radical than Woolf.[33] Comparing Woolf to Bowen, Maud Ellmann finds that the latter "relishes the narrative business of the realist, insofar as it releases her from the stifling rose-house of inner life into the world of cars and cocktail-shakers, typewriters and telephones – in short into the modern world."[34] Bowen's materialism was different from what Woolf repudiated in the work of Bennett, Galsworthy, and Wells, as it relates to psychology. Her characters have relationships with physical objects, such as furniture, and these stimulate thought and memory.

As with Woolf and Barnes, Bowen's characters work in combination. Heterosexual romance is often triangulated, with perilously innocent young heroines becoming matched with experienced women. *The Last September* demonstrates its heroine Lois's difficulty in defining a feeling as love, and her ultimate failure to do so in the case of a British soldier. Lois seems equally attracted to a visitor more mature than herself, Marda, who suggests Lois could do with experience and travel, settling only later for marriage (as Marda now intends to do). The heart seems only to have flourished in the past for the characters of *The Death of the Heart*, and especially Portia, an orphan brought to live with her half-brother Thomas and his wife Anna. Anna's past and present life (the latter closely observed by Portia for her diary) include numerous closely controlled flirtations. A child of her father's indiscretion with a woman of lesser social stature, Portia's memories of an early childhood in marginal places and off-season resorts, and her thoughts of both parents, suggest a superior culture of love.

Bowen sets novels such as *The Last September* and *The Heat of the Day* (1949) on the periphery of national crises – the Irish Civil War (*c.* 1920–2), and the worst bombings of London in the Second World War. The personal and political intersect in bewildering and trivial ways for Stella Rodney in *The Heat of the Day*. She awakes after a major bombing episode, wondering which neighborhoods and friends have survived. She has a series of betrayals in love, including suspicions that her current lover is a spy. Equally tenuous is the life of a middle-class soldier's wife on the home front, who is first found observing one of Stella's gentlemen friends. Her intersecting path provides connections across class and among women in a world that otherwise shows the fragmentation of modernism and modernity. Stella's son, the surprise inheritor of a ramshackle great house in Ireland, has the potential to transform Anglo-Irish relations, but his survival as an army inductee is as uncertain as history itself.

Zora Neale Hurston and Nella Larsen (treated more extensively elsewhere in this volume) turned modernist techniques toward questions of race, demonstrating another historical current of enormous significance, when we consider contemporary publications such as Alain Locke's *New Negro*, Nancy Cunard's *Negro* anthology (1937), and the role of the Harlem Renaissance in modernism. In *Passing* (1929), Larsen pursues the construction of whiteness and the psychology of black identification in a transatlantic frame. Hurston's *Their Eyes Were Watching God* (1937) centers on the cultural margins, moving through southern black communities. Its imagery reconnects sensually with nature. Protagonist Janie Crawford claims the horizon and a narrative voice, surviving a series of relationships (including her grandmother and three male partners) that impose standard gender expectations.

Though modernism was long considered apart from politics, women modernists experimented with consciousness, perception, the outsider's vision, transformative moments of being, and momentary connections with others, applying these to political concerns symptomatic of the twentieth century. Early sensitivity to the oppressions of gender and sexuality increasingly intersected with concerns of class, colonialism, militarism, fascism, and race, providing experimental models that can still be applied in our highly complex, global culture.

NOTES

1. May Sinclair, "The Novels of Dorothy Richardson," in *The Gender of Modernism*, ed. Bonnie Kime Scott (Bloomington: Indiana University Press, 1990), p. 445. Subsequent page numbers will be given parenthetically in the text.
2. May Sinclair, "May Sinclair," in *The Future of the Novel: Famous Authors and their Methods: A Series of Interviews with Renowned Authors*, ed. M. Starr (Boston: Small, Maynard, 1921), pp. 87–9.
3. May Sinclair, "The Poems of H. D.," in *The Gender of Modernism*, ed. Scott, p. 454.
4. Dorothy Richardson, "Foreword to Pilgrimage," in *The Gender of Modernism*, ed. Scott, p. 430.
5. Dorothy Richardson, "Women and the Future," in *The Gender of Modernism*, ed. Scott, pp. 412–13. Subsequent page numbers will be given parenthetically in the text.
6. D. Gillespie, "Dorothy Richardson," in *The Gender of Modernism*, ed. Scott, p. 394.
7. Virginia Woolf, "Romance and the Heart," in *The Essays of Virginia Woolf*, vol. III, *1919–1924*, ed. A. McNeillie (San Diego: Harcourt Brace Jovanovich, 1988), p. 367. Subsequent page numbers will be given parenthetically in the text.

8. Suzette Henke, "Modernism, Trauma, and Narrative Reformulation," in *Gender in Modernism: New Geographies, Complex Intersections*, ed. Bonnie Kime Scott (Urbana: University of Illinois Press, 2007), p. 561.

9. Jean Radford, *Dorothy Richardson* (Hemel Hempstead: Harvester, 1991), p. 23.

10. See Rachel Blau DuPlessis, *Writing beyond the Ending: Strategies of Twentieth Century Women Writers* (Bloomington: Indiana University Press, 1985).

11. Marianne DeKoven, "Gertrude Stein," in *The Gender of Modernism*, ed. Scott, p. 485.

12. Gertrude Stein, *Selected Writings of Gertrude Stein*, ed. C. Van Vechten (New York: Random House, 1990), p. 351.

13. DeKoven, "Gertrude Stein," p. 486.

14. Virginia Woolf, *The Letters of Virginia Woolf*, ed. Nigel Nicolson and Joanne Trautmann, 6 vols. (New York: Harcourt Brace Jovanovich, 1975–80), vol. III, p. 209.

15. Stein, *Selected Writings*, p. 517.

16. Elsewhere, I have used this date as an organizing principle. See Bonnie Kime Scott, *Refiguring Modernism*, vol. I, *The Women of 1928* (Bloomington: Indiana University Press, 1995). The year 1922 was a more male-dominated peak for "high" modernism, given the publication that year of James Joyce's *Ulysses* and T. S. Eliot's *The Waste Land*. That same year, though, Woolf published her first thoroughly experimental novel, *Jacob's Room*.

17. See L. A. DeSalvo, *Virginia Woolf: The Impact of Childhood Sexual Abuse on her Life and Work* (Boston: Beacon, 1989).

18. See Marianne DeKoven, *Rich and Strange: Gender, History, Modernism* (Princeton: Princeton University Press, 1991), pp. 105, 109–13, 138.

19. Katherine Mansfield, "A Ship Comes into the Harbour," in *The Critical Writings of Katherine Mansfield*, ed. Clare Hanson (Basingstoke: Macmillan, 1987), pp. 56–7.

20. Virginia Woolf, "Modern Fiction," *Essays of Virginia Woolf*, vol. IV, *1925–1928*, ed. A. McNeillie (Orlando, FL: Harcourt, 1994), p. 160. Subsequent page numbers will be given parenthetically in the text.

21. Virginia Woolf, "Mr. Bennett and Mrs. Brown," in *The Captain's Death Bed* (New York: Harcourt Brace, 1950), p. 96. Subsequent page numbers will be given parenthetically in the text.

22. Virginia Woolf, *A Room of One's Own* (Orlando, FL: Harcourt, 2005), p. 87. Subsequent page numbers will be given parenthetically in the text.

23. "Breaking the Sequence" became the title of an important study, Ellen G. Friedman and Miriam Fuchs's *Breaking the Sequence: Women's Experimental Fiction* (Princeton: Princeton University Press, 1989).

24. Virginia Woolf, *The Diary of Virginia Woolf*, vol. II, *1920–1924*, ed. A. O. Bell, assisted by A. McNeillie (New York: Harcourt Brace Jovanovich, 1978), p. 263.

25. Virginia Woolf, "A Sketch of the Past," in *Moments of Being: Unpublished Autobiographical Writings*, ed. J. Schulkind (New York: Harcourt Brace Jovanovich, 1976), p. 73.

26. Jane Marcus compares this work to Woolf's *Orlando* and Sylvia Townsend Warner's *Lolly Willowes* (1926), all within a fantasy genre in "A Wilderness of One's Own: Feminist Fantasy Novels of the Twenties – Rebecca West and Sylvia Townsend-Warner," in *Women Writers and the City*, ed. S. M. Squier (Knoxville: University of Tennessee Press, 1984), pp. 134–60.

27. During the early 1920s she wrote *Asphodel* (first published 1992), which laid the groundwork for *Bid Me to Live*. It experiments with repetition and narrative position and has formal kinship to Richardson and Stein. In 1927 she turned to its prequel *HERmione* (published 1981).

28. Djuna Barnes, *Nightwood* (New York: New Directions, 1961), p. 11.

29. Issues of fascism emerge as early as *Mrs. Dalloway*, according to some scholars. See M. Palowski, ed., *Virginia Woolf and Fascism: Resisting the Dictators' Seduction* (Basingstoke: Palgrave, 2001).

30. Virginia Woolf, *Three Guineas* (Orlando, FL: Harcourt, 2006), p. 126.

31. Virginia Woolf, *Between the Acts* (San Diego: Harcourt Brace Jovanovich, 1969), p. 189.

32. Elizabeth Bowen, Preface to *The Death of the Heart* (New York: Knopf, 1975), p. vii.

33. A. Bennett and N. Royle, *Elizabeth Bowen and the Dissolution of the Novel: Still Lives* (New York: St. Martin's Press, 1994), p. xix.

34. Maud Ellmann, *Elizabeth Bowen: The Shadow across the Page* (Edinburgh: Edinburgh University Press, 2003), p. 5.

2

MIRANDA HICKMAN

Modernist women poets and the problem of form

In *A Room of One's Own*, Woolf articulated the famous claim now so familiar that regrettably, it has lost some of its former luster and edge: "For we think back though our mothers if we are women."[1] Alicia Ostriker suggests that Woolf's claim compels in part because of her "mysterious" invented verb – we wonder what it is to "'think back'" through "something, another person, a set of people."[2] I would add that Woolf's verb also elicits the question of what it is to "think through" something or someone at all. In our time, as Ostriker suggests, it is the women writers of Woolf's own modernist generation through whom writers and critics, women and men, can now "think back." In 1986, Ostriker was reiterating with a difference what Woolf had emphasized in 1929: that it was "difficult to discover who our mothers are, much less think through them, thanks to a long history of criticism ... that veils them from us."[3] Fortunately, a wealth of watershed feminist recuperative criticism of the past three decades has now brought to wide critical awareness the women "makers of modernism," "forgotten" by mid-twentieth-century chronicles of modernism's development,[4] and has argued convincingly for their centrality to modernist practice. Thanks to pioneering critics such as Ostriker herself, Susan Stanford Friedman, Shari Benstock, and Rachel Blau DuPlessis,[5] we can now easily survey a canon of modernist women writers, think through them, and reconsider what they themselves thought by way of – in Woolf's formulation, "what food" sustained these "women as artists."[6]

Although Woolf highlights women predecessors who could offer such sustenance, deflecting the possibility that "great men writers" could do so, and while clearly these modernist women writers did draw upon female forerunners,[7] this chapter addresses ways in which modernist women also importantly thought by way of theories, movements, standards, and techniques closely associated with male contemporaries and near contemporaries, and accordingly, themselves came to be understood by way of ideas linked to their male comrades-in-art.[8] Addressing Mina

Loy, H. D., Marianne Moore, and Canadian modernist poet P. K. Page, this chapter highlights modernist women poets and their poetic form, but the contours of the arguments here could be used to trace the development of many modernist women fiction writers as well.

Responding to ideas and techniques connected with male modernists, in some cases "adapting them" to their own use,[9] shaped the careers of these modernist women poets and helped them to solve, or at least resolve upon provisional solutions to, a problem central to literary modernism 1910–45: finding poetic form adequate both to a new modern era and to modern efforts to challenge prevailing aesthetic and socio-political habits. This is what I mean by the pivotal modernist "problem of form." And the formal solutions these women poets advanced often carried important feminist ideological freight. Their engagements with male compatriots and the ideas associated with them often brought them greater recognition and legibility. But these engagements also came at a cost. In some cases, this price arose during their careers, as their work was misunderstood as a result of their contact with male contemporaries and/or techniques linked with them; and in some instances their reputations sustained trouble posthumously, as their associations with male moderns brought them in for misreadings, disparagement, or suspicion of complicity with forces that had kept women writers at the margins of modernism. This chapter explores the consequences of some of these engagements, consequences which can still hamper understanding of their poetic innovations. To overcome this pattern of compromised understanding, we might reread these costly interchanges so as to find ways to navigate more attentively through their poetic practice – focusing on areas of their poetry illuminated by their reckonings with ideas linked to prominent male moderns of their time.

In Loy's case, the early twentieth-century avant-garde movement of Italian Futurism, as exemplified by its leader, F. T. Marinetti, galvanized Loy in 1913–14 into a new modernist phase of her career, beyond the Pre-Raphaelite practice of her early days,[10] and offered both impetus and vital lexical, rhetorical, and conceptual resources for her work. Clearly indebted to Futurist typographical play and emphasis on the genre of the manifesto, for instance, are Loy's "Aphorisms on Futurism" (1914), her first published piece, and "Feminist Manifesto" (written 1914), published posthumously among Roger Conover's excellent collections of Loy's work from 1982 and 1996.[11] In 1914, Loy reported to Mabel Luhan being in the "throes of conversion" to Futurism;[12] that same year, she admitted to Carl Van Vechten having caught "war fever" from the bellicose Futurists.[13] Though she would shortly abandon Futurism, later skewering both Futurist men and ideas in satirical poems such as "Three Moments in Paris" (1914),

"The Effectual Marriage" (1915), and "Lions' Jaws" (1920), Loy would afterward acknowledge the Futurists' stimulating impact: to Luhan, she noted: "I am indebted to [Marinetti] for twenty years added to my life from mere contact with his exuberant personality."[14] Loy had clearly been compelled by Futurist challenges to cultural passéism as well as by their calls for a revitalization of language through *"parole in libertà"* – words in freedom.[15] Loy's commitment to dynamism also unmistakably shows Futurist influence, though Ellen Stauder reads Loy's Futurist-inspired dynamism as superseding the Futurist habit of conceptualizing objects and selves as grounded in stable essences with a more radical vision of objects and selves in process.[16]

As Elisabeth Frost notes, however, "Loy's brief immersion in Futurism clearly reveals the difficulty women experienced in forming alliances with the prominent figures – and philosophies – of avant-garde movements of the 1910s and 1920s."[17] Loy's brief infatuation with Futurist dynamism, bombastic rhetoric, charismatic masculinity, satirical technique, and the manifestic genre that, as Marjorie Perloff notes, the Futurists honed to an art form,[18] spurs critics who trace Futurism's imprint on Loy's work to insist on clarifying her complex relationship to Futurism – involving attraction, ambivalence, and eventual rejection – and in many cases to attempt to clear her from the charge of complicity with the Futurists' notorious endorsement of violence and "scorn for woman."[19] Biographer Carolyn Burke and critics such as Arnold, Kouidis, and Frost demonstrate how Loy's techniques escape Futurist misogyny and contribute to feminist work; they also emphasize Loy's later repudiation of the militarism she temporarily embraced, which "Psycho-Democracy" (1920) makes especially evident.[20]

But the effort to differentiate Loy's work from Futurism, while important, should not occlude how Loy's ambivalent responses to the Futurists shed important light on her work and thought – first, on the contours of her particular variety of feminism. Although Loy in later years clearly rejected Futurist militarism and misogyny, her early feminism exhibits Futurist-inspired conceptual and rhetorical aggression, together with a scorn for both images of women circulating in her culture and the ways that women sometimes conformed to these (see, for instance, "Feminist Manifesto," "Three Moments in Paris," and "The Effectual Marriage"). While Loy's textual signals often leave ambiguous how much irony to impute to her speakers, the critique in "Feminist Manifesto" of the restricted range of cultural roles available to women is clearly Loy's as well as the narrator's. Moreover, although – as Perloff stresses – Loy's experimental linguistic techniques both depart from and critique Marinetti's,[21] awareness of the inspiration Loy took both from Marinetti's theorizations of *parole in libertà* and the Futurist "typographical revolution"[22] illuminates techniques that became keynotes of Loy's poetic form – such as shouting capital letters, heterodox intralinear spacing that introduces unexpected gaps between words, and aposiopesis signaled through dashes. Like the prose of Stein (Loy's admiration for whom was reciprocated: see Loy's poem and essay on Stein, both entitled "Gertrude Stein," and Stein's praise of Loy in *The Autobiography of Alice B. Toklas*), Loy's work disrupts ordinary readerly procedures to stimulate new ways of processing language and thus, in Loy's view, new modes of consciousness. The staged interruptions of Loy's poetry, fostering readerly pauses, also contribute to the interrogative impact of her work: they invite readers to question statements advanced just before spatially induced caesurae.

And all this, in turn, generates Loy's signature effects of irony – deriving from readerly awareness of Loy's, and often also the speaker's, glittering ironic distance from received ideas, conventional practices, and traditional pieties. Also contributing to this effect is Loy's often outrageously heterodox diction – for instance, mischievously outlandish words (e.g. "sialagogues" and "mollescent" from "The Effectual Marriage") and ungainly abstract nouns, the latter of which read as a campy overwriting of the abstraction she regarded as a hallmark of Futurist discourse. In a review of 1918, Ezra Pound famously praised Loy's poetry for its "logopoeia," which he defined as "the dance of the intellect among words":[23] I would suggest that Loy's conjured perspective of wittily critical, often feminist, distance from common understandings and usages creates this effect of agile intellect. And as Elisabeth Frost notes, "like the other avant-gardists of her day" – and importantly guided by the Futurist example – "Loy believed that altering language could alter consciousness, thus changing identity itself." As a result, as Megan Simpson observes, Loy's "poetic innovations ... are inseparable from the feminist concerns that inform her entire writing project."[24] Accordingly, Loy's Futurist-inspired poetic form, and not only her Futuristic aggression and disdain for women as they were constructed in her environment, provided her with crucial wherewithal for staging feminist irony, and thus for her feminist promotion of transformations of consciousness.

H. D., meanwhile, is inevitably situated in critical commentary with respect to the poetic movement of Imagism, which emerged a few years after Futurism to become the earliest modernist movement in the Anglo-American context and, *pace* Hugh Kenner's dismissive assessment, remains widely read as germinal for later modernist poetry.[25] And H. D.'s association with Imagism, which has engendered many misunderstandings of her work, derived from her relationship to Ezra Pound. In London just before the First World War, Imagism was spearheaded by Pound in his by then typical role of avant-garde impresario – chiefly, he noted later, to gain H. D.'s work a hearing.[26] In January 1913, the first work framed as Imagist appeared in the pages of Harriet Monroe's *Poetry*, the journal instrumental to the development of many modernist careers, sparking awareness of the new movement and luring poet Amy Lowell from Boston to London to join this new band of experimentalists.

Although those involved with Imagism (others in the movement's nucleus included Richard Aldington and F. S. Flint) did not always agree on the movement's central tenets, their shared commitment to concise language, preference for concrete sensory particulars over abstract language, experiment with free verse and the examples of Japanese and Chinese poetry, and interest in conveying emotion indirectly by way of poetic images rather than lyric statement established a repertoire crucial to the development of modern poetry in ensuing years. Recently, commentators such as Pondrom and Kaufmann have credited H. D., rather than Pound, with providing the movement's aesthetic wellspring: Pound, they maintain, would not have known how to proceed, theoretically or practically, had H. D.'s austere free verse not shown him how.[27] As a result, we might read H. D.'s Imagism as neither revision of nor rejoinder to Pound's, but rather as an alternative non-Poundian way of playing out the possibilities of the repertoire of poetic techniques that have come to be encompassed by the Imagist moniker – a way that, even recently, has been misconstrued because of the tendency to define Imagism according to Pound's Imagist poems and theoretical commentary[28] and then to equate H. D.'s techniques with his. What Pound constructed as inspired by H. D., in other words, was not what she herself developed.

After the Imagist period 1912–17, the frequent critical reiteration of H. D.'s association with Imagism (despite her own many efforts to shed it) meant, on the one hand, that in many quarters she remained understood as merely Pound's protégé – the minor poet whom his scrawled flourish under her poems in the British Museum tea room ("*H. D., Imagiste*") catapulted to limited fame; and on the other, that critics either did not recognize, or would not validate, the ways in which H. D. later surpassed the Imagism of her first poetic collection, *Sea Garden* (1916). Fortunately, feminist criticism of the past thirty years has brought serious critical attention to H. D.'s later work such as her long poem, *Trilogy* (1944–6), written out of the circumstances of the Second World War, whose techniques H. D. herself stressed superseded the Imagist mode.[29] Feminist recuperative work has also featured H. D.'s epic *Helen in Egypt* (1961), in which, through revisionary mythmaking, H. D. transmutes received accounts of Helen of Troy toward a pacifist cultural vision. And beginning with Friedman's *Penelope's Web*, criticism has reckoned in illuminating ways with H. D.'s wealth of experimental prose fiction, much of it in autobiographical *romans à clef* written from the 1920s onward, in which, as Robert Spoo claims, H. D. develops a distinctive form of *écriture féminine*.[30] With its many repetitions, wealth of unexpectedly placed commas, abundance of wordplay and imagery, and ruminative circling, H. D.'s prose displays many of the same techniques as her later poetry.

But this turn to H. D.'s later work, to move her out of the "tiny and tidy Imagism box,"[31] should not preclude subtler understanding of her important early Imagist work. I should like to focus on one crucial aspect of H. D.'s early Imagist poetics that has not received sufficient recognition. My students often note the sense of disturbance that H. D.'s poems of *Sea Garden* create: either through the urgent supplication of her speakers, often pleading with absent god-figures (as in "Sea Gods"), or through scenes depicted, we are prompted to imagine violent force being visited upon a site. H. D. conjures rough weather affecting her featured seaside flowers by way of verbs connoting physical violence ("marred," "torn," "slashed"); gods appealed to will demonstrate their magnificence by "break[ing]" their adversaries ("Sea Gods"); her impressive "Storm" in the poem of the same name "crashes" and "crack[s] the live branch" (2); her speaker in "Sheltered Garden" calls for violent wind to destroy the realm in which the "life" of flowers and fruit (and by implication of the tropes used here, women) is "choke[d] out" (42). Through engagement with Imagism, H. D. develops a poetics of the sublime that features transformative violence – and in keeping with the discourse of the sublime, codes this violence as a welcome avenue toward renewal and greater knowledge. The positive coding of such poetically conjured violence is obvious in early poems such as "Sheltered Garden"; and other early poems such as "Envy" and "Eros" (also written in 1916, though not published in *Sea Garden*) likewise elevate violence. These poems associate violence with the power of love ("love must first shatter us," "Eros" VI, 21) and valorize god and goddess figures who have the power to destroy humans ("So the goddess has slain me," "Envy," IV, 1). Her early poems also valorize violence by implicitly praising its yield: though her flowers subjected to storms are "marred," they thereby become extraordinary blooms, proven capable of survival, and elevated by the system of value pervading her early poetry. Thus despite H. D.'s overt repudiation of the warlike commitments of many of her avant-garde male modernist cohorts in the 1910s, which she registers in an unpublished review in 1916 at the time of *Sea Garden*'s publication,[32] H. D. develops a rhetoric of violence out of her early Imagist work that continues in later work – recurring in late prose works such as the novella *Nights* (1935) and even appearing in the first portion of *Trilogy*, in the service of the poem's search for ways to redeem the destruction of war.

One might read such poetic violence as inscribing the experience of trauma, which H. D. certainly knew well through what she suffered during the First World War: the stillbirth of her child, the infidelity of her husband, the deaths of her brother and father. However it is related to the violence of the external environment that H. D. encountered, this poetics of sublime violence should be recognized as integral to H. D.'s Imagist poetics, and as important to what differentiates her Imagism from that of Pound and other Imagists. Pound's poem "Liu Ch'e," with its "wet leaf that clings to the threshold," exhibits what has come to be known as the signature Imagist metaphoric work: equating a complex emotional and intellectual condition ("an intellectual and emotional complex in an instant of time") with a sensory experience, often of a "natural object," and thus fostering a rich understanding of that multifoliate state.[33] The work of H. D.'s Imagist poems is different. To adapt Ostriker's comments on *Trilogy*, H. D.'s Imagist poems importantly perform the "work of persuasion,"[34] persuading us of the need for, and benefits of, an emancipatory transformation and the values it will serve, and doing so in part by imagining violence that answers cultural violence. H. D.'s sublime Imagist poetics responds to problems posed by a war-riven modern society that subjects women to various forms of cultural violence: her feminist poetic aims to help readers imagine their way out of such societal violence.

If H. D.'s case gestures toward the many women in modernist circles who engaged in sustained and complex relationships with Ezra Pound, at both gain and cost to their work and reputations (see Jayne Marek's *Women Editing Modernism*, especially the final chapter, for useful remarks on the dynamics between Pound and many women),[35] it is Marianne Moore's generative relationship with T. S. Eliot that I should like to feature next. As Celeste Goodridge notes, Eliot was an early admirer of Moore's work, offering in 1921, even before the *succès fou* of *The Waste Land* (1922) that assured his position as poetic and critical heavyweight, to bring out an edition of her poems. At this point, she would protest that her *oeuvre* was too scant to merit such a volume; but Goodridge observes that even by this time, Moore valued Eliot's temperament and critical standards, reading them as akin to her own.[36] Eliot's comparable offer in the mid-1930s to support her *Selected Poems* (1935), at a point when he had come to wield much more cultural influence than she (at this juncture, she readily accepted) would raise her stature to a new level. The Introduction by Eliot would have enormous impact on how Moore's poetry was understood,[37] putting into circulation a set of ideas through which Moore's work would be "thought" for years afterward: he praised her for having contributed to the "small body of durable poetry written in our time" with her "original sensibility," "alert intelligence," and "deep feeling."[38]

Although the version of Moore conjured by Eliot usefully foregrounds many aspects of Moore's poetics, it crystallizes an image of Moore that, even today, may stand in the way of recognition of her range. Eliot suggests that Moore's demanding poetry is best appreciated by those whose "alert intelligence" matches hers. Laudable also is her "reticent" "sensibility," which generates a poetic that takes objects of the natural world – flora and fauna – as the "best release for the major emotions" (9). For Eliot, such reticence indicates welcome sensitivity, marking those who can feel, fortunately, in ways apart from those generally "accepted" (9). Although he makes no explicit mention of it, we cannot but detect the resonance with the very personal idea foundational to his famous "Impersonal theory of poetry" from "Tradition and the Individual Talent": "only those who have ... emotions know what it is to want to escape from these things."[39] He implies that Moore's "reticent" "sensibility" is kindred to his own, bespeaks "deep feeling," and gives rise to the kind of impersonal poetic he admires. He also credits Moore with "startling" readers into attending to objects they would not ordinarily notice – and praises the skill and "elegance" of her "complicated, formal patterns" that courageously buck the early twentieth-century free verse trend (10).

Even if we decide not to question the validity of these comments or the standards underwriting them, or not to read in them a desire to tame Moore into an unthreatening tidy spinster (my students tell me that the Cynthia Ozick era of Eliot-bashing is past), Eliot's observations still miss a great deal of what Moore's poetry offers. Eliot's influential remarks helped to sustain the myth of Moore as "elegant" and "discreet" that played a considerable part in her approval by many male contemporaries and still circulates today; they also contributed to the occlusion of important aspects of her poetic.[40] Accordingly, today we might reread Eliot's powerful comments, acknowledge how thinking through them has affected, and perhaps in some cases adversely limited, views of Moore's poetry, and use them anew to highlight her poetry's dominant characteristics. Eliot's term "reticent," for instance, challenges us to ask how well this characterization accommodates the lavish, even byzantine, inventories of Moore's major poems such as "The Steeple-Jack," "The Jerboa," and "Marriage." Perhaps because of his investment in the image of Moore as gentle scientist fascinated by the world's tiny cells, Eliot does not recognize the at times breathtakingly weird tentacular energy of Moore's poems, as they race metonymically away from their putative central subjects in what feels like a burst of intellectual adrenaline: like the strawberry plant invoked in the opening line of "Nevertheless," they seem to run underground and surface at unexpected places. (And this they do even if one does not factor in Moore's legendary bent for destabilizing revision of her poems.)[41] The "reticent" "sensibility" and "detail" Eliot stresses simply do not capture her sprawling associative catalogs, charged with the "gusto" she praised and the distinctive mobile energy suggested by what William Carlos Williams called her "anthologies of transit."[42] Eliot doesn't register her talent for spiky satire, as evinced in poems such as "To a Steam Roller," "He Wrote the History Book," or "Marriage." Emphasizing Moore's penchant for visual detail (8), he bypasses the way that the lofty aerial perspective and sometimes frenetic energy of her poems derives from massive collections of not visual, and not even always sensory, but rather often conceptual details. And importantly, when he credits her poems with powers of description, he does not note that, rather than stemming from a description of one environment, her copious details and quotations are gathered, magpie-style, from a bewildering array of disparate sources ("Marriage" provides an especially good example), the obscurity and occasional mundanity of which, I would suggest, implicitly thumb a nose at attemptedly magisterial displays of learned sources from other major moderns such as Eliot himself.

However, Eliot does emphasize Moore's "light rhyme" (10–11), a practice which provides an important inroad to her off-beat poetic of combined appreciation and critique, as well as her poetic exhortations – by way of form as well as theme – to acts of heightened attention. Light rhyme involves rhyming a stressed syllable with one of secondary stress, and as Eliot explains it, is a form of the practice whereby rhymes suggest a pattern of emphasis different from patterns signaled by a poem's sense and metrics: it involves rhyming, and thus stressing, syllables left less- or un-stressed by meter and/or sense. Eliot's spotlight on this practice in turn illuminates other techniques whereby Moore accords weight to that which otherwise isn't weighted. In particular, her syllabic meter generates lineation that then elevates syllables that ordinarily would remain unaccented or only slightly emphasized: for Moore, as for Woolf in "Modern Fiction," "the accent falls differently."[43] And this gives rise to Moore's implicit critique, by way of form, of ordinary patterns of emphasis, and her concomitant advocacy of alternative perspectives – which, cued by Woolf, I read as feminist. I would also suggest that, in addition to serving other objectives, Moore's circuitous poetic evokes a strategy of feminist dodging, wily avoidance of expectations that can often rush in on a woman, affecting how she is read and received, when she is positioned as this or that kind of female.

The work of major Canadian modernist poet P.K. Page links both to Eliot and back to Imagism as developed by Pound. Page published until almost the year of her death in 2010, but here I focus on her markedly modernist work of the 1940s and 1950s, written before a nearly decade-long period during which she published no new poetry. Page's work has been situated in the context of Canadian modernism by commentators such as Brian Trehearne and Dean Irvine:[44] her early work clearly emerged from a dialogue with techniques of poets by then marked as modernist – such as the Imagists, Eliot, and Auden – and reckoned with a problem of form that would become a signature problematic of late modernism: how to reconcile a bent for intricate Imagistic play, directed toward the articulation of heterodox perspectives, with a political commitment to social commentary that often called for more plainspoken poetic expression. Page encountered this generative problem in Montréal in the 1940s a few years after those British and American poets with whom it is closely associated (e.g. Auden, Pound, Muriel Rukeyser), during a decade that Brian Trehearne identifies as one of "modernist consolidation in Canadian literature."[45]

Page showed a predilection for modernist technique, especially in the way she amassed images in her poetry – conveying emotion and attitude through them rather than through direct statement, displaying the impact of Poundian Imagism – and in the way she guided her early poetry by T.S. Eliot's concepts of "impersonality" and the "objective correlative."[46] Like many Canadian contemporaries, Page contended with what Trehearne terms the "Imagist legacy" (60). And from the outset, Page's work with imagery, inflected with Eliotic-inspired impersonality, led her into some trouble. Page's reworking of Imagist strategy involved an abundance of images, introduced one after another, sometimes creating an effect of destabilizing rapid succession: as a result, her poems can feel choked with too many different, even incompatible or conflicting images. I think here of her famous poem about women office workers during wartime, "The Stenographers," appearing in *As Ten, as Twenty* (1946), and the later "Portrait of Marina," from *The Metal and the Flower* (1954).

But rather than regard this signature aesthetic of accumulation as a drawback, as did early commentators like John Sutherland and as have more recent critics such as Rosemary Sullivan (Sutherland suggested that Page's "overwhelming" "abundance of images" compromised her attempts at social commentary, and Sullivan reads her "capacity for image-making" as "eclips[ing] her capacity to generate sympathy for the subjects her portraits depict"),[47] I would credit Page with a valuably provocative post-Imagist technique of

Imagistic "extravagance"[48] that foregrounds the poet's effort to find a suitable Imagistic lexicon. This effect of restless artifice, even excessive fertility, can play productively into her poems' thematics: in "The Stenographers," the images contribute to a combined effect of feeling buffeted, not able to stay in any one perspective long enough, and feeling bottled in by too much. This, in turn, fosters understanding of the plight of the stenographers, themselves unable to hold on to anything for long, whether memories, the lunch hour, the "brief bivouac of Sunday" (1), or the soldiers who take them out for a quick joyride; and themselves overwhelmed by too many memories, tears, and unwelcome duties.

The way Page uses her arresting Imagism in "Portrait of Marina" permutes the technique to even more brilliant effect. As in many other early poems, here she uses images to capture, and critique, the plight of women in some way socially trapped, in this case a spinster daughter tyrannized by her seafarer father. In a climactic moment, the poem climbs to a startling array of organic and inorganic imagery (sun glinting on water, antlers, candelabra on which Marina's tears are "perilously hung" [40]) to capture the pain of the migraines from which Marina suffers, shooting from her "unlovely head" (38). By the time we reach the culminating statement, "too many mirrors dizzied her and broke" (48), we ourselves have been "dizzied" by a welter of disparate poetic images, a surfeit characteristic of Page. And as the images of breakage communicate Marina's brokenness, they break into our thought: the sudden coincidence between Marina's experience and our own commands our attention in a compelling moment of poetic empathy.

I frame the arguments about Page this way in order to reply to critical concerns about the costs of her Imagist-inspired imagery, as well as to concerns Page herself raised about how such startling images, rich and strange, threatened her poems' capacity to register the sympathy of a speaker for a subject portrayed and engender such sympathy in readers. In one of the last poems Page wrote before her silence, the self-critical "After Rain," she suggested that her propensity for being "seduced" by sights into producing "myriad images" stifled her capacity for feeling, indicating, or encouraging sympathy for her poetic subjects. But drawing upon the concept of surrealist force that many critics have attributed to Page's poetic,[49] I would emphasize the power of what happens in "Portrait of Marina." With the sudden weird flowering of the surrealist-accented Imagism, in a feminist move, Page elicits keen awareness of the sharp unbearability of Marina's pain. As with Loy, H. D., and Moore, we can use aspects of Page's work foregrounded by her associations with prominent male moderns – in her case Pound and Eliot – to move toward new ways of thinking about her poetic form and the projects it serves. Like the other modernist women poets addressed in this brief survey, Page enlists techniques closely associated with male moderns, here Imagism and impersonality, creating versions of them different from those of Pound and Eliot, toward her own strong solution to the modernist problem of form.

NOTES

1. Virginia Woolf, *A Room of One's Own and Three Guineas* (Oxford: Oxford University Press, 1992), p. 99.
2. Alicia Ostriker, "What Do Women Poets Want?: H. D. and Marianne Moore as Poetic Ancestresses," *Contemporary Literature* 27.4 (1986), 475–92.
3. *Ibid.*, 478.
4. For "the forgotten and silenced makers of modernism" see the dedication to Bonnie Kime Scott's anthology *The Gender of Modernism* (Bloomington: Indiana University Press, 1990), which surveys the work of women and men modernists, and which both registers and contributes to the feminist re-mappings of modernist canons.
5. For landmark examples of early feminist recuperative criticism leading up to Scott's anthology, see Susan Friedman's groundbreaking work on H. D., such as "Who Buried H. D.?: A Poet, Her Critics, and Her Place in 'The Literary Tradition,'" *College English* 36.7 (1975), 801–14; *Psyche Reborn: The Emergence of H. D.* (Bloomington: Indiana University Press, 1981); and *Penelope's Web: Gender, Modernity, H. D.'s Fiction* (Cambridge: Cambridge University Press, 1990). See also work on H. D. by Rachel Blau DuPlessis in *H. D.: The Career of that Struggle* (Sussex: Harvester, 1984); and Alicia Ostriker's commentary on H. D. in *Writing Like a Woman* (Ann Arbor: University of Michigan Press, 1980). Shari Benstock's magisterial *Women of the Left Bank* (Austin: University of Texas Press, 1986) surveys the activity of women modernists in Paris 1900–40 such as Djuna Barnes, Gertrude Stein, H. D., and Jean Rhys.
6. Woolf, *Room*, p. 68.
7. For commentary on the influence of Sappho on such women modernists as H. D. and Amy Lowell, for instance, see Susan Gubar, "Sapphistries," *Signs* 10.1 (1984), 43–62.
8. This chapter takes a cue from the landmark work of Sandra M. Gilbert and Susan Gubar in *No Man's Land*, vol. 1, *The War of the Words* (New Haven: Yale University Press, 1988), in which they describe the "battle of the sexes" they read as pervading the literary environment of the late nineteenth and early twentieth centuries. Building on their commentary on the "resentment with which such men as … T. S. Eliot, D. H. Lawrence, [and] Ernest Hemingway reacted to what they perceived as unprecedented female power" (p. 66) in modernist contexts, this chapter addresses the effects of how these women modernist poets, working out of the climate Gilbert and Gubar portray, made use of ideas closely associated with their male contemporaries.
9. Woolf, *Room*, p. 99.

10. Ellen Stauder, "The Irreducible Surplus of Abstraction: Mina Loy on Brancusi and the Futurists," in *Mina Loy: Woman and Poet*, ed. M. Shreiber and K. Tuma (Orono, ME: National Poetry Foundation, 1998), pp. 369–72, esp. p. 370.

11. Loy, *The Last Lunar Baedeker*, ed. Roger Conover (Charlotte, NC: Jargon Society, 1982); and *The Lost Lunar Baedeker*, ed. R. Conover (New York: Farrar, Straus, and Giroux, 1996).

12. Conover, ed., *Lost*, p. 180.

13. *Ibid.*, p. 179.

14. *Ibid.*, p. 180.

15. See F.T. Marinetti, "Destruction of Syntax – Imagination without Strings – Words in Freedom" (1913), in *Futurist Manifestos*, ed. U. Apollonio (Boston, MA: MFA Publications, 1970), pp. 95–106.

16. See Virginia Kouidis, *Mina Loy: American Modernist Poet* (Baton Rouge: Louisiana State University Press, 1980), pp. 56–7 and Stauder, "Irreducible," esp. p. 372.

17. Elisabeth Frost, *The Feminist Avant-Garde in American Poetry* (Iowa City: University of Iowa Press, 2003), p. 30.

18. Marjorie Perloff, *The Futurist Moment: Avant-Garde, Avant-Guerre, and the Language of Rupture* (Chicago: University of Chicago Press, 1986), ch. 3.

19. See Marinetti, "The Founding and Manifesto of Futurism 1909," in *Futurist Manifestos*, ed. Apollonio, p. 19.

20. See Carolyn Burke, *Becoming Modern: The Life of Mina Loy* (New York: Farrar, Straus, and Giroux, 1996); E. Arnold, "Mina Loy and the Futurists," *Sagetrieb* 8 (1989), 83–117; Frost, *The Feminist Avant-Garde*, ch. 2, esp. p. 31; Kouidis, *Mina Loy*; Stauder, "Irreducible," esp. p. 374. For commentary on Loy's relationship to Futurist eugenicist theories, see Aimee Pozorski, "Eugenicist Mistress and Ethnic Mother: Mina Loy and Futurism, 1913–1917," *MELUS* 30.3 (2005), 41–69.

21. Perloff, "English as a 'Second' Language," in *Mina Loy*, ed. Schreiber and Tuma, p. 137.

22. For the Futurist "typographical revolution," see Marinetti, "Destruction of Syntax," 95–106.

23. Ezra Pound, "A List of Books – 'Others [Anthology for 1917],'" *Little Review* 4 (March 1918), 54–8.

24. Frost, *The Feminist Avant-Garde*, p. 32; Megan Simpson, *Poetic Epistemologies: Gender and Knowing in Women's Language-Oriented Writing* (Albany: State University of New York Press, 2000), p. 52.

25. Hugh Kenner, *The Pound Era* (Berkeley: University of California Press, 1971), p. 173. For claims about Imagism's influence, see C. Pondrom, "H.D. and the Origins of Imagism," in *Signets*, ed. Susan Stanford Friedman and Rachel Blau DuPlessis (Madison: University of Wisconsin Press, 1990), p. 86; Louis Dudek, *The Theory of the Image in Modern Poetry* (St. John's: Memorial University of Newfoundland, 1981), p. 265; J. Gage, *In the Arresting Eye: The Rhetoric of Imagism* (Baton Rouge: Louisiana State University Press, 1981).

26. Kenner, *Pound Era*, p. 177.

27. See Pondrom, "Origins," pp. 85–109; and M. Kaufmann, "Gendering Modernism," in *Unmanning Modernism: Gendered Rereadings*, ed. E.J. Harrison and S. Peterson (Knoxville: University of Tennessee Press, 1997), pp. 59–72.

28. See Pound, "A Retrospect," in *The English Modernist Reader 1910–1930*, ed. P. Faulkner (Iowa City: University of Iowa Press, 1986), pp. 59–71.

29. See letter from H. D. to Norman Holmes Pearson, undated, 1943, in *Between History and Poetry: The Letters of H. D. and Norman Holmes Pearson*, ed. D. Hollenberg (Iowa City: University of Iowa Press, 1997), p. 31.

30. See Robert Spoo, "H. D. Prosed," in *The Future of Modernism*, ed. Hugh Witemeyer (Ann Arbor: University of Michigan Press, 1997), p. 202.

31. See Ostriker, *Writing Like a Woman*, p. 7.

32. H. D., "Responsibilities" (1916), *Agenda* 25.3–4 (1987–8), 51–3.

33. Pound, "A Retrospect," pp. 60, 65.

34. Alicia Ostriker, "No Rule of Procedure: The Open Poetics of H. D.," in *Signets*, ed. Friedman and DuPlessis, pp. 336–51.

35. Jayne Marek, *Women Editing Modernism: "Little" Magazines and Literary History* (Lexington: University Press of Kentucky, 1995).

36. Celeste Goodridge, *Hints and Disguises: Marianne Moore and Her Contemporaries* (Iowa City: University of Iowa Press, 1989), pp. 100–26, esp. pp. 101 and 116.

37. See S. Kineke, "T. S. Eliot, Marianne Moore, and the Gendered Operations of Literary Sponsorship," *Journal of Modern Literature* 21.1 (1997), 121–36.

38. T. S. Eliot, "Introduction," *Selected Poems* (London: Faber and Faber, 1935), p. 12. Subsequent references to pages from this work will be cited parenthetically in the text.

39. T. S. Eliot, "Tradition and the Individual Talent," in *Selected Prose of T. S. Eliot*, ed. Frank Kermode (New York: Harcourt Brace Jovanovich, 1975), pp. 38, 43.

40. For Moore as "elegant" and "discreet," see Adrienne Rich, "When We Dead Awaken: Writing as Re-Vision," *On Lies, Secrets, and Silence: Selected Prose 1966–1978* (New York and London: W. W. Norton, 1979), p. 39. For evidence of the admiration Moore enjoyed from male contemporaries, see C. Tomlinson, ed., *Marianne Moore: A Collection of Critical Essays* (New York: Prentice Hall, 1969); on Moore as "acceptably masculine," see Kineke, "Gendered Operations," 129.

41. Robin Schulze's scholarship valuably highlights the many versions of Moore's poems and the implications of her signature revisions.

42. Moore, "Humility, Concentration, and Gusto," *Predilections* (New York: Viking Press, 1955), pp. 12–20; and Williams, "Marianne Moore," *Dial* 78 (May 1925), 393–401.

43. Woolf, "Modern Fiction," in *Modernism*, ed. L. Rainey (Malden, MA: Blackwell, 2005), p. 898.

44. Brian Trehearne, *The Montreal Forties: Modernist Poetry in Transition* (Toronto: University of Toronto Press, 1999), pp. 41–105 and Dean Irvine, "The Two Giovannis: P. K. Page's Two Modernisms," *Journal of Canadian Studies* 38.1 (2004), 23–45.

45. Trehearne, *Montreal Forties*, p. 48.

46. See S. Djwa, "P. K. Page: A Portrait of the Artist as a Young Woman," *Journal of Canadian Studies* 38.1 (2004), 9–22, esp. 19.

47. John Sutherland, "P. K. Page and *Preview*," *First Statement* 1.6 (1942), 7–8; Rosemary Sullivan, "'A Size Larger Than Seeing': The Poetry of P. K. Page," *Canadian Literature* 79 (1978), 32–42.

48. For "extravagance," see M. Wilson, "Other Canadians and After," *Tamarack Review* 9 (1958), 77–92.

49. See Trehearne, "P. K. Page and Surrealism," *Journal of Canadian Studies* 38.1 (2004), 46–64.

3

PENNY FARFAN

Women's modernism
and performance

As a young journalist in New York in 1914, Djuna Barnes voluntarily underwent forcible feeding in order to write about the involuntary experiences of hunger-striking British suffragists. In "How It Feels to Be Forcibly Fed," she recalls being bound to the operating table and held down at the head, hips, and feet by three men while the doctor inserted the feeding apparatus through her nose; and although she states that "it is utterly impossible to describe the anguish" of the experience,[1] she proceeds to describe it with extraordinary vividness and power:

> If I, playacting, felt my being burning with revolt at this brutal usurpation of my own functions, how they who actually suffered the ordeal in its acutest horror must have flamed at the violation of the sanctuaries of their spirits.
>
> I saw in my hysteria a vision of a hundred women in grim prison hospitals, bound and shrouded on tables just like this, held in the rough grip of callous warders while white-robed doctors thrust rubber tubing into the delicate interstices of their nostrils and forced into their helpless bodies the crude fuel to sustain the life they longed to sacrifice.[2]

In summing up her experience, Barnes observes, "For me it was an experiment. It was only tragic in my imagination. But it offered sensations sufficiently poignant to compel comprehension of certain of the day's phenomena."[3]

Most often regarded as an example of Barnes's "stunt" journalism, along the lines of her reports on being hugged by a gorilla and rescued by a fireman,[4] "How It Feels to Be Forcibly Fed" has received little attention from performance historians. With its self-conscious use of theatrical discourse, however, and as a striking example of "performative journalism,"[5] Barnes's article encapsulates many of the dimensions, strategies, and concerns that characterize the intersection of women's modernism and performance and thus serves as a useful starting point for this chapter.

"Playacting" / identification / politics / community

Barnes was not a suffragist, but "playacting" at being one caused her to experience very real "sensations" that "compel[led] comprehension of certain of the day's phenomena" – specifically, militant suffragism, but also the less topical, more fundamental relationship between gender and power. In an early study of the work of Henrik Ibsen as exemplary of new trends in modern drama, George Bernard Shaw wrote:

> In the new plays, the drama arises through a conflict of unsettled ideas rather than through vulgar attachments, rapacities, generosities, resentments, ambitions, misunderstandings, oddities and so forth as to which no moral question is raised. The conflict is not between clear right and wrong: the villain is as conscientious as the hero, if not more so: in fact, the question that makes the play interesting (when it *is* interesting) is which is the villain and which the hero. Or, to put it another way, there are no villains and no heroes.[6]

Gay Gibson Cima has pointed out that the moral ambiguity of modern drama posed significant challenges to the performers who brought it to life onstage: in contrast to their work in nineteenth-century melodrama, for example, early actors in Ibsen's drama "had to keep an open mind toward their characters' morality" and "be able to understand (if not necessarily to accept) what was sometimes an unconventional, and perhaps even an unacceptable, evaluation of a character's guilt and responsibility."[7] Literalizing acting theorist and director Constantin Stanislavski's notion of the "magic if"[8] – what would I do, how would I feel in a particular character's given circumstances? – Barnes's "experiment" with "playacting" generated genuine feelings of pain, outrage, and violation. In a 1908 essay on Sarah Bernhardt, Virginia Woolf speculated that "each part [an actress] plays deposits its own small contribution upon her unseen shape."[9] One such "deposit" is evident in "How It Feels to Be Forcibly Fed," in which, through her visceral account of her experience, Barnes attempts to bring her readers to a similar state of identification, representing even her own voluntary submission to forcible feeding as a kind of rape of body and spirit and, in doing so, raising questions about the moral authority of a legal system that would allow such treatment of imprisoned women and about the purported criminality of militant suffrage activism relative to such legally sanctioned violation.

The moral ambiguity that Barnes pointed toward, that Shaw regarded as characteristic of modern drama in the Ibsen tradition, and that challenged easy identifications on the part of performers and spectators alike is evident in the work of many modernist women playwrights. In Gwen Pharis

Ringwood's *Still Stands the House* (1938), for example, in which a portrait of a dead father presides over the stage action in a way that is reminiscent of Ibsen's *Hedda Gabler* (1890), the middle-aged, unmarried Hester has devoted her life to housekeeping for her widowed father and to raising her motherless younger brother on the family's isolated western Canadian farm. When she learns that her brother, to whom their father has left the farm, plans to sell it and move closer to town, she descends into murderous madness. Unable to accept her brother's unilateral decision, which she sees as the negation of the purpose of her dutiful life, she contrives to send him and his pregnant wife out to meet their deaths in a bitter prairie blizzard. In the play's final image, Hester sits alone onstage, entombed in the cold, still house as it is shrouded by snow, at once pitiable in her predicament as a woman with no control over her own destiny in a male-dominated world and monstrous in the act to which that predicament has driven her.

In Sophie Treadwell's 1928 play *Machinal*, real-life murderer Ruth Snyder, convicted with her lover of killing her husband, is transformed into a generic everywoman figure – "an ordinary young woman, any woman"[10] – while expressionist dramaturgical and theatrical techniques are deployed to draw spectators into the subjective experience that might lead to such an action. For example, Young Woman's thoughts about her unappealing and unloved future husband's interest in her are expressed in an increasingly desperate stream-of-consciousness monologue – "George H. Jones – Fat hands – flabby hands – don't touch me – please – fat hands are never weary – please don't – married – all girls – most girls – married – babies" – and Treadwell's stage directions call for "the sound of steel riveting" as the lights dim on Young Woman's honeymoon night.[11]

Susan Glaspell's *Trifles* (1916) is also concerned with a woman who commits murder, but in this case, the killer, Mrs. Wright, never actually appears on stage. Instead, the play centers on Mrs. Hale and Mrs. Peters, who visit the farm house where the crime has occurred and piece together what happened through their sympathetic engagement with the objects of Mrs. Wright's domestic life – the "trifles" that the male investigators regard as unimportant as they search for a motive that would incriminate Mrs. Wright in the murder of her husband. Choosing not to reveal what they discover on the grounds that John Wright's abuse of his wife drove her to murder and that her life with him has been punishment enough, Mrs. Hale and Mrs. Peters become in effect the "jury of her peers" (as Glaspell entitled a 1917 short story adapted from the play) that would be unavailable to Mrs. Wright in the male-dominated court of law in which she faces trial. In this way, *Trifles* dramatizes the formation of a proto-feminist community that raises questions about the justice of the legal system.

In Glaspell's play, personal identification becomes the basis for political action, however covert, while Barnes's "How It Feels to Be Forcibly Fed" resonated in its performative dimensions with the spectacular activism of the suffrage campaign with its rallies, demonstrations, parades, pageants, and plays, among them *Votes for Women* (1907) by former Ibsen actress Elizabeth Robins. In Robins's play, the protagonist Vida Levering is a revisionist version of the conventional figure of the "woman with a past"[12] in that her personal experience of unwed pregnancy and illegal abortion has given rise to her passionately committed suffrage activism. *Votes for Women* includes a suffrage rally scene similar to an actual rally that Robins herself attended and that converted her to the suffrage cause; and this staged rally, during which the speakers address the audience within the play and, through them, the theatre audience, made explicit the theatre's potential as a forum for political debate.

A number of other suffrage plays followed *Votes for Women*, but modernist women writers put drama to work in the service of other political causes as well. Edna St. Vincent Millay's *Aria da Capo*, for example, premiered in 1919 in the aftermath of the First World War and was described by reviewer Alexander Woollcott as "a study of heart-breaking tragedy considered as an interlude between the laughters of fluffy satiric comedy."[13] The play begins with a scene of frivolous banter between stock comic characters Pierrot and Columbine, but is then interrupted by Cothurnus, Masque of Tragedy, who forces two young shepherds to engage, against their initial friendly impulses, in a squabble over territory and resources that leads them ultimately to kill each other. When Pierrot and Columbine return to the stage and ask for the dead bodies to be removed before they resume their comic play, Cothurnus advises them to "hide them from the house, / And play the farce. The audience will forget."[14] Woollcott wrote of the ending of Millay's "bitterly ironic" play, with its return to the beginning – the "*aria da capo*" to which the title refers – "And so on and so on, as the curtain slowly falls, the same old idle chatter, over and over again, forgetful of the dead youths lying there under the table."[15] Brenda Murphy has noted that Millay updated the traditional forms of the Harlequinade and the pastoral dialogue by modernizing Pierrot and Columbine's costumes and making comic references to cubism and atonal music, and that, in doing so, she "established the context of modernity."[16] As a result, in Woollcott's view, "no mother from a gold-starred home, who saw the war come and go like a grotesque comet and who now hears the rattlepated merriment of her neighbors all the more distinctly because of the blank silence in her own impoverished home – surely no such mother will quite miss the point of 'Aria da Capo.'"[17]

Another aspect of modernist women's use of the theatre for political ends was enacted in the work of Lady Augusta Gregory as folklorist, playwright, founding member of the Irish Literary Theatre (1899–1901), and co-founder in 1903 and a director for many years of the Irish National Theatre Society, which became known as the Abbey Theatre in 1904. In Gregory's assessment of her contribution to Irish politics:

> though Ireland is always with me, and I first feared and then became reconciled to, and now hope to see even a greater independence than Home Rule, my saying has been long, "I am not fighting for it, but preparing for it." And that has been my purpose in my work for establishing a National Theatre, and for the revival of the language, and in making better known the heroic tales of Ireland.[18]

In a play such as *The Rising of the Moon* (1907), then, Gregory's nationalism was expressed not only in her sympathetic portrayal of an escaped Fenian who is aided in his evasion of capture by a police sergeant who was a nationalist in his youth, but in her incorporation of rebel ballads and her deployment of a dialect she called "Kiltartan," by which she attempted to translate into English the speech patterns and characteristics of spoken Irish.

Whereas Gregory's plays supported a nationalist cultural agenda, Georgia Douglas Johnson used drama to address the issue of lynching in the American South. In her play *Safe* (c. 1929), for example, an African American woman gives birth to a baby boy just as an offstage mob lynches a young black man for standing up to his boss in a dispute about wages. Hearing the victim cry out for his mother as he is dragged to his death, Liza chooses to kill her newborn son in order to keep him "safe – safe from the lynchers!"[19] Although the government-sponsored Federal Theatre Project's director Hallie Flanagan stated at the inception of the program in 1935 that the theatre "must become conscious of the implications of the changing social order,"[20] one of the FTP's readers wrote in a report on *Safe* that "the glaring weakness of utter exaggeration is too bright – and it fails not because the idea is not dramatic, but because it follows from an absurdity – that they lynch Negro boys 'Down South' for defending themselves from thieves. In fact, the crime that produces lynching is vastly fouler."[21] As Winona Fletcher has remarked, "Clearly this reader [had] fallen victim to the myth that 'only rape produced lynching down South' and expect[ed] the playwright to protect this myth by ignoring the truth."[22] Along with Johnson's other anti-lynching plays, *Safe* remained unpublished and unproduced during her lifetime.

The example of Johnson points toward the importance and complexity of community for modernist women playwrights and theatre artists. Djuna

Barnes's exposure to the suffrage movement through her work on "How It Feels to Be Forcibly Fed" undoubtedly contributed to the feminist and queer insights that informed her later work, including such plays as *The Dove* (1923) and *To the Dogs* (1923), but it is also worth noting that Barnes was a member of the Provincetown Players (1915–22), a small but highly influential non-commercial theatre company that was formed to foster the development of American drama. Closely associated with the rise to prominence of playwright Eugene O'Neill, the Provincetown Players also included not only Barnes but Glaspell, Millay, Treadwell, and many other women who were integrally involved in all areas of theatre production. As Cheryl Black has observed of the company's early years, "At a time when women playwrights were rare, women directors rarer, and women scenic designers nearly unheard of, Provincetown's female membership excelled in all these functions."[23] This unprecedented involvement of women in all aspects of the company's operations, Black suggests, fostered an atmosphere of receptiveness to women's ideas and support for women's work that made it "perhaps the most important platform for feminist drama in America before the 1960s."[24]

In London, the Pioneer Players (1911–20), founded by director/designer Edith Craig, provided a similar forum for women's work in all areas of theatre production. Notably, such key company members as Craig, Christopher St. John, and Cicely Hamilton had previously been involved in staging suffrage drama, and although the company's mandate was not restricted to feminist issues but was instead "to produce plays dealing with all kinds of movements of interest at the moment" and "to assist social, political, and other Societies by providing them with plays as a means of raising funds,"[25] it staged a number of plays by women, including, for example, St. John's *The First Actress* and Hamilton's *Jack and Jill and a Friend* in 1911, and Glaspell's *Trifles* in 1919 and *The Verge* during a brief revival of the company in 1925.

Such enabling connections among women modernists engaged in playwriting, theatre production, and performance were not limited to political causes and cultural organizations, but transpired through social and personal networks as well. For example, Georgia Douglas Johnson's home in Washington, DC was a gathering place for writers of the Harlem Renaissance, including playwrights Angelina Weld Grimké and Zora Neale Hurston, while Natalie Barney's salon in Paris was a venue for the presentation of works by such modernist writers as Barnes and Gertrude Stein, as well as dance artist Isadora Duncan. In a less direct, more circuitous network of productive affiliation, Ringwood, based in and writing about western Canada, found inspiration in the work of Gregory and other Irish playwrights of the early twentieth century. As she later recalled, "The Irish theatres' depiction of the fisherfolk, the farmers, the myth and history and political conflict of a non-urban and non-industrial people had a relevance to my own experience and life that was not apparent in the London and Broadway plays that I read."[26] Ringwood's interest in Irish drama was undoubtedly sparked in part by her exposure to the American little theatre and folk drama movements through her graduate studies at the Carolina Playmakers School at the University of North Carolina at Chapel Hill, where she wrote *Still Stands the House*. These movements had themselves been influenced by the Abbey Theatre's tour of the United States in 1911, so that Alain Locke, as a leading advocate of African American drama, stated in 1925, "Harlem has the same role to play for the New Negro as Dublin has had for the New Ireland."[27]

Such "tangling," as Bonnie Kime Scott has called the "rich set of connections and common concerns" among late nineteenth- and early twentieth-century writers and artists, has contributed to the expansion of the field of modernist studies beyond its conventional periodization and style to encompass a more varied range of responses to modernity.[28] In theatre and performance studies, this tangling has problematized easy distinctions between, for example, the sentimentalism of *Votes for Women*, the folk realism of *The Rising of the Moon*, *Trifles*, *Safe*, and *Still Stands the House*, and more formally experimental works such as *Aria da Capo* and *Machinal*.

Representation / parody / presence

Noting Barnes's self-reflexive concern both with performance and with the gender dynamics of looking and being looked at, Barbara Green has suggested that "How It Feels to Be Forcibly Fed" is as much about "the issue of representation" as it is about suffrage activism.[29] A concern with exposing the politics of representation and reworking dominant representational conventions distinguishes Barnes's *To the Dogs*, as well. The dramatic action of the play is framed by the female character Helena Hucksteppe posing with her back to the audience, but whereas Joan Retallack has observed that *To the Dogs* "seems to be symbolically guarded from development by [this] sentinel posture,"[30] Helena's pose functions as a refusal of the mastering gaze not only of the male character Gheid Storm but also of theatre audiences accustomed to traditional conventions of plot and character that position spectators to identify with the male protagonist in his pursuit of the female object of his desire.[31] Retallack notes that "nothing really happens" between Helena and Gheid and suggests therefore that Barnes was at heart a novelist whose early exploration of dramatic form was a "misalliance,"[32] but when Gheid asks, "What are you trying to say?" Helena might in fact be speaking for Barnes when she answers, "I'm saying it."[33] In *To the Dogs*, Barnes was not "trying" to conform to the dramatic conventions of plot and character that Retallack finds lacking in her work; on the contrary, her refusal of those conventions *is* the meta-theatrical action of her play. Gheid describes Helena as "a queer woman,"[34] and his thwarted expectation of sexual mastery – he enters Helena's house, uninvited, through the window – is analogous to the play's impenetrability if conventional (hetero-normative) expectations of dramatic form, like Gheid's conventionally masculine expectations of women, are not left to "go to the dogs." In Barnes's meta-theatrical queering of the gender and sexual politics of representation, the ruin of such conventions is arduous for both playwright and heroine: *To the Dogs* went unproduced, and Helena, having resisted Gheid's advances, admits to being "tired."[35] This difficult refusal does not constitute failure, however, but is instead an act to be celebrated: "To the dogs!"

Women artists' self-reflexive critical engagement with dominant represen-tational conventions was not restricted to avant-garde drama such as that of Barnes but extended to popular performance forms as well. Josephine Baker's most notorious early performances in Paris were situated within meta-performative scenarios that staged the constructedness of racist and colonial ideologies of the black female body. The culminating moment of *La Revue nègre*, for example, in which Baker made her Paris debut in 1925, took the form of a kind of play-within-a-play in which Baker, topless in a skirt of feathers, and Joe Alex, also in feathers, played the roles of stage performers in a Harlem nightclub whose act was a sexually suggestive "African" "*Danse Sauvage.*" An equally famous performance at the Folies-Bergère the following year was also self-consciously framed, as Baker's topless, banana-skirted character Fatou climbed down a tree in the jungle and into the dreams, so to speak, of a sleeping colonial explorer. Baker once remarked, "The white imagination sure is something . . . when it comes to blacks,"[36] but while her sardonic comment makes clear her critical distance from the racist and colonialist representations produced by that imagina-tion, the question of whether her parodic repetition of primitivist tropes succeeded in establishing critical distance from those tropes has been the subject of debate. For Petrine Archer-Straw, for example, "Baker's perfor-mance in *La Revue nègre* reinforced stereotypes of blacks at a time when Europe's blurred and limited image of them as Africans was changing to accommodate an increased awareness of urban African-American cul-ture,"[37] while for Michael Borshuk, Baker:

was able to diminish the negative power of governing stereotypes and discursive impositions by situating herself at the exaggerated limits of those distorted representations, thus revealing the illegitimacy of white-concocted notions of Negro primitivism and eroticism by situating them within the self-consciously illusory spectacle of the stage.[38]

This debate over the effects of Baker's performing body signals the role of the audience in the making of meaning, and indeed, for Gertrude Stein, the role of the audience was central in the theatre, which she regarded as being less about representation than about present experience. As she explained in her lecture "Plays" (1935), "Everybody knows so many stories and what is the use of telling another story. What is the use of telling a story since there are so many and everybody knows so many and tells so many."[39] Instead, Stein suggested, plays, like all art, should "live in the actual present, that is the complete actual present, and . . . completely express that complete actual present."[40] In this sense, she came to discover, a play is like a "landscape" in that it exists in the audience's perceptual experience of the relations among the various elements of which it is composed.[41] In her short first play, *What Happened: A Five Act Play*, written in 1913, Stein dispensed with plot, clearly defined characters, line assignments, and stage directions and instead offered "lively words"[42] – "A tiger a rapt and surrounded overcoat securely arranged with spots old enough to be thought useful and witty quite witty in a secret and in a blinding flurry"[43] – with which she sought to express what happened "without telling what happened, in short to make a play the essence of what happened."[44] As Bonnie Marranca has written, "What happened was the theatre experience itself. In other words, the creation of an experience was more important than the representation of an event."[45] Thus, Marranca explains, in Stein's earliest dramatic explorations and through the many plays and operas that followed, including *Four Saints in Three Acts* (1927), she "shifted attention from the text to the reader (or spectator). In every sense, the perceiving intelligence took precedence over the art object whose status as an autonomous, self-contained totality was diminished. The observer and the art object were not separate but interdependent, making art and life indistinguishable."[46]

Corporeality / performance / everyday life

In "How It Feels to Be Forcibly Fed," Barnes extended her feminist critique beyond the immediate issue of the suffrage campaign in part through her ironic use of theatrical discourse to blur the distinction between performed role and lived experience. At the end of the essay, she writes of her ordeal:

It was over. I stood up, swaying in the returning light; I had shared the greatest experience of the bravest of my sex. The torture and outrage of it burned in my mind; a dull, shapeless, wordless anger rose to my lips, but I only smiled. The doctor had removed the towel about his face. The little, red mustache upon his upper lip was drawn out in a line of pleasant understanding. He had forgotten all but the play. The four men, having finished their minor roles in one minor tragedy, were already filing out at the door.[47]

Although Barnes describes nearly choking in the course of the operation, by the end of it, the doctor experiences comfortable continuity between his everyday reality and his "playacting" role as medical representative of a coercive male political establishment. Barnes, however, experiences discontinuity between self and role; whether swallowing or smiling, she performs under duress. The corporeality of her "playacting" "experiment" thus enables her to understand not only the extreme political experiences of the English suffragists but also the more mundane gender politics that inform the performance of everyday life and that necessitate that she herself "only smile" at the doctor at the end of her ordeal, despite the "dull, shapeless, wordless anger" that she is in fact feeling. In essence, then, Barnes's "performance" was an actual experience of the power vested in male subjects to bring resistant women into line.

This recognition of the performing body as liminal zone between aesthetic practice and everyday life was a central feature of modernist women's thinking about and engagement in performance, so that the corporeal intersection of performed role and performing subject functioned both as a way to understand the mundane practices of everyday life and as a strategic method for intervening in those practices. For example, the sexually dissident women recovered from history and brought to the stage in Cicely Hamilton's suffrage-era *Pageant of Great Women* provided opportunities for queer identification on the part of some of the performers who played them, including Hamilton, Christopher St. John, and the *Pageant*'s director Edith Craig in the role of cross-dressed painter Rosa Bonheur. Thus, in addition to raising awareness of women's achievements throughout history in order to demonstrate their fitness for full and responsible citizenship as recognized through the right to vote, the *Pageant* participated in the formation of lesbian identity as it emerged into public view in the early twentieth century.[48]

If Craig, St. John, and Hamilton used theatricalized historical characters to articulate offstage identities, Isadora Duncan extended her onstage reforms into her performance of everyday life. Duncan viewed ballet dancers as "articulated puppet[s]" and "deformed skeleton[s]" and, in her own work, sought instead to "dance the freedom of woman."[49] Consequently, whereas ballerinas wore pointe shoes and costumes that corseted their upper bodies, Duncan performed barefoot in unrestrictive, flowing tunics; whereas ballets were organized around plots involving identifiable characters and appropriate scenic locales, Duncan's generally plotless dances avoided conventional theatrical role-playing and were backed only by blue velvet curtains; whereas ballet was constituted of highly codified steps and gestures that clearly required special training and considerable strength, Duncan's dances were composed of simple movements that created the illusion of unchoreographed spontaneity; whereas ballet sought to transcend gravity, Duncan continually acknowledged its force; and whereas ballets were choreographed by ballet masters external to the performance, Duncan danced her own dances alone. But Duncan's commitment to what she regarded as the emancipation of the dancing female body was integrally linked to her sense of the need for a more fundamental liberation of women's bodies. "Preach[ing] freedom of the mind through freedom of the body,"[50] she insisted on – and bodied forth – women's right to wear unconstraining clothing, to reject what she regarded as the confinement and servitude of conventional marriage, to take lovers, and to have children outside of marriage.

The performance of self was a key aspect of the work of Elsa von Freytag-Loringhoven as well. "The Baroness," as she was known (having in fact married a baron), was a poet and visual artist but was perhaps most famous for her extraordinary self-presentations in the streets and studios of Greenwich Village. As the artist George Biddle recalled:

> I met her in my studio in the spring of 1917. Having asked me ... whether I required a model, I told her I should like to see her in the nude. With a royal gesture she swept apart the folds of a scarlet raincoat. She stood before me quite naked – or nearly so. Over the nipples of her breast were two tin tomato cans, fastened with a green string around her back. Between the tomato cans hung a very small bird-cage and within it a crestfallen canary. One arm was covered from wrist to shoulder with celluloid curtain rings, pilfered from a furniture display in Wannamaker's. She removed her hat, trimmed with gilded carrots, beets, and other vegetables. Her hair was close cropped and dyed vermillion.[51]

Other found elements incorporated into the Baroness's spectacular assemblage-ensembles included a bustle with a battery-operated tail-light, a cancelled postage stamp stuck to her cheek, a coal scuttle hat, and a tea-ball necklace. For Jane Heap, writing in *The Little Review* in 1922, the Baroness was "the only one living anywhere who dresses dada, loves dada, lives dada";[52] but as Eliza Jane Reilly has pointed out, while the Baroness indeed "shared the Dadaist contempt for the pretensions and hypocrisy of the gatekeepers of high art," her "confrontational style and her razor-sharp insight into sexual politics"[53] made her, in Irene Gammel's words, "a living icon for feminists in Greenwich Village,"[54] among them not only Heap but also her *Little Review* co-editor Margaret Anderson, photographer Berenice Abbott, and Djuna Barnes. With her performative interventions into the practice of everyday life, Freytag-Loringhoven was, as Gammel has written, the "embodiment of avant-garde experimentation with female sexual self-representation."[55]

For ethnographer, playwright, and novelist Zora Neale Hurston, the notion of an underlying sense of "drama" provided a way both to explain and to transvalue distinctive aspects of African American culture ranging from the use of "action words" (for example, "cook-pot")[56] and other linguistic embellishments, to courtship and fighting rituals, to the ongoing evolution of a living folklore. As Hurston explains in "Characteristics of Negro Expression" (1934), "Every phase of Negro life is highly dramatized. No matter how joyful or sad the case there is sufficient poise for drama. Everything is acted out. Unconsciously for the most part of course. There is an impromptu ceremony always ready for every hour of life. No little moment passes unadorned."[57]

In Virginia Woolf's final novel, *Between the Acts* (1941), the embodied art of theatre, requiring live actors and a community of spectators, serves as a metaphor for the permeable boundaries between and influences across aesthetic productions and lived experience and thus is a device for meta-textual speculation on the social function of art, including, implicitly, Woolf's own writing.[58] The fact that Woolf is believed to have drawn inspiration for *Between the Acts* in part from the work of Edith Craig,[59] who staged community pageants and founded a theatre in an ancient barn at her mother Ellen Terry's farm in Kent, not far from Woolf's house in Sussex, is suggestive of the significance that one of the most canonical of modernists saw in the exploration of drama and performance by women artists in the early twentieth century.

Drama and performance have generally been under-represented in accounts of the development of modernism,[60] while women's contributions have been insufficiently recognized within accounts of the development of modern theatre, drama, and performance. As the ways in which women explored the intersection of modernism and performance are increasingly understood,[61] the contours and concerns of the fields of modernist studies and theatre, drama, and performance studies are inevitably being reshaped. What Djuna Barnes's "How it Feels to Be Forcibly Fed" exemplifies, then, and what was being played out in the sampling of modernist plays and performances that I have discussed in this chapter was a moment in history when women artists engaged, through playwriting and performance, with key aspects of modern social, political, and cultural life and when performance offered a way both to understand that life and to intervene in its complex modes of enactment.

NOTES

1. Djuna Barnes, "How It Feels to Be Forcibly Fed," in *New York*, ed. Alice Barry (London: Virago, 1990), p. 177.
2. *Ibid.*, p. 178.
3. *Ibid.*, pp. 174–5.
4. See, for example, Phillip Herring, *Djuna: The Life and Work of Djuna Barnes* (New York: Viking, 1995), p. 89.
5. Barbara Green, "Spectacular Confessions: 'How It Feels to Be Forcibly Fed,'" *Review of Contemporary Fiction* 13.3 (Fall 1993), 70.
6. George Bernard Shaw, "The Technical Novelty in Ibsen's Plays," in *Dramatic Theory and Criticism: Greeks to Grotowski*, ed. Bernard F. Dukore (Fort Worth, TX: Holt, Rinehart and Winston, 1974), p. 642.
7. Gay Gibson Cima, *Performing Women: Female Characters, Male Playwrights, and the Modern Stage* (Ithaca, NY: Cornell University Press, 1993), p. 42.
8. Constantin Stanislavski, *An Actor Prepares*, trans. Elizabeth Reynolds Hapgood (New York: Theatre Arts, 1980), p. 56.
9. Virginia Woolf, "The Memoirs of Sarah Bernhardt," in *Books and Portraits: Some Further Selections from the Literary and Biographical Writings of Virginia Woolf*, ed. Mary Lyon (London: Hogarth, 1977), p. 201.
10. Sophie Treadwell, *Machinal*, in *Plays by American Women: 1900–1930*, ed. Judith Barlow (New York: Applause, 1981), p. 173.
11. *Ibid.*, pp. 186, 200.
12. Sheila Stowell, *A Stage of Their Own: Feminist Playwrights of the Suffrage Era* (Ann Arbor: University of Michigan Press, 1992), pp. 18–19.
13. Alexander Woollcott, "Second Thoughts on First Nights: There Are War Plays and War Plays," *New York Times* (December 14, 1919): sec. 8: 2.
14. Edna St. Vincent Millay, *Aria da Capo*, in *15 American One-Act Plays*, ed. Paul Kozelka (New York: Washington Square, 1961), p. 96.
15. Woollcott, "Second Thoughts," sec. 8: 2.
16. Brenda Murphy, *The Provincetown Players and the Culture of Modernity* (Cambridge: Cambridge University Press, 2005), p. 145.
17. Woollcott, "Second Thoughts," sec. 8: 2.
18. Augusta Gregory, *Seventy Years: Being the Autobiography of Lady Gregory*, ed. Colin Smythe (Gerrards Cross: Colin Smythe, 1974), p. 54.
19. Georgia Douglas Johnson, *Safe*, in *Strange Fruit: Plays on Lynching by American Women*, ed. Kathy A. Perkins and Judith L. Stephens (Bloomington: Indiana University Press, 1998), p. 115.
20. Hallie Flanagan, qtd. in Winona L. Fletcher, "From Genteel Poet to Revolutionary Playwright: Georgia Douglas Johnson," *Theatre Annual* (1985), 50.
21. Qtd. in *ibid.*, 55.
22. *Ibid.*, 55.

23. Cheryl Black, *The Women of Provincetown, 1915–1922* (Tuscaloosa: University of Alabama Press, 2002), p. 3.
24. *Ibid.*, p. 147.
25. Pioneer Players, First Annual Report, qtd. in Christine Dymkowski, "Entertaining Ideas: Edy Craig and the Pioneer Players," in *The New Woman and Her Sisters: Feminism and Theatre 1850–1914*, ed. Vivien Gardner and Susan Rutherford (Ann Arbor: University of Michigan Press, 1992), p. 231.
26. Gwen Pharis Ringwood, qtd. in George Ryga, preface, *The Collected Plays of Gwen Pharis Ringwood*, ed. Enid Delgatty Rutland (Ottawa: Borealis, 1982), p. xvi.
27. Alain Locke, qtd. in James V. Hatch, "The Harlem Renaissance," in *A History of African American Theatre*, by Errol G. Hill and James V. Hatch (Cambridge: Cambridge University Press, 2003), p. 216.
28. Bonnie Kime Scott, introduction, *Gender in Modernism: New Geographies, Complex Intersections* (Urbana: University of Illinois Press, 2007), p. 14.
29. Green, "Spectacular Confessions," 84.
30. Joan Retallack, "One Acts: Early Plays of Djuna Barnes," in *Silence and Power: A Reevaluation of Djuna Barnes*, ed. Mary Lynn Broe (Carbondale: Southern Illinois University Press, 1991), p. 47.
31. See Laura Mulvey, "Visual Pleasure and Narrative Cinema," in *Art After Modernism: Rethinking Representation*, ed. Brian Wallis (New York: New Museum of Contemporary Art, 1984), pp. 361–73; and Teresa de Lauretis, "Desire in Narrative," in *Alice Doesn't: Feminism, Semiotics, Cinema* (Bloomington: Indiana University Press, 1984), pp. 103–57.
32. Retallack, "One Acts," pp. 47, 52.
33. Djuna Barnes, *To the Dogs*, in *At the Root of the Stars: The Short Plays*, ed. Douglas Messerli (Los Angeles: Sun & Moon, 1995), pp. 137–8.
34. *Ibid.*, p. 140.
35. *Ibid.*, p. 146.
36. Josephine Baker, qtd. in Phyllis Rose, *Jazz Cleopatra: Josephine Baker in Her Time* (New York: Doubleday, 1989), p. 81.
37. Petrine Archer-Straw, *Negrophilia: Avant-Garde Paris and Black Culture in the 1920s* (New York: Thames and Hudson, 2000), p. 107.
38. Michael Borshuk, "An Intelligence of the Body: Disruptive Parody through Dance in the Early Performances of Josephine Baker," *EmBODYing Liberation: The Black Body in American Dance*, ed. Dorothea Fischer-Hornung and Alison D. Goeller (Münster, Germany: LIT, 2001), p. 41.
39. Gertrude Stein, "Plays," in *Last Operas and Plays*, ed. Carl Van Vechten (Baltimore: Johns Hopkins University Press, 1995), p. xliv.
40. *Ibid.*, p. xxxvi.
41. *Ibid.*, pp. xlvi–lii.
42. *Ibid.*, p. xxxix.
43. Gertrude Stein, *What Happened*, qtd. in *ibid.*, p. xliv.
44. Stein, "Plays," p. xliv.
45. Bonnie Marranca, "Introduction: Presence of Mind," in Stein, *Last Operas and Plays*, p. ix.
46. *Ibid.*, p. x.
47. Barnes, "How It Feels," p. 179.

48. Penny Farfan, *Women, Modernism, and Performance* (Cambridge: Cambridge University Press, 2004), pp. 78–84.

49. Isadora Duncan, *My Life* (New York: Liveright, 1927), p. 75; Isadora Duncan, "The Dance of the Future," in *The Art of the Dance*, ed. Sheldon Cheney (New York: Theatre Arts, 1928), pp. 56, 63.

50. Isadora Duncan, *Isadora Speaks*, ed. Franklin Rosemont (San Francisco: City Lights, 1981), p. 53.

51. George Biddle, qtd. in Robert Reiss, "'My Baroness': Elsa von Freytag-Loringhoven," *Dada/Surrealism* 14 (1985), 87.

52. Jane Heap, qtd. in Rudolf E. Kuenzli, "Baroness Elsa von Freytag-Loringhoven and New York Dada," in *Women in Dada: Essays on Sex, Gender, and Identity*, ed. Naomi Sawelson-Gorse (Cambridge: MIT Press, 1998), p. 442.

53. Eliza Jane Reilly, "Elsa von Freytag-Loringhoven," *Women's Art Journal* 18.1 (1997), 31, 29.

54. Irene Gammel, "Parading Sexuality: Modernist Life Writing and Popular Confession," in *Confessional Politics: Women's Sexual Self-Representations in Life Writing and Popular Media*, ed. Irene Gammel (Carbondale: Southern Illinois University Press, 1999), p. 48.

55. *Ibid.*, p. 53.

56. Zora Neale Hurston, "Characteristics of Negro Expression," in *The Gender of Modernism: A Critical Anthology*, ed. Bonnie Kime Scott (Bloomington: Indiana University Press, 1990), p. 175.

57. *Ibid.*, p. 175.

58. Farfan, *Women, Modernism, and Performance*, pp. 89–101.

59. Jane Marcus, "Some Sources for *Between the Acts*," *Virginia Woolf Miscellany* 6 (Winter 1977), 1–3.

60. Penny Farfan and Katherine E. Kelly, "Staging Modernism: Introduction," *South Central Review* 25.1 (Spring 2008), 1–11.

61. See, for example, Katherine E. Kelly, ed. *Modern Drama by Women 1880s–1930s: An International Anthology* (London: Routledge, 1996); Farfan, *Women, Modernism, and Performance*; and Katherine E. Kelly, "Gender and Collaboration in Modern Drama," in *Gender in Modernism*, ed. Scott, pp. 677–95.

4

JAYNE MAREK

Magazines, presses, and salons in women's modernism

Women's modernism as reflected in the operations of magazines, presses, and salons is a topic at once expansive and specific. Certainly it is open to a variety of approaches. To borrow playfully from Virginia Woolf, the topic may indicate "women and what they are like"; or it might mean "women and the fiction that they write" as produced by certain publishing concerns for particular readers; or it might mean discussions in social salons by or about women and their writings; again, it might signify an interlocking pattern of women, the salons that they convene, and the publications they run or in which they appear. This final approach – finding all of these aspects "inextricably mixed together" – means that a single chapter about women, modernism, presses, and salons "should never be able to come to a conclusion" due to the unavoidable complexity in any matter that involves sex.[1]

It is now a truism of modernist scholarship that small presses and "little" magazines fostered the aesthetic innovations that later became canonized as literary modernism. Women's work in such venues necessarily contributed to the development of modernist aesthetics, despite social attitudes of the time that tended to ignore or belittle aspects of the feminine. Experimental writings by Gertrude Stein, Dorothy Richardson, H. D., Marianne Moore, Mina Loy, Virginia Woolf, Djuna Barnes, Zora Neale Hurston, and other women provoked and responded to fiction and poetry by Ford Madox Ford, James Joyce, Ezra Pound, T. S. Eliot, Langston Hughes, Jean Toomer, D. H. Lawrence, and other men. The success of small magazines and presses was undergirded by the more ephemeral phenomenon of salons, which may be broadly construed as intellectual and artistic gatherings arranged for the express purpose of spreading new ideas, drawing attention to fresh and significant work, and (not least) of pleasing and stimulating the *salonniers*.

How can one recapture the sense of conversation, rivalry, and above all newness that animated the exchange of ideas in the early twentieth century? To what degree was salon culture affected by gender? Further, how can one characterize a "female" orientation in tasks such as editing and publishing?

The answers – now as then – reflect the complexity of the material to be assessed. Modernist studies regularly cross borders among disciplines, not to mention distinctions of nationality, genre, so-called "high" and "low" culture, and gender. The period's many disruptions and rejections of former boundaries may make the formerly radical transgressions of modernist women seem mundane, the barriers they scaled less formidable. Such thinking misreads the historical record. Scholars must not overlook the extent of modernist women's efforts to cope with the biases of their culture. The many persistent dissonances in modernist history show that interdisciplinary critical studies must continue to raise questions of gender's effects on the literary record.

One such question involves the nature of women's activities as women artists theorized, enacted, and conveyed modernist aesthetics. Conventional scholarship has tended to treat the history of publications, especially books, as relatively distinct from the history of salons of like-minded artists and intellectuals. Published records, being much easier to assess, have predominated in critical histories. Especially for women, who have been less visible to historiography, it is difficult to pin down the effects of amorphous movements of authors and aficionados through salons, that is, through temporary and non-material exchanges that occurred in conversations. Little better is the case of ephemeral publications, especially those circulated in only a few dozen or a few hundred copies. The transitory nature of many small publications may lead one to fear that, for some aspects of the historical record, there is no there there. Considering salons, little magazines, and book publishers together gives a stronger sense of how the more fleeting aspects of modernist developments affected the documents of the permanent record.

Modernist works have always sent mixed signals about certain material aspects of culture. One such aspect is place. Physical locations created the imaginative backdrop for modernist works, even as authors, artists, musicians, and publishers tended to group themselves in particular cities. The abstract "Hellas" that informed H. D.'s Imagist and post-Imagist poetry and the globally disparate settings in Marianne Moore's poetry composed imagined landscapes out of mythological or historical fragments. Virginia Woolf's London (notably in *Mrs. Dalloway*) or Nella Larsen's Chicago, on the other hand, drew on an essential cosmopolitan center, important as a city in itself and as a signal of contemporary consciousness. As Cristanne Miller notes, "Many modernist writers were conscious of the relevance of location ... Modernist narratives elevated various cities almost to the level of character."[2]

Location, location, location – the mantra of business and real estate also applies to modernist developments. Miller emphasizes that specific locations "significantly inflected modernist women's performances of subjectivity, gender, race, and religion in their texts and their lives" – and, in its turn, modernism can be reread according to its "distinctive and distinctively gendered forms" that reflect settings.[3] For the most part, the hotbeds of change, and the location of many female-focused salons, were the cities: Paris, London, New York, and Berlin, the "great modern metropolises" now "regarded as central to the inception of modernism."[4] One may easily draw connections between the kinetic energy of such cities and the eclectic artistic styles of the modernist avant-garde. Cosmopolitanism and progressivism in all forms of endeavor often went hand in hand. The modernist emphasis on movement, on depicting flux and dynamism in literary language, was well served by cities that attracted practitioners of the new. Salon culture flourished in cities that had a high concentration of both creative innovators and society patrons who could afford to nurture their favorite artists and authors. The global context of change in the early twentieth century, and persistent cultural misogyny, meant that women had to work hard as they developed into arbiters of the public sphere.

Salon culture, already well established in Europe, shifted its form and function in the post-Enlightenment European culture from which Anglo-American modernism developed. According to Jürgen Habermas, the salon society of the nobility had transformed by the eighteenth century into a bourgeois coffeehouse culture of male merchants and intellectuals who debated the value of literature, art, politics, and economic ideas.[5] One outgrowth of these debates was an explosion of publications that fundamentally linked commodity culture to an ideology that valued public opinion. The very idea of "personhood" – self-reflection and self-preoccupation – was conveyed through publication. Yet while Habermas comments that the previous salon culture of the elites was "essentially shaped by women," he does not pursue gender as an important factor in his analysis.[6]

Salon culture and publication represented two notable fields of the post-Enlightenment shift toward a social ideology of individualism. Even though women did not enter the field of publishing with a significant presence until the modernist era, in terms of access to formative and avant-garde ideas women were firmly established as proprietors of salons. London, Paris, and New York all boasted legendary salons and publishing concerns run by women. Salons provided a focused forum that accelerated the social processing of new ideas in circulation at the time. For an experimental author, friendly discussion groups such as salons often provided the only substantive responses from readers or listeners who were willing to indulge the author's methods. Women's salons – or those in which women predominated – gave female artists, authors, dancers, musicians, and other creative thinkers acceptance that was less mediated by presumptions about gender and more premised on active exchange and testing of ideas. Personalities reigned – indeed, they constituted the whole point of salon culture. To succeed with a salon required a particular set of attributes: along with independent means, women *salonniers* needed to live in an accessible location, preferably with plenty of international comings and goings. These women also needed to have networks and connections that would reliably bring in interesting people. Women *salonniers* needed to be good listeners, and, finally, be the kind of people who wished to help others make the most of their ideas, whether this meant providing an introduction, sponsoring a program, offering financial backing, even providing meals and shelter at times. The success of a regular salon depended on creating an atmosphere of lively acceptance and exchange, with the leader exhibiting an intangible quality of spirit that drew people in, assured them of her attention, and testified to her profound interest in a wide range of ideas.

A few of these leaders seemed to stand in the place of the old aristocracy, for instance Lady Ottoline Morrell, who presided over large gatherings of deliberately cultivated visitors at her homes in London and the English countryside. Other women, such as Virginia Woolf and Vanessa Bell of the Bloomsbury circle, happened into salon culture as a result of lifestyle and found it to be a personally and professionally stimulating way of engaging with modernist ideas. The salon cultures developed by Gertrude Stein, Mabel Dodge, and Natalie Barney went a step further, clearly leaning toward the progressive and idiosyncratic.

Barney's book of memoirs, *Adventures of the Mind* (1929), asks, "Are there still patrons for writers? Are we interested in them to the point of making it easier for them to stay alive so that their work may benefit?"[7] Barney's words indicate her opinion that it was the obligation of "a small sincere number of readers and writers joined together by the laws of exchange" to help creative artists as "two indispensable parts of the one whole," and, further, express the underlying purpose of her salon as an effort to provide support for "the best minds" – "Let them be consumed in the most efficient way, to their best production, so that we can profit from them!"[8] These comments serve as a reminder of the purpose and importance of salons and the energy they generated for the women who ran them.

Ottoline Morrell set out to amass a salon around herself beginning around 1907. The Morrells had recently moved to a large house at 44 Bedford Square, and Ottoline borrowed the formula that had worked for many London *salonniers*: she met and read about scores of people with an interest in the arts, and she invited as many as she could to attend her Thursday evenings. Her striking appearance and outlandish clothing added cachet to her sincere appreciation for excellent talk among diverse guests. Between 1908 and 1915 in London, Ottoline Morrell "came to be a combination of friend, critic, patron, muse, and goddess."[9] After 1915, her salon culture continued at Garsington, a spacious country estate. For a few of Ottoline's regulars, such as the painter Augustus John and writers Lytton Strachey, Siegfried Sassoon, D. H. Lawrence, W. B. Yeats, and T. S. Eliot, she gave gifts, arranged commissions, provided housing and connections, and otherwise sponsored and encouraged them, sometimes for a considerable period. Ottoline Morrell's influence in fostering modernism in England arose directly from her extensive social contacts and her personal artistic inclinations; it is unfortunate that many literary histories dismiss her as an eccentric because of the gossip spread about her by some of her visitors. That may be the cost of hosting a successful salon.

Both Ottoline Morrell and the Bloomsbury group benefited from their frequent associations and mutual acquaintances, despite the vexed relationship between Ottoline and Virginia Woolf. Bloomsbury, a London neighborhood, came to represent the best-known social group during the modernist era. Reflecting a number of prior and subsequent cliques such as the Friday Club, the Apostles of Cambridge, and the Memoir Club, this association of friends and family members in London included many of the figures essential to the innovative aesthetics of the period, such as Virginia and Leonard Woolf, Vanessa and Clive Bell, Roger Fry, E. M. Forster, Lytton Strachey, and Duncan Grant. Discussions, readings, and exhibitions formed the core of the group's activities, and Bloomsbury group members actively produced articles, books, paintings, and designs that helped establish their distinctive postimpressionist ethos. Already by 1910, the group was seen (and criticized) as an influential circle that inspired both satire and envy. Its exchanges influenced Virginia Woolf's writing style, which sometimes explicitly conflated thought with a conversational tone.[10] Bloomsbury also provided Virginia and Leonard Woolf with more opportunities to secure and then sell manuscripts they published through their Hogarth Press. The Bloomsbury group remained a significant force in modernist arts and letters for many years, and its reputation as an indulgent, self-interested clique was moderated in part by the seriousness and success of the Hogarth Press.[11]

As a magnet for artistic people from many nations and the capital of America's postwar expatriates, Paris was the location of Gertrude Stein's famous salon, located at 27, Rue de Fleurus. Initially, the apartment was a gathering place for acquaintances of Gertrude Stein and her brother Leo Stein, both of whom had begun to purchase innovative modern art. Paintings crowded together on the walls, hung at all heights, created an environment uniquely suited to conversation about modern aesthetics and the latest artistic innovations. When Leo left to establish his own home and Alice B. Toklas moved in, Gertrude and Alice created a particularly eclectic salon on Saturday evenings that welcomed not only painters but writers, photographers, journalists, collectors, students, and bon vivants of many stripes. The Rue de Fleurus salon was well established by 1906 and continued for many years, numbering among its notable visitors the authors Sherwood Anderson, Carl Van Vechten, and Ernest Hemingway and artists Henri Matisse, Francis Picabia, Arthur Dove, William Glackens, Marsden Hartley, and especially Pablo Picasso. Stein enjoyed exercising her power in intellectual exchange with some of the most remarkable artistic minds of the era. The salon provided a way to have satisfying intellectual exchanges on a regular basis and probably allowed her visitors, at least, to come away with a better sense of the aesthetic rationales for Stein's writings.

Natalie Clifford Barney, also in Paris and a friend of Stein and Toklas, was the leading figure in another salon noted for its visible embrace of lesbian culture. Her Friday afternoon gatherings at 20, rue Jacob, featured one or two special guests each week. Barney focused on bringing together writers who represented an exciting diversity, especially in the heady 1920s, as she deliberately courted "an intellectual, international elite, an understanding across diverse languages."[12] Among the "elite" were the dancer Isadora Duncan and writers Colette, Rainer Maria Rilke, Anatole France, Djuna Barnes, Rabindranath Tagore, and Paul Valéry; these and others benefited from the cross-pollination of ideas and from Natalie's diligence and energy. She helped make many connections among authors, do translations, place publications, and nurture the authors' egos. As a writer who realized the limitations of her own work, Barney put her energies into creative exchange in several senses. In 1927, she set up an Académie des Femmes as a response to the then-male Académie-française.[13] The Académie des Femmes helped establish women's significance in modern letters; inductees included Stein, Colette, Barnes, Elisabeth de Gramont, and Mina Loy.[14]

A sometime friend of Gertrude Stein, Mabel Dodge created her salon at the outskirts of Greenwich Village. Dodge convened groups of progressive thinkers, activists, artists, and authors in a salon that met from 1913 to 1915. She also contributed her energies to progressive social and artistic causes. One of her earliest contributions came from her volunteer work to help organize the 1913 Armory Show of postimpressionist art, at which she distributed printed copies of Gertrude Stein's written "cubist" portrait of Dodge, which – due to the notorious strangeness of the artworks and of Stein's verbal style – brought instant celebrity.[15] Dodge represented the "New Woman" figure of the times, and her interest in radical ideas helped her populate her salon with political figures such as Emma Goldman, Margaret Sanger, and Bill Haywood, arts professionals such as Bobby Jones, and authors Max Eastman and Lincoln Steffens.

Dodge sometimes took friends with her on visits to her villa in Italy, where she was when the First World War broke out; this experience led to her interviewing soldiers and their wives for a piece in the political little magazine *The Masses* that drew the interest of the newly formed Woman's Peace Party.[16] This conjunction suggests that the greatest value of Dodge's salon arose from her ability to have one foot in the world of money and privilege and one foot in the world of radical populism or, later, in the spiritual traditions of the Pueblos. After the First World War, she settled in Taos, New Mexico, married Tony Luhan, and continued her involvement in progressive causes, notably Native rights. By the 1920s, she had formed an art colony that enjoyed a number of significant visitors, such as authors Mary Austin, Willa Cather, Dorothy Brett, D. H. Lawrence, Jean Toomer, and Robinson Jeffers, painters Georgia O'Keeffe and John Marin, the photographer Ansel Adams, and the composer Leopold Stokowski. This array of contacts signifies Mabel Dodge Luhan's enduring legacy to modernism as a muse and supporter of important twentieth-century artists.

African American literary salons, especially on the East Coast, often included women as members. "In just about every good-sized city," writes David Levering Lewis, "earnest little bands of part-time Afro-American culture-nurturers" formed literary groups and sometimes sponsored publications.[17] A group in Philadelphia produced the magazine *Black Opals*, and Boston's Quill Club published its own organ, the *Saturday Evening Quill*, to which Quill Club members Dorothy West and her cousin Helene Johnson contributed.[18] In New York City, a salon formed around Jessie Redmon Fauset, the literary editor for the NAACP's journal *The Crisis*, who fostered the talents of many members of the New Negro, or Harlem, Renaissance. Carolyn Wedin Sylvander notes that "Fauset was an important figure in two kinds of social event – the testimonial dinner or benefit and the private at-home cultural soiree"; Fauset's personal generosity allowed her to connect with younger as well as established writers, to provide encouragement and advice, and to cultivate a welcoming literary climate.[19]

The most famous African American woman's literary salon was in Washington, DC, where poet Georgia Douglas Johnson convened a regular gathering on Saturday nights that David Levering Lewis characterizes as "a freewheeling jumble of the gifted, famous, and odd."[20] Literary visitors included many authors and poets: Angelina Weld Grimké, Zora Neale Hurston, Alain Locke, Jessie Fauset, Alice Dunbar-Nelson, Sterling Brown, Anne Spencer, Langston Hughes, and Countee Cullen. Johnson's evenings began after the death of her husband in 1925 and lasted, by her account, about ten years, attracting considerable attention especially from New York members of the New Negro Renaissance.[21] Johnson herself characterized the salon as the place "where many of the splendid young writers of the present-day received their ... inspiration."[22]

The "inspiration" found in women's salons nurtured modernist imagination into new forms, first as talk and then as material culture. Verbal culture as in salons is essentially subjective, non-material, constantly being modified, and as difficult to record as dance. Print culture, which some women chose as their métier, on the other hand, is material, fixed in individual forms, and may be considered objective. The eclectic nature of experimentation during this era meant that one of modernism's necessary tasks was to define itself, and – as an outgrowth of salons' exchange of ideas – print culture provided essential demonstrations of the modernist ethos.

Getting into print requires sustained labor and money, another form of the social economics that undergird salons. Even as salon culture depends on the existence of an educated bourgeois class with the leisure time for regular discussions, magazines and presses require both funding and an educated readership that represents particular commercial demands. All of these elements influenced the modernist work that made it into print. Some recent critical analyses of modernist culture have considered the economics of providing access to avant-garde ideas. Lawrence Rainey insists that the ideologies of modernist innovations cannot be detached from the context of commercial factors that mediated the emergence of new literature and art, in part through wealthy patrons' investment in limited-edition books that, through their rarity, validated the mythology of their status as avant-garde masterpieces.[23] Of necessity, modernist artists and writers developed "new strategies for reputation building" around the presentation of their works and ideas to a public "ranging from patron-*salonniers* to mass audiences, or from patron-investors, dealers, and speculators to a broader (if numerically restricted) corpus of critics and educated readers."[24]

Commercial interests did not obviate many modernists' interest in making radical changes in the larger culture as well as in the arts. While the period's social attitudes often displayed sexism, ethnocentrism, and racism, some magazines specifically included art and writings from women and from African American, Hispanic, Jewish, immigrant, or Asian contributors. Multiplicity remains modernism's predominant heritage in literary arts and is most obviously seen in the forms and contents of little magazines.

Little magazines run by women dominate much of early Anglo-American modernism. The quintessential example is *Poetry, A Magazine of Verse*, founded in Chicago in 1912 by Harriet Monroe. Its now-legendary status was far from a sure thing when it began, since Monroe was determined to solicit new work from many kinds of poets and to pay for it. Unlike many little magazines, *Poetry* began on relatively stable financial footing, as Monroe had lined up underwriters to support the magazine for five years from its inception, thereby giving herself time to develop the poetry renaissance she envisioned. Her famous "open-door policy" brought in reams of submissions. Although she had her preferences, Monroe printed a wide range of poems and launched many literary careers; most notably, *Poetry* introduced Imagism to the United States and gave space to extensive debates about the value and aesthetics of free verse. Many now-familiar names appeared in *Poetry*: H. D., Marianne Moore, Robert Frost, Carl Sandburg, T. S. Eliot, Amy Lowell, D. H. Lawrence, Langston Hughes, and scores more. Other early magazines that followed in *Poetry*'s footsteps were ultimately more radical in their contents – for instance, *Others* and *The Seven Arts* – but Monroe's journal established poetry's position as a precursor for significant subsequent developments in American modernism.

Another woman-run magazine was *The Little Review*, founded in 1916 (also in Chicago) by Margaret Anderson. Her eclectic interests allowed the magazine to focus on a range of topical issues (among them feminism, anarchism, psychoanalytic theory) as well as on the aesthetics of the new. Jane Heap joined as co-editor in 1916, bringing a background in visual arts, a remarkable ability with words, and an openness to spirituality that added depth and extended the range of the magazine. *The Little Review* moved to New York in 1917 and then to Paris in 1922, where it continued sporadically under Heap's direction until 1929, promoting more visual and sculptural as well as literary aspects of the avant-garde. Over the years, contributors such as Gertrude Stein, Marianne Moore, Djuna Barnes, Ezra Pound, James Joyce, William Carlos Williams, Ben Hecht, Hart Crane, and even Elsa von Freytag-Loringhoven established *The Little Review*'s spirit of curiosity and experimentation.

England's *The Egoist* (formerly *The New Freewoman*) grew into a literary periodical from its origins as a radical suffragist organ. Founder Dora Marsden eventually ceded the editorship to Harriet Shaw Weaver, whose connections with writers such as Rebecca West, H. D., James Joyce, Richard Aldington, May Sinclair, Ezra Pound, and T. S. Eliot directly shaped the literary contents. By 1914, the journal was running articles about Imagist poetry and had been serializing Joyce's *A Portrait of the Artist as a Young Man*; it continued to grow in influence, presenting an Imagist number in 1915 and offering early publication or critical notice for a number of emerging authors including Marianne Moore, Wyndham Lewis, Amy Lowell, and Dorothy Richardson, until its cessation in 1919.

This triumvirate of little magazines under women's direction was "of major importance over a long period for most of the writers" essential to modernism, since "periodical publishing – however small, specialist, erratic, or partisan – is where writers turn if they're young or experimentalist," and since "the chance of an audience is compelling and overriding."[25] Little magazines of many types benefited from women's editorial contributions: Kay Boyle of *This Quarter*, Emily Clark of *The Reviewer*, Katherine Mansfield of *Rhythm* and *Blue Review*, Lola Ridge of *Broom*, Marianne Moore of *The Dial*, and H. D. and Bryher of *Close Up*, among others.

If one rethinks modernism from the point of view of women's contributions, notably those of black women as analyzed by scholar Hazel Carby, then Anglo-American modernism as well as the New Negro or Harlem Renaissance received a major charge of energy from black women before the turn of the twentieth century.[26] The early example of Pauline Hopkins, editor for four years of the *Colored American Magazine* (1900–4), had echoes in later literary editorships, for instance of Jessie Redmon Fauset at *The Crisis* (1919–26) and *The Brownies' Book* (1920–1) and of Dorothy West at *Challenge*, later renamed *New Challenge* (1934–7). The social politics associated with literary modernism appeared in high relief in the pages of these journals.

Fauset's progressive ideas appeared in her many *Crisis* editorials, biographical profiles, and features detailing the political situations of blacks in many parts of the world. In *The Brownies' Book*, a spinoff children's magazine, Fauset as editor included many didactic as well as creative pieces designed to instill pride and knowledge in young African Americans. In the following decade, Dorothy West founded her magazine as a direct response to the atrophy of publishing opportunities for blacks during the Depression. West printed both established and newer writers in an attempt to keep the New Negro Renaissance flowing, which, for a time, she was able to do. Of equal pertinence were West's socialist sympathies, evident in a number of pieces in *Challenge* and the last issue, *New Challenge*, which featured the radical "Blueprint for Negro Writing" by co-editor Richard Wright.

Other African American periodicals showed similar editorial orientations in women's contributions or under women's direction. Alice Dunbar-Nelson for a time ran a politically oriented newspaper, *The Wilmington Advocate*, with her husband in Delaware and wrote commentaries and reformist articles for other black publications, such as *The Pittsburgh Courier* and *The Messenger*. Gwendolyn Bennett's arts column in *Opportunity* magazine, "The Ebony Flute," chronicled literary, musical, theatrical, and social events during 1926–8 at the height of the New Negro Renaissance; although conversational in tone, the column nevertheless was specifically directed toward spreading information about events in Harlem to other black artists' groups.[27] While not overtly political, Nora Douglas Holt's journal *Music and Poetry* (1921) was radical in its approach: Holt espoused seriousness and respect for black musical performers and composers, gave equal time to male and female professionals, and was unapologetic in her support for classical music at a time when jazz, blues, and folk music idioms dominated the New Negro Renaissance.

Disparate in location, orientation, and tenure, these magazines nevertheless gave women a stable yet malleable platform from which to launch their own, and others', ideas and writings. The modernist era still found women editors, in themselves, to be unexpected, but in fact women in publishing, by their presence and through their choices, were creating the necessary critical mass to call attention not only to women's literature and criticism but also to literary modernism more broadly.

As with little magazines, literary presses and imprints varied from the temporary – convened to meet a specific need – to the enduring. Books from publishing concerns run by women ultimately had immense impact on literary modernism. Sylvia Beach's production of the full text of *Ulysses* is the touchstone example of a one-time publication that profoundly affected the modernist canon.[28] Portions of *Ulysses* had appeared in *The Little Review* in 1919–20, but, when one of those issues with allegedly "obscene" material in it was noticed by an attorney who contacted the New York Society for the Suppression of Vice, there was a trial at which editors Margaret Anderson and Jane Heap were fined; despite their scorn for the court's stodginess, they decided not to publish any more of the book. However, the case led Joyce's supporters in England and France to investigate other means of producing the book. Sylvia Beach, one of Joyce's admirers, was the owner of the Paris bookstore Shakespeare and Company and close friends with Adrienne Monnier, who ran another book shop, La Maison des Amis des Livres. Both shops were predicated on building up the literary community in Paris, and Beach took the next logical step when she decided to publish *Ulysses* in its entirety. She used her bookstore connections to help publicize the venture; she read proofs and helped persuade the printer to accommodate Joyce's many manuscript changes and additions.[29] The book caused a sensation when it ultimately appeared in 1922.

Jane Heap, for her part, continued as editor of *The Little Review* in France after Margaret Anderson left the magazine; Heap's experience led her to try to place Gertrude Stein's voluminous experimental novel, *The Making of Americans*.[30] A number of misunderstandings had arisen with the original Parisian publisher, Robert McAlmon of Contact Editions, and he and Stein were quarreling about costs, payment, and distribution abroad. Heap took the initiative to contact Albert and Charles Boni and nearly succeeded in having Boni buy 1,000 sets of printed sheets for binding in the United States;

however, further disagreements between McAlmon and Stein led to only a limited number of copies being bound and sold.[31] Nevertheless, Heap's intervention raised Stein's profile among publishers in America and England and reinforced her commitment to the avant-garde. As Robert Crunden points out, *The Making of Americans* seems "a literary counterpart to Picasso's analytic cubism," to mental processes in general, to cinema, and to America particularly as "a space that is filled with moving," in Stein's own words.[32]

Other American women were engaged with independent publishing concerns. Caresse Crosby, an American who lived for years in Europe, edited and helped produce manuscripts for the Black Sun Press, which she ran with her husband, Harry Crosby, in Paris from 1927 into the 1930s after Harry's death; Black Sun printed work by Joyce, Lawrence, Kay Boyle, Hart Crane, Ezra Pound, and others.[33] More visibly, the Boston author Amy Lowell shrewdly used her poetic interests and personal fortune to launch Imagism as a valid poetic form in America. She oversaw the collection and printing of the three-volume *Some Imagist Poets* (1915–17), which accomplished the astonishing goal of drawing attention to recent innovations in poetry during the chaotic years of the First World War. Publishing *Some Imagist Poets* was no small feat. The volumes were intended to be jointly compiled, with each of the six contributors choosing her or his own poems in consultation with the others. However, the start of the First World War immediately complicated the practical work of collecting, sharing, discussing, and finally producing the texts, and Lowell found herself doing the lion's share of the work as well as staking the publication. The initial volume drew the ire of Ezra Pound, who had printed an earlier anthology, *Des Imagistes*, and did not like the direction he thought Imagism was headed; Lowell had to respond to Pound, her publisher, and the other contributors as well as manage the editing, publicity, and distribution of books, printed sheets, and royalties. Fortunately, H. D., then living in England, helped Lowell mend fences with the English Imagists, and the volumes ended up launching Imagism as a viable poetic form in America.[34]

Harriet Monroe of *Poetry* magazine also produced several influential anthologies titled *The New Poetry*. Monroe collaborated with her first co-editor, Alice Corbin Henderson, on the first two volumes in 1917 and 1923. Placed with Macmillan, the first edition became a best-seller, tapping the market for poetry that *Poetry* magazine had helped to create among reading groups, libraries, and universities. By the time the third and final version of *The New Poetry* appeared in 1932, the books had influenced countless subsequent anthologies and helped place into the canon many of the modern authors whose works *Poetry* had printed.

Despite the usual pressures of time and money, some book publishers managed to stay in operation for a number of years. The most substantial footing was gained by Leonard and Virginia Woolf's Hogarth Press. Established in 1917, Hogarth Press was a mutual effort by husband and wife to find a physically and intellectually absorbing hobby that would provide distraction from the demands of writing. Virginia Woolf, in particular, wished to have a steadying focus to help her combat mental illness; helping to run a small private press seemed ideal for a woman who had, in her youth, enjoyed bookbinding.[35] Virginia and Leonard both set type, pulled pages, and bound the texts, and Leonard applied his management skills to the economic side – ensuring that the press turned a profit from the first, despite modest sales.[36] The Woolfs' literary connections extended from Virginia's early contacts, established by her father Sir Leslie Stephen's status as author, through the Bloomsbury circle. This high profile allowed Hogarth Press to attract manuscripts from a long list of notables, including economist John Maynard Keynes, psychologist Sigmund Freud, and authors Katherine Mansfield, T. S. Eliot, E. M. Forster, Robert Graves, Edwin Muir, and H. G. Wells. Hogarth Press usually produced several hand-set books per year, but the press's success quickly forced the Woolfs to engage commercial typesetters and printers to produce most of Hogarth's long list of titles (over 450 books were produced from 1917 up to Virginia's death in 1941).[37]

Also in England, Harriet Shaw Weaver of *The Egoist* developed the Egoist Press, which produced on a small scale but was responsible for numerous works of interest – notably James Joyce's *A Portrait of the Artist as a Young Man* (for which Weaver initially established the press), T. S. Eliot's *Prufrock and Other Observations*, H. D.'s *Hymen*, and the Poets' Translation Series that helped establish Imagism's classical roots. Winifred Ellerman, known as Bryher, sponsored a number of publishing concerns. One of the earliest was through Weaver's press; Bryher and H. D. compiled the first book of Marianne Moore's poems, with Bryher financing the Egoist Press's publication of the book.[38] Bryher's money also supported her first husband Robert McAlmon's Contact Editions, the film journal *Close Up* (which she co-edited with her second husband Kenneth Macpherson and the poet H. D., her longtime companion), the later periodical *Life and Letters To-Day*, and her Brendin Publishing Company.[39]

Nancy Cunard's Hours Press, established at Réanville, France, in 1928, introduced Samuel Beckett to the literary world and produced a number of fine editions of established writers; Cunard's other lasting legacy to twentieth-century literature was her monumental anthology *Negro*, completed three years after Hours Press production was discontinued in 1931.[40] At about that time, Gertrude Stein and Alice B. Toklas developed Plain Editions in Paris as a way to make up for the absence of publishers willing to take Stein's work on a regular basis.[41] Previously, Stein had used small publishers for occasional works, at one point subsidizing her *Geography and Plays* (1922) herself.[42] Plain Editions allowed more of Stein's works to reach print, and Stein was pleased to achieve some distribution, at least, in Parisian bookstores and abroad. Later, Stein had no more need to self-publish owing to the success of *The Autobiography of Alice B. Toklas* in 1933.

The dramatic publication histories of *Some Imagist Poets*, *The Making of Americans*, *The New Poetry*, and *Ulysses*, among other signatures of the modernist period, indicate the highly visible status of independent publishers and limited editions and suggest that some of the texts' inherent "coding" involves satisfaction and accomplishment by women who knew their publishing interests would fly in the face of convention. While women generally had less access to institutions of capital and were seldom considered to be real players in the game of literary value judgments, much valuable literature would not have been published or produced if not for women's contributions of time, enthusiastic readership, and especially material support and labor. Women with both money and marketing acumen – and women in the right place to make the connections that brought them exciting new manuscripts – were those likelier to make a significant impact through informal connections, patronage of artists, and sponsored publishing.

The modernists' fiery rhetoric about what they wished to accomplish, taken in itself, does not sufficiently demonstrate why their new approach was able to sustain itself and eventually to reshape the canon of twentieth-century literature. Nor do most dicta of the period indicate how gender roles particularly inflected literary productions. Yet behind the printed pages that eventually codified modernism in its signal texts, the existence of these works in itself demonstrates women's private connections and personal dedication to a culture of ideas that made it possible for radically new literature to reach the public.

Margaret Anderson, long stigmatized for her unabashed flaunting of "female" traits, provides a fitting coda. In the first volume of her autobiography, Anderson wrote about her decision to found *The Little Review* as born of the realization that "nothing inspired [was] going on" despite her deep desire "that life be inspired every moment."[43] Anderson then realized that "the only way to guarantee this is to have inspired conversation every moment" – that, in fact, she would need to create the right medium: "if I had a magazine," she mused, "I could spend my time filling it up with the best conversation the world has to offer."[44] The little magazines and small presses run by modernist women, like the salons and coteries, provided direct links between "inspired conversation" and the public dissemination of new ideas.

Modernism benefited from such direct links between conversation and publication, and Anderson's remarks signal the excitement that resulted as the new ideas took verbal and material shape – an excitement shared and appreciated by all subsequent students of modernism.

NOTES

1. Virginia Woolf, *A Room of One's Own* (1929; Harmondsworth: Penguin, 1975), pp. 5–6.
2. Cristanne Miller, *Cultures of Modernism: Marianne Moore, Mina Loy, and Else Lasker-Schüler* (Ann Arbor: University of Michigan Press, 1995), pp. 2–3.
3. *Ibid.*, p. 2.
4. *Ibid.*, p. 1.
5. Jürgen Habermas, *The Structural Transformation of the Public Sphere*, trans. Thomas Burger (Cambridge: MIT Press, 1989), p. 33.
6. *Ibid.*, pp. 28, 33.
7. Natalie Clifford Barney, *Adventures of the Mind*, trans. John Spalding Gatton (New York: New York University Press, 1992), p. 116.
8. *Ibid.*, p. 117.
9. Sandra Jobson Darroch, *Ottoline: The Life of Lady Ottoline Morrell* (New York: Coward, McCann, & Geoghegan, 1975), p. 62.
10. Hermione Lee, *Virginia Woolf* (London: Chatto & Windus, 1996), p. 269.
11. J. H. Willis, *Leonard and Virginia Woolf as Publishers: The Hogarth Press, 1917–41* (Charlottesville: University Press of Virginia, 1992), p. 400.
12. Barney, *Adventures of the Mind*, p. 115.
13. *Ibid.*, pp. 13–14, 117.
14. Suzanne Rodriguez, *Wild Heart: A Life. Natalie Clifford Barney's Journey from Victorian America to Belle Epoque Paris* (New York: HarperCollins, 2002), pp. 252–5.
15. Lois Rudnick, *Mabel Dodge Luhan: New Woman, New Worlds* (Albuquerque: University of New Mexico Press, 1984), pp. 66–9.
16. *Ibid.*, p. 102.
17. David Levering Lewis, *When Harlem Was in Vogue* (New York: Vintage, 1982), p. 156.
18. Dorothy West, *Where the Wild Grape Grows* (Amherst: University of Massachusetts Press, 2004), pp. 16–17.
19. Carolyn Wedin Sylvander, *Jessie Redmon Fauset, Black American Writer* (Albany, NY: Whitston, 1981), p. 77.
20. Lewis, *When Harlem Was in Vogue*, p. 127.
21. Gloria T. Hull, *Color, Sex, and Poetry: Three Women Writers of the Harlem Renaissance* (Bloomington: Indiana University Press, 1987), pp. 165–6.
22. *Ibid.*, pp. 166–7.
23. Lawrence Rainey, *Institutions of Modernism: Literary Elites and Public Culture* (New Haven: Yale University Press, 1998), pp. 39, 99.
24. *Ibid.*, p. 4.
25. Gillian Hanscombe and Virginia L. Smyers, *Writing for Their Lives: The Modernist Women 1910–1940* (London: Women's Press, 1987), p. 189.

26. Hazel V. Carby, *Reconstructing Womanhood: The Emergence of the Afro-American Woman Novelist* (New York: Oxford University Press, 1987), p. 7.
27. Abby Arthur Johnson and Ronald Maberry Johnson, *Propaganda and Aesthetics: The Literary Politics of African-American Magazines in the Twentieth Century* (Amherst: University of Massachusetts Press, 1991), pp. 55–6.
28. Rainey, *Institutions of Modernism*, pp. 42–76.
29. Noel Riley Fitch, *Sylvia Beach and the Lost Generation: A History of Literary Paris in the Twenties and Thirties* (New York: Norton, 1983), pp. 102–40.
30. Jayne Marek, *Women Editing Modernism: "Little" Magazines and Literary History* (Lexington: University Press of Kentucky, 1995), pp. 95–9.
31. James R. Mellow, *Charmed Circle: Gertrude Stein and Company* (New York: Praeger, 1974), pp. 316–20; Hugh Ford, *Published in Paris: American and British Writers, Printers, and Publishers in Paris, 1920–1939* (New York: Macmillan, 1975), pp. 65–8.
32. Robert M. Crunden, *American Salons: Encounters with European Modernism 1885–1917* (New York: Oxford University Press, 1993), pp. 180–1.
33. Geoffrey Wolff, *Black Sun: The Brief Transit and Violent Eclipse of Harry Crosby* (New York: Vintage, 1985), pp. 174–5, 313.
34. Marek, *Women Editing Modernism*, pp. 103–6.
35. Willis, *Leonard and Virginia Woolf as Publishers*, pp. 4–6.
36. *Ibid.*, pp. 15–16.
37. *Ibid.*, pp. 404–5.
38. Hanscombe and Smyers, *Writing for Their Lives*, pp. 207–12.
39. George Bornstein, *Material Modernism: The Politics of the Page* (Cambridge: Cambridge University Press, 2001), pp. 110–13.
40. Ford, *Published in Paris*, pp. 276–8.
41. Mellow, *Charmed Circle*, pp. 348–50.
42. Ford, *Published in Paris*, p. 233.
43. Margaret Anderson, *My Thirty Years' War* (1930; New York: Horizon Press, 1969), p. 35.
44. *Ibid.*

5

Gender in women's modernism

In her 1928 essay *A Room of One's Own*, Virginia Woolf championed the ideal of the "androgynous mind," claiming that "It is fatal to be a man or woman pure and simple; one must be woman-manly or man-womanly."[1] Though delivered by means of a seemingly conversational, even whimsical rhetoric, Woolf's proclamation is nonetheless one of the most revolutionary statements by a modernist woman writer advocating the overthrow of the traditional patriarchal gender roles that rendered women unequal and inferior in the perceptions of Western societies. The concept, however, was not *sui generis*; rather, it was the culmination of various movements advancing the cause of women's rights that had been growing since the Enlightenment, through philosophers such as Mary Wollstonecraft, Marion Reid, and John Stuart Mill. Woolf sought not only to subvert long-standing gender conventions restricting women's ability to move beyond the limitations of the domestic sphere but also, albeit more subtly, to challenge the validity of what Adrienne Rich would term "compulsory heterosexuality."[2]

Early feminists argued for the education of women and against the legal restrictions that rendered most women little more than their husbands' chattel. Eventually women's suffrage movements arose in Britain, the United States, and other nations.[3] While concerned primarily with gaining women's right to vote, they advocated women's property and marital rights as well. As these efforts gained momentum in the 1880s and 1890s, the ideal of the "New Woman" emerged as a preferable alternative to the Victorian "feminine ideal" espoused by Sarah Stickney Ellis's conduct books and in Coventry Patmore's poem "The Angel in the House," the latter of which apotheosized the figure Woolf would later claim to "kill" in self-defense in her essay "Professions for Women" (1931):

> She was intensely sympathetic. She was immensely charming. She was utterly unselfish. She excelled in the difficult arts of family life. She sacrificed herself daily. If there was chicken, she took the leg; if there was a draught she sat in it

– in short she was so constituted that she never had a mind or wish of her own, but preferred to sympathize always with the minds and wishes of others. Above all – I need not say it – she was pure.[4]

The New Woman, on the other hand, clearly had a mind and wishes of her own. She defied traditional gender roles by seeking an education equal to that available to men as well as an occupation in which she could put her education to use and earn an independent income. Accordingly, she would be free to marry for love rather than economic security – if, that is, she chose to marry or have children at all. She challenged the norms that religion and society considered ordained by God and nature, cast off the restrictive corsets and crinolines that hampered a woman's bodily movements – in some extreme cases daring to don quasi-masculine attire – and sought to participate in the political processes that affected her life and liberty. Some of the most radical New Women favored free love as the solution to marriage inequality and sexual mores that fostered a double standard for men and women.

Her advocates were freethinking writers and activists of both sexes, notably the members of the Fabian Society, a British socialist intellectual group whose membership included Edward Carpenter, George Bernard Shaw, H. G. Wells, Annie Besant, Emmeline Pankhurst, Havelock Ellis, Leonard and Virginia Woolf, and Bertrand Russell, among others. Similar groups of intellectuals and social activists arose elsewhere, one notable example being the Heterodoxy Club, founded in Greenwich Village in 1912 by suffragist Marie Jenney Howe. Its members included Emma Goldman, Helen Hull, Henrietta Rodman, Crystal Eastman, and, perhaps most notably, Charlotte Perkins Gilman.[5] It was Eastman who, as Mary P. Ryan observes, "issued the new woman's sexual manifesto in no uncertain terms":

> Feminists are not nuns. That should be established. We want to love and be loved, and most of us want children . . . But we want our love to be joyous and free – not clouded with ignorance and fear.[6]

Considering the number of authors among the members of these associations, it is hardly surprising that the New Woman soon became a significant figure in literary plots. In addition to her numerous writings on the subject of women's rights, Gilman is responsible for two works of fiction that are staples of the feminist canon, her story "The Yellow Wallpaper" (1892) and the utopian novel *Herland* (1915). In the former, a semi-autobiographical protest against the misguided medical treatment given to women with psychological disorders, an unnamed woman suffering from post-partum depression is confined – virtually incarcerated – by her physician husband and forced to endure a "rest cure." Accordingly, she is confined to bed and deprived of any work or activity that could excite her mental state. The treatment proves a hindrance rather than a help, and in her solitude she seeks mental stimulation by obsessively and imaginatively observing the wallpaper in her room, eventually falling prey to psychosis and seeking fellowship with the imaginary woman who, she believes, dwells within its patterns. In the end, wishing to hide her obsession from her husband, she strips the wallpaper from the wall so as to "free" the woman. Once her husband discovers what she is doing, he faints in shock – an oddly "feminine" expression of distress – and the story concludes with her repeatedly circling the room, continually walking over him and proclaiming her escape. The story makes painfully evident that the traditional roles of wife and mother, combined with a lack of patriarchal compassion or insight, can be so destructive to a woman's psyche that for some women the only liberation possible is an escape into madness.

In contrast with dysfunctionality of "The Yellow Wallpaper," *Herland* suggests the seemingly unlimited potential of women in a utopian society free from the restrictions of traditional patriarchal gender roles and, thanks to parthenogenesis, from any need of any male assistance in reproducing. Seen from the perspective of one of three American male explorers who accidentally discover an unknown, all-female society, the novel extols the New Woman's ideals and sets them against the limited roles of women in early twentieth-century America. To the narrator's amazement, the inhabitants of Herland, undisturbed by the presence of the male sex for centuries, are skilled workers and administrators who display advanced scientific and mathematical knowledge, practice population control, cultivate the land thoughtfully to insure an ample food supply, and live free from war. Their national policy is dictated by consideration of the greater good of their society as a whole. All the women are, moreover, strong in both mind and body. The three men are taken captive but treated respectfully until they are assimilated, with varying degrees of success, into this otherwise homosocial culture. The men nonetheless insist on introducing elements of American culture, including marriage and heterosexual relationships. Though two of the men manage, with difficulty, to adjust to the concept of sexual equality, the third is banished as he is unable to overcome his need for sexual domination. Through allegorical characters, Gilman effectively condemns many of the gender and sexual practices of her own nation and society while imagining what could be if women were allowed to live to their full potential.

As attractive as the concept of the New Woman might be to many women and not a few men, it inevitably met resistance, as Gilman's story suggests, from the forces of patriarchal tradition, particularly those vested in the religious and medical professions. The New Woman stood in direct contradiction to the scriptural dictum demanding women be submissive to their husbands, thus the concept of sexual equality was anathema to many clergy-men and believers, a blasphemous rejection of a divinely ordained order of nature. At the same time, while the medical sexologist Havelock Ellis (whose wife, Edith Lees, with whom he had an "open marriage," was openly lesbian) was sympathetic to the cause of the New Woman, other medical men, such as Richard von Krafft-Ebing, reinscribed the notion that submission was an innate and therefore natural condition for women, while Cesare Lombroso and Guglielmo Ferrero argued in *La donna delinquente* [*The Female Offender*] (1895) that women who deviated from the prescribed social norms were degenerate and prone to criminal behavior. Many physicians regarded women who derived pleasure from sexual activity, rather than regarding it as an unpleasant duty necessary to please a husband and bear children, as disordered and dangerous. Religious tradition, unproven medical theories, and no small amount of social hysteria combined to portray women seeking not only equality but also sexual pleasure in their relationships as threats to the very foundations of Western civilization.[7]

While most discussions of the New Woman focused almost exclusively on new models of heterosexuality, lesbianism was nonetheless tacitly implicated in both the ideals of the various fin-de-siècle feminist movements and the fears these concepts provoked in the more conventionally minded. In effect, a woman who was free to love as she chose might choose to love another woman and, consequently, women might readily dispose of any need for men other than for reproductive purposes. Further complicating matters was the lack of specific distinction, at that time, between biological sex and gender; "masculine" and "feminine" behaviors were believed to be simply part of the natural order, while the concept of sexuality was only rudimentally understood by sexologists, much less by most ordinary individuals. Moreover, lesbianism maintained a certain degree of invisibility, not simply as a concept so dangerous as to be unspeakable, but also because of a lack of cultural awareness that it existed at all. Sexual acts between men had been criminalized in Britain by means of the Labouchère Amendment to the Criminal Law Amendment Act of 1885 and sensationalized a decade later by the trials of Oscar Wilde, who was imprisoned as a result of the afore-mentioned legislation. No similar law, however, existed in Britain regarding sexual contact between women. An apocryphal story maintains that Queen Victoria personally lined through passages pertaining to female homosexu-ality in the Labouchère Amendment as a result of her belief that women possessed an essential innocence and lack of sexual desire that would obviate the possibility of such conduct. In reality, the legislators themselves chose not to criminalize lesbianism as to do so would acknowledge its existence and draw the attention of women who would otherwise remain ignorant of it.[8]

Lesbianism, however, was not unknown in nineteenth-century literature, even if it was more often the subject of male-authored fantasy than a representation of love and desire between actual living women. Exotic and dangerous women, often cross-dressed or vampiric, seduced or otherwise engaged in erotic gambols with innocent and rather more ordinary women – arguably for the pleasure of the male voyeuristic gaze – in works such as Théophile Gautier's *Mademoiselle de Maupin* (1835), Honoré de Balzac's *The Girl With the Golden Eyes* (1835), Charles Baudelaire's *Les Fleurs du mal* (1857), Algernon Charles Swinburne's "Anactoria" (1866), Paul Verlaine's *Scenes of Sapphic Love* (1867), Pierre Louÿs's *The Songs of Bilitis* (1894), and Aleister Crowley's "The Lesbian Hell" (1898). Even in more ostensibly realistic texts as Thomas Hardy's *Desperate Remedies* (1871) or Émile Zola's *Nana* (1880), the lesbian figure is one of irremediable decadence.[9] Even Olive Chancellor, the protagonist of Henry James's *The Bostonians* (1886) and one of the few conceivably sympathetic lesbian characters in male-authored nineteenth-century fiction, is a controlling man-hater who seems more neurasthenic than libidinous. While James grants Olive a certain tragic dignity in the end, she nonetheless retains a trace of the aforementioned stereotypes. While she is too lacking in erotic energy to be vampiric in the usual sense, she nonetheless plots to take possession of Verena Tallent, her love object, in a relatively cold, bloodless manner, virtually purchasing the younger woman from her father – only to lose her to her vastly more unpleasant and controlling cousin, the chauvinistic Basil Ransom.

Gertrude Stein's *Q.E.D.* (1903) is one of the first modernist novels to represent lesbianism forthrightly without recourse to exotic stereotypes, titillating eroticism, or other forms of sensationalism. Heavily influenced by James, Stein's first novel details a triangulated lesbian relationship based on her own problematic affair with a fellow student who was also involved with another woman student. The analytical and earnest Adele, Stein's autobiographical character, seeks to understand the attraction she feels towards the capricious Helen, even as their relationship comes under the scrutiny of Helen's lover, the sophisticated and wildly jealous Mabel. Adele and Helen declare their love and seem on the verge of consummating it, but Mabel intervenes, informing Adele that her relationship with Helen is financial as well as sexual. Adele, heretofore naïve regarding the dynamics of sexual relationships, is appalled and enters into a wildly oscillating cycle of conflicting emotions. She finally decides to forego her finer sensibilities and pursue Helen romantically, but the latter, fatigued by Adele's indecision, rejects her, leading to Adele's final, frustrated acknowledgement that the situation is "very near being a dead-lock."[10]

Stein relocated to Paris soon after writing *Q.E.D.*, and the novel remained unpublished until after her death. She subsequently reconfigured the plot of *Q.E.D.* across racial and sexual lines to create "Melanctha," one of the stories comprising *Three Lives* (1909). In doing so, Stein recast her autobiographical character Adele as Jeff Campbell, a young African American doctor who is attracted to Melanctha, an educated mulatta who "was always seeking peace and quiet, and she could always only find new ways to be in trouble," much like Helen.[11] Their relationship does not progress beyond circular discussions in which Jeff extols the middle-class values of "living good and being regular," while Melanctha protests that he is unable – or unwilling – to comprehend the lure of less socially acceptable epistemologies.[12]

Changing the category of social marginalization from sexuality to race is hardly unproblematic; nonetheless, the seemingly endless argument between the two main characters, here greatly magnified and more wrought with frustration by means of Stein's by now characteristic use of repetition, is virtually the same case for middle-class sexual repression that Adele fecklessly posits as a safeguard against the lesbian temptations that Helen represents. The heterosexual masquerade that Stein imposes on "Melanctha" – suggestions of homoerotic bonds between the protagonist and her female friends notwithstanding – is arguably as significant as the racial one. As Lillian Faderman observes, Stein understood that, at that point in time, any unambiguous representation of lesbianism "was *inaccrochable* unless she could disguise it. She was determined to tell the truth, but willing to compromise enough to 'tell it slant.'"[13] The literary sex change to which Stein resorted was employed by other lesbian authors at the time, most famously Virginia Woolf in her rendering of her lover Vita Sackville-West in *Orlando* (1928), Sackville-West in her own quasi-autobiographical novel *Challenge* (1923), and, arguably, Willa Cather in *My Ántonia* (1918). Moreover, as subsequently demonstrated by the censorship trial of Radclyffe Hall's *The Well of Loneliness*, the power of governmental agencies to impose legal sanctions against works deemed to be offensive was still a formidable force in keeping lesbianism invisible to the public eye. Accordingly, Stein relied on a double discourse of encoded references accessible only to the *cognoscenti* and further occluded by means of relentless repetition and wordplay. In "Miss Furr and Miss Skeene" (1922), for example, she suggests a lesbian relationship between the eponymous characters by stating that "they were regular in being gay, they learned little things that are things in being gay, they learned many little things that are things in being gay, they were gay every day, they were regular, they were gay, they were gay the same length of time every day, they were gay, they were quite regularly gay."[14] The intentional nonsense of these phrases would easily discourage further examination by those hunting for obscenity.

Gertrude Stein would seem an unlikely embodiment of the New Woman ideal. Her now-iconic image, with her close-cropped hair and little to suggest any traditional outward sign of femininity, would suggest that she achieved a degree of personal androgyny that allowed her to separate the fact of biological sex from all socially imposed gender roles. Even so, Stein was among the first to reap the rewards the New Woman sought. She graduated from Radcliffe College, where she studied psychology under William James, and attended medical school at Johns Hopkins. A family inheritance allowed her to live independently and follow a career of her own choosing, and if the New Woman was free to choose when and whom she would marry, Stein did precisely that, in this case taking a woman, Alice B. Toklas, as her "wife." Remarkably, her narrative of their relationship, *The Autobiography of Alice B. Toklas* (1933), brought her an extraordinary degree of celebrity rather than opprobrium, thanks in part to its faux-naïve charm, as well as its considerable circumspection regarding the sexual aspect of their life together.

The achievement of Willa Cather, Stein's near contemporary and a fellow American, followed a similar trajectory, even if their works were, both stylistically and in setting, worlds apart. Sandra M. Gilbert and Susan Gubar note that Cather "[found] it necessary to separate herself from the didacticism of the feminist movement and from what she viewed as a fatally feminized literary matrilineage."[15] Even so, her own life, as well as those of many of her female protagonists, achieved the objectives to which the New Woman aspired. Adamant in her desire for an education, Cather attended the University of Nebraska, where she adopted masculine attire, wore her hair short, and at times referred to herself as "William Cather, Jr.," suggesting a sense of gender dysphoria, even as she began her first relationships with other women. From her provincial beginnings, which play a significant role in the *bildüng* of her most notable characters, she eventually moved to New York, where she became the managing editor of *McClure's Magazine*. In her subsequent career as a novelist, she attained tremendous popularity and was one of the best-selling American authors of the early twentieth century.

Most of her novels focus to some degree on the concept of success and failure in America for individuals of either sex and of various class or ethnic backgrounds. An examination of two of her major novels, *The Song of the Lark* (1915) and *My Ántonia* (1918), will reveal the extent to which her more successful female characters are those who eschew traditional gender roles. The former work chronicles the ascent of Thea Kronborg, the daughter of a Swedish immigrant family, from a small frontier town to international acclaim as an operatic diva.[16] Her success is the result of a strong work ethic and a single-minded determination as she devotes herself to learning and eventually mastering her art. So extraordinary is her dedication that she often seems coldly aloof in her interactions with others. She manifests no particular "feminine" sentimentality toward her family, and, with the exception of a brief interlude with her admirer Fred Ottenburg (whose attraction to her is magnified by seeing her in boyish garb), she shows no interest in romantic pursuits. Indeed, her eventual marriage to Fred is related in a single sentence in the concluding pages and seems, at that point, little more than an afterthought of scant importance.

In *My Ántonia*, another immigrant woman realizes her own form of success, albeit one far removed from the glamour of the operatic stage. The niceties of lady-like behavior are luxuries that Ántonia Shimerda, the eldest daughter of an impoverished Bohemian settler family in Nebraska, cannot afford in the wake of her father's apparent suicide. In order to help support her family, "Tony" engages in physical labor, often dressed in boy's clothing, and gradually loses the refinement she once had, much to the chagrin of the narrator, her childhood friend and erstwhile admirer Jim Burden. To some extent, Jim is the more "feminized" of the two, lacking Ántonia's physical and psychic strength. Indeed, he exhibits a certain sexual squeamishness, as he is again disturbed when the adolescent Ántonia begins to exhibit a sexualized femininity replacing her earlier tomboyishness and, as a girl of the working class, is perceived as free and easy by her social betters. As the object of the male gaze, she barely escapes rape by her employer and is later impregnated by a man who abandons her at the altar, even as the more privileged Jim leaves Nebraska to study at Harvard. At this juncture, social and gender expectations of success or failure would seem a matter of inevitability for the respective characters; twenty years later, however, when Jim returns to Nebraska, he discovers a vital and content Ántonia, now married to a fellow immigrant and the mother of a large family. Through hard work, she and her husband have developed a prosperous farm and a happy home. Their relationship, however, is clearly based on companionship rather than passion, unlike Jim's own now loveless marriage.

In an abstract discussion of the art of fiction, Cather stated that "It is the inexplicable presence of the thing not named, of the overtone divined by the ear but not heard by it, the verbal mood, the emotional aura of the fact or the thing or the deed, that gives high quality to the novel or the drama, as well as to poetry itself."[17] Various critics have argued that lesbianism, or homoerotic desire in general, is "the thing not named," present in its seeming absence, in Cather's novels.[18] Sexual passion is represented solely as a heterosexual construct, and even then as a destructive force that brings disaster to men and women alike – for every Thea Kronborg or Ántonia Shimerda, Cather presents a nearly parallel character who fails disastrously. The eponymous heroine of *Lucy Gayheart* (1935), a budding artist who could aspire to the greatness of a Thea Kronborg, is undone when her romantic fantasies eclipse her art, while Marian Forrester, the *grande dame* of *A Lost Lady* (1923), falls prey to her own venal sexuality. Myra Henshawe, the protagonist of *My Mortal Enemy* (1926), seeks the privileges and comfort to be gained through the performance of traditional femininity but ultimately loses all by using sexuality and marriage so as to achieve her desires through her husband rather than through her own work. Men, too, are undermined by their heterosexual desires, particularly those who romantically idealize the perceived femininity of their love objects, only to suffer disillusionment or fall into feminized roles themselves. These male characters, particularly those from whose narrative viewpoint the female protagonist is seen, can be interpreted as literary cross-dressers who, like Stein's Jeff Campbell, allow the lesbian author to represent the female protagonist by means of an eroticized gaze. In Judith Butler's assessment, they perform "a translation into the masculine gender" that would not be acceptable to a mainstream audience if mediated by means of an unambiguously female consciousness:

> The prohibition that is said to work effectively to quell the articulation of lesbian sexuality in Cather's fiction is ... precisely the occasion of its constitution in exchange. It is perhaps less that the legibility of lesbianism is perpetually endangered in Cather's text than that lesbian sexuality within the text is produced as a perpetual challenge to legibility.[19]

The First World War and professions for women

Because of the resistance of patriarchal culture, many of those who aspired to the freedoms embodied by the New Woman found the attainment of those ideals elusive. Many female protagonists, regardless of their particular sexuality or gender identity, either perished or eventually capitulated to the demands of tradition and society in the fictions of diverse modernist women writers including Edith Wharton, May Sinclair, Willa Cather, Virginia Woolf, Nella Larsen, Jean Rhys, Dorothy Richardson, and Elizabeth Bowen, among others. But if male-dominated institutions long restricted women's ability to explore unconventional gender roles and express their sexuality, political infighting among the governments of the world's most powerful nations, the highest echelons of the patriarchy, eventually – and ironically – necessitated the entrance of women into occupations that had previously been the sole province of the male sex.

In *Three Guineas*, Virginia Woolf, writing on the verge of the Second World War, recalled the moment when the commencement of the First World War provided women with an unprecedented opportunity to set aside restrictive domestic roles and the idea that "Marriage was the only profession open to her":

> How else can we explain that amazing outburst in August 1914, when the daughters of educated men ... rushed into hospitals ... drove lorries, worked in fields and munitions factories ... So profound was her unconscious loathing for ... the private house with its cruelty, its poverty, its hypocrisy, its immorality, its inanity that she would undertake any task however menial, exercise any fascination however fatal that enabled her to escape.[20]

For some this escape would prove only temporary; many had to relinquish their exciting new occupations to make way for men returning to the workforce once the war had ended. However, the staggering casualties wrought by increasingly lethal military technologies resulted in significant demographic shifts, particularly in Britain and Europe and, to a lesser extent, in the United States. The loss of a large number of men of marriageable age meant that marriage, "the only profession open" to women before the war, was now closed to many of them. The friendship and works of Vera Brittain and Winifred Holtby illustrate the impact of the war on the lives of young women. The two met at Somerville College, one of the first Oxford colleges founded for women, soon after the war. Both women had personally experienced the horrors of combat, Brittain as a Voluntary Aid Detachment nurse and Holtby as an enlistee in the Women's Auxiliary Army Corps. Brittain's brother and her fiancé were both killed in battle, while Holtby's sweetheart was wounded. After they graduated from Somerville, the two women lived together for five years, until Brittain's marriage, establishing themselves as writers and activists for feminist and pacifist causes.[21] Brittain's volumes of memoirs, *Testament of Youth* (1933) and *Testament of Friendship* (1940), respectively recounting her war experiences and her relationship with Holtby, provide an insight into the multifarious ways in which the First World War drastically changed not only the lives of many British women but social constructions of gender as well.

The taste of liberation that many felt, combined with the postwar cynicism of the "Lost Generation," resulted in shifting sexual mores. Sociologist Jeffrey Weeks observes that "amongst certain strata of the population the 1920s saw a relaxation of some sexual taboos: the new feminists spoke of sexual pleasure, birth control was more openly advocated, progressive intellectuals espoused sex reforms, while homosexuality caused a certain fashionable *frisson*."[22] These issues appear with increasing frequency and frankness in women's literature of the 1920s. Complexly intertwined themes of war and female self-realization, particularly in terms of gender and sexuality, feature prominently in Radclyffe Hall's best-known fictions. "Miss Ogilvy Finds Herself" (written as a short story in 1926; later published in book form in 1934) begins with the demobilization of an ambulance corps unit. As the erstwhile driver Wilhelmina Ogilvy mournfully watches, her vehicle is unceremoniously dispatched to postwar obsolescence. Before the war, Miss Ogilvy's talents for management were unfulfilled because of her sex, and she felt no desire for marriage and children. The war had provided her with an opportunity to escape "the bad joke that Nature seemed to have played her" and allowed her a highly romanticized taste of "manly" pursuits and military bravado.[23] Her return to civilian life and her family leaves her increasingly depressed and disoriented. During the course of a solitary exploration of a local cave, she falls asleep and has an atavistic dream of herself as a primitive warrior, the protector of "his" land and woman. In an odd narrative twist and shift in point of view, the story concludes with Miss Ogilvy found dead in the cave the following day, presumably having found herself and departing a world that held no place for her.

"Miss Ogilvy Finds Herself" presents a rather forlorn prospect of what it meant to be a lesbian in the postwar years as well as a problematic conflation of gender and sexuality. Miss Ogilvy is not simply a woman who desires other women; rather, she is a personification of Krafft-Ebing's theory of sexual inversion, in effect a male consciousness trapped in a female body, seeking to perform masculine gender roles and desiring women as would a heterosexual man. This theory is dubious, however, as it posits sexual inversion as an essential trait and does not allow for the fluidity of socially constructed gendered behavior. Moreover, as it does not differentiate gender from biological sex or distinguish homosexuality as a phenomenon unto itself, it would seem to obviate the possibility of love and desire between two non-"inverted" women. "Miss Ogilvy Finds Herself" can be seen, however, as an experimental practice piece for Hall's highly controversial novel, *The Well of Loneliness* (1928), in which the overly simplistic ideas about sex, gender, and sexuality that inform the former work become much more complicated.

Stephen Gordon, the long-suffering protagonist of *The Well of Loneliness*, is marked from birth by her otherness in a variety of ways. She is given a masculine name by parents who wanted a son, seemingly predestining her to be a disappointment and, by way of compensation, masculine. At an early age she demonstrates a deep aversion to feminine activities and attire. She also becomes passionately infatuated with a female servant while still a small child and reacts with rage and melancholy upon discovering the woman's romance with a male servant. Given her parents' respective reactions – her father indulges her while her mother recoils from her – one might easily conclude that Stephen's masculinity is a gendered performance in response, identifying with the benevolent father and rebelling against the disapproving mother. Her earlier attraction to a female servant, moreover, could be readily attributed to a Freudian polymorphous perversity, which is arguably the norm for small children. Hall, however, conflates gender and biological sex in representing Stephen as a "narrow-hipped, wide-shouldered little tadpole of a baby, that yelled and yelled ... as though outraged to find itself ejected into life," suggesting that her difference is essential rather than socially constructed.[24] Considering that Stephen is born on Christmas day and ultimately plays the self-effacing martyr of society, Hall would seem to suggest that her character's sex, gender, and sexuality are part of a divinely ordained, messianic destiny.

Seeking to understand his unusual daughter, Sir Phillip Gordon, a minor aristocrat, studies the writings of Karl Heinrich Ulrichs, Richard von Krafft-Ebing, and other sexologists whose influence on Hall is apparent. He dies, however, without discussing these ideas with either his daughter or wife, and thus Stephen's adolescence is one of constant mother-daughter strife, particularly after Stephen's affair with a married woman is revealed. Upon reaching adulthood, Stephen settles in London and subsequently Paris, pursues a career as a writer, and begins to meet other homosexuals, male and female alike, including Jonathan Brockett, a gay man thought to be based on Noël Coward, and Valerie Seymour, a character based on the American expatriate Natalie Barney. Stephen, who ironically exhibits a certain degree of moralistic prudery, takes little comfort in lesbian and gay society, finding her fellow queers pathetic, revolting, and decadent. It is only with the onset of the First World War that Stephen finds a situation in which she feels she belongs when, like Miss Ogilvy, she joins an ambulance corps. Her service at the front, during which she is wounded and decorated for valor, allows her to engage in the masculine endeavors she craves. It also brings her love, in the character of Mary Llewellyn, a younger, feminine member of the corps.

After the war, Stephen and Mary commence a marriage-like relationship. Mary is soon drawn to the community around Valerie Seymour. Stephen, however, disdains the homosexual *demimonde*, which she fears will make Mary coarse and worldly, and instead futilely seeks the acceptance – on her own terms – of "respectable" upper-middle-class society. Distressed that she cannot give Mary a "normal" life, Stephen manipulates Mary into a marriage with her friend Martin Hallam. The novel concludes with Stephen, having accomplished this most extraordinarily self-abnegating and self-destructive feat, crying out, "Acknowledge us, O God, before the whole world. Give us also the right to our existence!"[25]

That Mary, whose own wishes seem beside the point, can so readily be reassimilated into institutional heterosexuality evinces Hall's basic misunderstanding of female homosexuality. Stephen's own self-assessment is distorted by reading Krafft-Ebing's description of inverts in his *Psychopathia Sexualis* (1886), which she finds in her father's library, causing her to imagine herself as one of "thousands of miserable, unwanted people, who have no right to love, no right to compassion because they're hideously maimed and ugly."[26] Hall herself was more inclined to Havelock Ellis's theory that inversion was not a pathological condition but rather a natural variation. Her acceptance of this theory, though, was such that she conceptualized only the masculine lesbian as the true, essential "invert"; feminine lesbians, according to this line of thinking, were not inverts themselves but rather "normal" women attracted to the masculinity of their female lovers. More recent critics have suggested that Stephen is not actually a lesbian but instead transsexual, a concept unknown to Hall.[27]

From an aesthetic point of view, *The Well of Loneliness* is hardly a great novel; Virginia Woolf quite aptly described it as a "meritorious dull book."[28] While courageous in its unambiguous approach to an unspeakable issue, the book is melodramatic and sentimental, and Hall's prose is often pedestrian and tedious. Stylistically, it is redolent of the Victorian era and evinces little if any association with modernist aesthetics or sensibilities. As such, it would hardly seem to merit the critical attention that has been given it, were it not for its historical legacy. It was possibly the first novel to present love between women in an unambiguous manner, and the notoriety surrounding its banning made it a *cause célèbre*. *The Well of Loneliness* was not, however, the only significant lesbian novel published in 1928. Virginia Woolf's *Orlando* appeared in press as the trial to ban Hall's work was taking place. Why the one novel incurred censorship and the other did not is a matter of representation and stylistics. Hall had no wish to be unambiguous in her presentation of marginalized sexuality – indeed, she intended to draw attention to it – and her novel was banned primarily for the one sentence that marks the consummation of Stephen's relationship with Mary: "And that night they were not divided."[29] Woolf, on the other hand, understood that to be silenced could render one's message ineffectual, and thus she resorted to ambiguity, fantasy, humor, and modernist experimentalism to shape her literary gift of love to *Orlando*'s inspiration, Vita Sackville-West.

Orlando, Woolf's whimsical protagonist, is born during the reign of Elizabeth I and has relationships with many women during his youth and early adulthood, until he awakes one morning in the eighteenth century to discover that he has changed – quite literally – into a woman. Orlando treats the matter nonchalantly, but thereafter discovers the world as women experience it. In the early twentieth century, by which time she is in her thirties, she marries Marmaduke Bonthrop Shelmerdine (based on Sackville-West's husband Harold Nicolson, who was gay). She recognizes "Shel" as her androgynous equal and counterpart:

> "You're a woman, Shel!" she cried.
> "You're a man, Orlando!" he cried.[30]

Woolf's point is not to represent these characters as hermaphroditic or inter-sexual, but rather, in keeping with her concept of the androgynous mind, to emphasize that the biological sex of the body does not determine the gender or the sexuality of the body, and that men and women alike need to create a blend of the best qualities of masculinity and femininity.

The "lesbianism" of the text is presented ambiguously. The female Orlando has flirtations with other women and recalls with some passion the affair that she had with Sasha, the Russian princess, while still a man. Overall, the novel's rhetoric is comparable to an inside joke – the sophisticated reader appreciates Woolf's sly feat of speaking the unspeakable, while an uninitiated audience is able to see only a quirky story about a character who has lived over three hundred years while aging only thirty and who changed sexes somewhere along the line. In effect, the story is so fantastic that anything could be possible, and a censor would be hard pressed to single out anything particularly obscene without looking ridiculous in the attempt.

Woolf's entire *oeuvre* is significant in its treatment of sex, gender, and sexuality, perhaps more than that of any other modernist woman writer. Many of her novels include women who are at odds with traditional gender roles and the institution of marriage. Rachel Vinrace in *The Voyage Out* (1915) is distressed to discover the meaning of heterosexuality and marriage and symbolically dies before she can wed her fiancé. The sexually repressed title character of *Mrs. Dalloway* (1925), on the other hand, marries for safety following an episode of lesbian panic, yet remains haunted decades later by memories of her youthful love for another woman.[31] Progressing further with the anti-wedlock plot, Lily Briscoe in *To the Lighthouse* (1927) resists the insistence of Mrs. Ramsay, the maternal figure with whom she is enamored, that she must marry, and she is ultimately able to arrive at a degree of self-awareness that transcends the demands of tradition. Woolf also understood the social resistance any woman who broke with convention would inevitably encounter. Lily Briscoe, along with Doris Kilman in *Mrs. Dalloway* and Miss La Trobe in *Between the Acts* (1941) – three apparently lesbian characters – demonstrate the lack of acceptance and the struggle to achieve self-sufficiency afflicting women outside of the marriage plot. Nor did Woolf confine her exploration of gender and sexuality to women. Her most sympathetic male characters such as St. John Hirst in *The Voyage Out*, Septimus Warren Smith in *Mrs. Dalloway*, and Neville in *The Waves* (1931) – all arguably homosexual – are at odds with traditional masculinity and are to some extent "man-womanly."

In an earlier version of what would eventually become the essay "Professions for Women," Woolf predicted that "In fifty years I shall be able to use all this very queer knowledge [the imagination is] ready to bring me. But not now":

> I cannot make use of what [the imagination] tell[s] me – about womens [*sic*] bodies for instance – their passions – and so on, because the conventions are still very strong. If I were to overcome the conventions I should need the courage of a hero, and I am not a hero.[32]

The works of a vast multitude of women writers in the second half of the twentieth century evince the accuracy of Woolf's predictions. That they were able to do so is due, in great part, to the modernist women writers who blazed a trail before them.

NOTES

1. Virginia Woolf, *A Room of One's Own* (New York: Harcourt Brace, 1929), p. 104.
2. Adrienne Rich, "Compulsory Heterosexuality and Lesbian Existence," in *Blood, Bread, and Poetry: Selected Prose 1979–1985* (New York: W. W. Norton, 1986), p. 23.
3. While most historical attention has been focused on the United States and the United Kingdom, neither of these nations was the first to extend the right to vote to women. They were preceded by New Zealand (1893), Australia (1902), Finland (1906), Norway (1913), Denmark (1915), Iceland (1915), and the Netherlands (1917). Austria, Czechoslovakia, Poland, and Sweden, along with the United Kingdom, extended suffrage in 1918. Germany and Luxembourg followed in 1919, as did the United States in 1920.
4. Virginia Woolf, "Professions for Women," in *The Death of the Moth and Other Essays* (New York: Harcourt Brace, 1942), p. 237.
5. On the Heterodoxy Club, see Judith Schwarz, *Radical Feminists of Heterodoxy: Greenwich Village, 1912–1940* (Norwich, VT: New Victoria Publishers, 1986); see also Sandra Adickes, *To Be Young Was Very Heaven: Women in New York Before the First World War* (New York: Macmillan, 2000), pp. 33–44, 59–68, 87–97. For a comprehensive study of modernist feminist movements in both the United States and Britain, see Lucy Delap, *The Feminist Avant-Garde: Transatlantic Encounters of the Early Twentieth Century* (Cambridge: Cambridge University Press, 2007).
6. Mary P. Ryan, *Mysteries of Sex: Tracing Women and Men Through American History* (Chapel Hill: University of North Carolina Press, 2006), p. 216.

7. For an overview of the most influential writings of medical sexology, see Regina Barreca, *Desire and Imagination: Classic Essays in Sexuality* (New York: Plume, 1995).

8. See Lesley A. Hall, *Sex, Gender and Social Change in Britain since 1880* (New York: Palgrave Macmillan, 2000), pp. 39–40.

9. See Lillian Faderman, *Surpassing the Love of Men: Romantic Friendship and Love Between Women from the Renaissance to the Present* (New York: William Morrow, 1981), pp. 277–94.

10. Gertrude Stein, *Fernhurst, Q.E.D., and Other Early Writings* (New York: Liveright, 1973), p. 133.

11. Gertrude Stein, *Three Lives* (New York: Vintage, 1936), p. 93.

12. *Ibid.*, p. 124.

13. Faderman, *Surpassing the Love of Men*, p. 405.

14. Gertrude Stein, "Miss Furr and Miss Skeene," in *Geography and Plays* (Madison: University of Wisconsin Press, 1993), p. 17. The origin of the vernacular use of "gay" as a synonym for "homosexual" is unknown; however, Stein's story might well mark the first written example of the usage.

15. Sandra M. Gilbert and Susan Gubar, *No Man's Land: The Place of the Woman Writer in the Twentieth Century*, vol. II, *Sexchanges* (New Haven: Yale University Press, 1989), p. 174.

16. Thea Kronborg is based, with some artistic license on Cather's part, on the Swedish-American soprano Olive Fremstad (1871–1951). For a discussion of Fremstad as a lesbian icon, see Terry Castle, "In Praise of Brigitte Fassbaender: Reflections on Diva Worship," in *En Travesti: Women, Gender Subversion, Opera*, ed. Corinne E. Blackmer and Patricia Juliana Smith (New York: Columbia University Press, 1995), pp. 20–58.

17. Willa Cather, "The Novel *Démeublé*," in *Not Under Forty* (Lincoln: University of Nebraska Press, 1988), p. 50.

18. On gender and sexuality in Cather's novels, see Sharon O'Brien, *Willa Cather: The Emerging Voice* (Oxford: Oxford University Press, 1987); Judith Butler, *Bodies That Matter* (New York: Routledge, 1993), pp. 143–66; Marilee Lindemann, *Willa Cather: Queering America* (New York: Columbia University Press, 1999); Hermione Lee, *Willa Cather: Double Lives* (New York: Vintage, 1989); Jonathan Goldberg, *Willa Cather and Others* (Durham, NC: Duke University Press, 2001).

19. Butler, *Bodies That Matter*, pp. 144–5.

20. Virginia Woolf, *Three Guineas* (New York: Harcourt Brace, 1938), pp. 38–9.

21. The nature of the relationship between Brittain and Holtby has long been a matter of speculation, despite Brittain's denial of lesbianism. For an examination of the complexity of their relationship as well as their works, see Jean Kennard, *Vera Brittain and Winifred Holtby: A Working Partnership* (Hanover: University Press of New England, 1989). It should be noted that Holtby presented a sympathetic representation of a lesbian couple in her novel *The Crowded Street* (1924).

22. Jeffrey Weeks, *Sex, Politics and Society*, 2nd edn. (London: Longman, 1989), p. 199.

23. Radclyffe Hall, *Miss Ogilvy Finds Herself* (New York: Harcourt Brace, 1934), p. 12.

24. Radclyffe Hall, *The Well of Loneliness* (1928; New York: Anchor, 1990), p. 13.

25. *Ibid.*, p. 437.
26. *Ibid.*, p. 204.
27. See Jay Prosser, "'Some Primitive Thing Conceived in a Turbulent Age of Transition': The Transsexual Emerging from *The Well*," in *Palatable Poison: Critical Perspectives on* The Well of Loneliness, ed. Laura Doan and Jay Prosser (New York: Columbia University Press, 2001), pp. 129–44; and Judith Halberstam, "'A Writer of Misfits': 'John' Radclyffe Hall and the Discourse of Inversion," in *Palatable Poison*, ed. Doan and Prosser, pp. 145–61. The essays in *Palatable Poison* comprise possibly the most extensive examination of Hall's novel to date.
28. Virginia Woolf, *The Letters of Virginia Woolf*, vol. III, *1923–1928*, ed. Nigel Nicolson and Joanne Trautmann (New York: Harcourt Brace, 1978), p. 520.
29. Hall, *The Well*, p. 313.
30. Virginia Woolf, *Orlando* (New York: Harcourt Brace, 1928), p. 252.
31. On the narrative function of lesbian panic in Woolf's novels, see Patricia Juliana Smith, *Lesbian Panic: Homoeroticism in Modern British Women's Fictions* (New York: Columbia University Press, 1997), pp. 17–73.
32. Virginia Woolf, "Speech before the London/National Society for Women's Service, January 21, 1931," in *The Pargiters: The Novel-Essay Portion of* The Years, ed. Mitchell A. Leaska (New York: Harcourt Brace, 1978), p. xxxix.

6

THADIOUS M. DAVIS

Black women's modernist literature

Although the shift into a modern mode happened for all African Americans with Emancipation, the major turn to modernist literature for African American women occurred with the second generation to come of age after the end of slavery. For these women born just before or just after the turn of the twentieth century, literature was more often an avocation than a vocation. The economic pressures on all descendants of enslaved people and the social strictures separating blacks into ever more limited spaces meant that a career as a writer was virtually an impossibility, yet black women persisted in writing, and in doing so with an acute consciousness of their raced and gendered location in a social ground constituted out of spatial and relational structures.

The all-important room of one's own that Virginia Woolf desired for herself and other women artists in her era, black women writers during this same period configured simply as "elbow room," by which they placed an added emphasis on the body itself. During the New Negro or Harlem Renaissance, a progressive period for African American writers following the First World War, Georgia Douglas Johnson publicly spoke of that small space when she was featured in *Opportunity Magazine*'s 1927 "Contest Spotlight":

> I write because I love to write ... If I might ask of some fairy godmother special favors, one would sure be for a clearing space, elbow room in which to think and write and live beyond the reach of the Wolf's fingers. However, much that we do and write about comes just because of the daily struggle for bread and breath – so perhaps it's just as well.[1]

Johnson articulated eloquently the common plight facing black women and men writers even in the heyday of the "vogue" in New Negro writing, the need for the economic resources to do the work of an artist, but she called attention particularly to the narrow spaces of confinement in which black women artists worked. One result, then, is the preoccupation with issues of space; these issues, whether related to labor and means of production or to social ranking, turn on the inequities of race construction and gender stratifications.

Yi-Fu Tuan sees space as freedom and place as security, but considers that both are "basic components of the lived world" and often taken for granted.[2] Tuan's thinking about space enables a reading of black women modernists, who struggled to achieve the openness and freedom of space, but from the vantage point of security and stability which for too long and too often were not components of black life.

Dialogue between the past and the present as a way of approaching futurity was especially significant for black women artists. Shoulder to shoulder with black men from the middle passage through enslavement and emancipation, black women moved into the modern era with this historical awareness. As a result they understood that they were still pressed against both the bodies and the needs of black men, who personified the conception of achieving futurity through racial uplift. Elise Johnson McDougald, writing in Alain Locke's landmark 1925 anthology, *The New Negro*, catalogs the progress made by black women in employment and education; nonetheless, she concludes with the dominant thinking: "She is measuring up to the needs of her family, community and race, and radiating a hope throughout the land. The wind of the race's destiny stirs more briskly because of her striving."[3] For black women the erasure of their specific concerns as women within their racial identity remained one of their greatest challenges and problems.

In acknowledging the precarious position of black women as historical subjects, Anne Spencer wrote in her self-introduction in Countee Cullen's poetry anthology *Caroling Dusk* (1927): "I write about some of the things I love. But I have no civilized articulation for the things I hate. I proudly love being a Negro woman – its [sic] so involved and interesting. *We* are the PROBLEM – the great national game of taboo."[4] Spencer makes her claim a national issue without articulating the specifics of the problem and taboo. Black women writers, much like Spencer, finding themselves without elbow room often simply reverted either to eliding what they could not express or to struggling to make visible in some symbolic context what they desired to bring to expression. Spencer, for example, could not resist representing the social relations governing women's lives: "It is dangerous for a woman to defy the gods; / To taunt them with the tongue's thin tip," because "The gods own the searing lightning, / The drowning waters, tormenting fears, / The anger of red sins," and "are Juggernaut." Her advice to women in this poem, "Letter to My Sister," originally entitled "Sybil Warns Her Sister," is unequivocal: "Lock your heart, then quietly, / And lest they peer within, / Light no lamp when dark comes down / Raise no shade for sun; / Breathless must your breath come through / If you'd die and dare deny / The gods their god-like fun."[5] Whether "gods" is a trope for "men," "patriarchy," or "authority" is left to speculation; however, there is no misreading the dire warning to women who dare to speak or write their thoughts. Spencer's cryptic poetry with its strong metaphysical bent evokes the compressed spaces of Emily Dickinson's poems and Gwendolyn Brooks's early work, especially in its delicate playfulness and subtle wit.

What Spencer signifies is more than a singular condition of constriction adversely affecting her individual writing. She recognized that modernity involved visuality. In the early twentieth century, black women artists sought a space of visibility, though ironically not in isolation from others, but instead within society. Elbow room surfaces repeatedly as a desire to be seen and represented within the public sphere for modern black women, such as Spencer, Johnson, Marita Odette Bonner, Jessie Fauset, Nella Larsen, and Zora Neale Hurston, who sought enabling space within the close quarters, whether familial, societal, or geographical, in which they functioned.

On the eve of the Harlem awakening, Georgia Douglas Johnson published her first book of poems, *The Heart of a Woman* (1918). The title poem stands out and suggests a theme similar to Paul Laurence Dunbar's caged bird symbolism in his poem "Sympathy":

> The heart of a woman falls back with the night,
> And enters some alien cage in its plight,
> And tries to forget it has dreamed of the stars
> While it breaks, breaks, breaks on the sheltering bars.[6]

This poem and a few later ones reveal Johnson's ability to uncover the emotional reality of a black woman in the new era, or as W. E. B. Du Bois noticed, "her revelation of the soul struggle of a woman of the race."[7] Her poem "Lethe" implies this ongoing struggle: "I seek a little tranquil bark / In which to drift at ease / Awhile." Johnson chafed under the constrictions of physical and psychological space necessary to create art or to construct subjectivity: "I used to abide / In the narrowest nest in a corner / My wings pressing close to my side."[8] She links space to freedom and place to security that is not necessarily comforting in much the way Tuan conceives of the two concepts.

Contesting "place" fixity and recognizing overlapping gender and race concerns, Johnson exhibited an understanding of how power relations operated in everyday life. Her modern sensibility is frequently obscured by her sentimental literary language, which Marita O. Bonner described as "the heavy ornateness of the good old language of the nineteenth century."[9] Bonner, who wrote short stories and plays, would be remembered best by late twentieth-century readers for her essay, "On Being Young – A Woman – and Colored" which evokes a heightened awareness of the lack of subjective space for black women artists quite similar to Johnson's. Bonner expressed her own discomfort at the debilitating strictures placed on black women who remained "motionless on the outside" but who "decide that something is wrong with a world that stifles and chokes; that cuts off and stunts; hedging in, pressing down on eyes, ears and throat."[10]

Although Johnson's books of poetry, *Bronze* (1922) and *An Autumn Love Cycle* (1928), garnered praise, her most notable awards were for her plays. *Plumes* won a first prize in 1927 from *Opportunity* and *Blue Blood* an honorable mention in 1926. These, the best-known of her twenty-eight plays, demonstrate her most innovative accomplishment as a playwright: situating black women at the center of her plays at a time when black men held the major place as protagonists on stage. By giving black women a prominent space in tackling social problems, Johnson dismantled hierarchies of power and reconstituted social relations. She portrayed lynching from the perspective of its impact on the black family and its women members. In *A Sunday Morning in the South*, *Safe*, and *Blue-eyed Black Boy*, Johnson shifted from the spectacle of the male lynch victim to the visible, traumatized living, the mothers, sisters, wives, or daughters left behind. She relocated gender issues to the foreground in representing truths about black women's lives under assault from a vicious and violent annihilation of black bodies and the concomitant destruction of black families. Although the ideologies of the dominant culture remained formidable, Johnson figured black resistance as detectable, persistent, and embodied in her women characters who challenged fixity of beliefs and attitudes while undermining conceptions of the social field as certain or inevitable.

Without ever achieving elbow room, but defying her "genteel poverty," Johnson created a cosmopolitan salon for black artists in her Washington home. Her "Saturday Nights" of talk, readings, and performances nurtured the work of prominent artists, including Jean Toomer, Langston Hughes, Zora Neale Hurston, Waring Cuney, May Miller, Sterling Brown, Angelina Grimké, Alice Dunbar-Nelson, and Bruce Nugent. Her guests included well-known white modernist authors Vachel Lindsay, Edna St. Vincent Millay, H. G. Wells, Waldo Frank, and Rebecca West, who were invested in making modern art "new" and in black contributions to that project. Johnson also provided the space for intergenerational exchanges: Du Bois, James Weldon Johnson, and Charles S. Johnson, for example, frequented Johnson's meetings and each had access to publishing outlets in New York. In her home cross-racial and cross-generational relations occurred within a social structure that could subvert power relations and transform the place of struggling black writers. Her expansive sense of an artistic community influenced Alain Locke in his critical formulations in key texts including *The New Negro* (1925) and *Plays of Negro Life* (1927).

Georgia Douglas Johnson's productive yet constricted career bears similarities to that of Jessie Redmon Fauset, one of the visible New Negro modernists and author of four novels, *There Is Confusion* (1924), *Plum Bun* (1929), *The Chinaberry Tree* (1931), and *Comedy: American Style* (1933). "Black women's work remains a fundamental location where the dialectical relationship of oppression and activism occurs," as Patricia Hill Collins observes, so that "understanding the intersection of work and family in Black women's lives is key to clarifying the overarching economy of domination."[11] A "race woman" active in the National Association for the Advancement of Colored People and literary editor of its organ, *The Crisis*, Fauset was a "New Woman," who spent her adult life working as an editor or teacher, both before and after her marriage in 1929.

The issue of gender intersecting with work was especially pertinent to Fauset's historical and political consciousness. In her journalistic pieces and in her speech at the 1921 Second Pan-African Congress in London, she reminded audiences of gender and its intersection with race as affecting black women's class location, which for black women was intricately connected with their opportunities for decent work. In configuring work as the way to change negative attitudes toward black women, Fauset may have influenced key points Du Bois made in "The Damnation of Women," published in 1920, the year after she joined him in editing *The Crisis*: "The future woman must have a life work and economic independence. She must have knowledge. She must have the right of motherhood at her own discretion." Du Bois warned against "abolish[ing] the new economic freedom of women": "We cannot imprison women again in a home or require them all on pain of death to be nurses and housekeepers."[12]

In *There Is Confusion*, Fauset responds to Du Bois by attributing to a daughter, Joanna Marshall, rather than to a son in the upwardly mobile family, the positive personality traits to succeed in a race-conscious world. Joanna not only has ambition, drive, and intelligence, but she also stands in sharp contrast to Peter Bye whose irresponsibility and shiftlessness she modulates into positive traits. Joanna and all of the black women in the text, particularly Maggie Ellersley who rises in class position based on her evolving work options, confront racism and sexism in the area of work, but all, including a large caste of working-class women who are housekeepers, laundresses, boarding house operators, and seamstresses, are represented as dignified and removed from predictable stereotypes. Opportunities for employment divide black women into rigidly stratified classes and place them in subordinate positions, but

Fauset depicts Joanna (a dancer) and Maggie Ellersley (a businesswoman) as successful in their endeavors.

Fauset's attention to work is as well an extension of the feminist concerns of Heterodoxy, the group of committed feminists who met in Greenwich Village from 1912 to 1940. Grace Nail Johnson, wife of James Weldon Johnson, was the only black member of Heterodoxy, but the club's feminist ideology filtered into the circles of black women in New York through interaction with members of Heterodoxy: Charlotte Perkins Gilman, whom Du Bois quotes in "The Damnation of Women"; Zona Gale, who wrote the introduction to Fauset's *Chinaberry Tree*; Fannie Hurst, who employed Zora Hurston for a time and wrote *An Imitation of Life*, one of the best-known novels of passing. Fauset's protagonist Angela Murray in *Plum Bun* is an emergent artist, whose artwork and Greenwich Village Bohemian crowd underscore Fauset's inclusion of Heterodoxy's New Woman ideology.

In her thematics of "the new," Fauset produces "modern" treatments of irreverent and taboo subjects (sexuality, incest, promiscuity, miscegenation, illegitimacy), and she attacks the arbitrariness and destructiveness of gender, class, and race constructions. One major component of her gendered modern work is the construction of a visible, textual, and reproducible African American feminine. Given the historical materiality of African American women and their exclusion from "the feminine," though not from the sexualization of women's bodies, Fauset may be read as locating black women in the space of femininity and within textual representation of the feminine. She refuses to focus on abject black bodies. She writes femininity as constructed in social spaces: work, home, community. Both Sarah "Sal" Strange and her daughter Laurentine in *The Chinaberry Tree* are models of the feminine constituted within the private home, though Sal was once the mistress of a prominent white man who fathered Laurentine and left her well-off at his death. Sal's niece Melissa, secretly the product of her mother's affair with a married man, is also a representative of modern black femininity, but constructed within the public community. Fauset draws these women as "moral," upright, hardworking, talented, "proper," beautiful, and "modern" in their attitudes, behaviors, and appearances.

In denying the power of the past and social conventions or circumstances to determine the value of her characters' lives, Fauset develops their subjectivity within innovative women-centered spaces. Laurentine, for example, is a gifted "modiste," an artist who creates a design for lounging pajamas, signifying the increasing fluidity of women's identity, and a businesswoman who uses her entrepreneurial skills to enervate static images and traditional roles of women. Aided first by her white half-sisters and then by her black women clients, she revamps her domestic sphere into a workplace with women wage-laborers in her employ. Her younger cousin, Melissa, experiments with potential identities and has "the modern young person's scorn for unnecessary formulae."[13] Melissa attempts to overcome the societal restrictions that arbitrarily define black femininity. She refuses to accept black women's bodies as mere commodities, even though she positions herself within an emerging commodity culture and its new inventions that are changing women's lives, including domesticity and reproduction ("Melissa ... had the modern girl's own clear ideas on birth control").[14] Melissa may hold romantic notions, but she also observes that in her marriage, she has no intention of being "an inviolate shrine which sounds to me mighty darn useless."[15] While marriage for both Melissa and Laurentine functions as a companionate reward for their positive traits and stellar conduct, it is the larger community of women that initiates and fosters the self-knowledge necessary for such marriages.

In the public sphere, Fauset creates women-centered heterotopias, spaces that Foucault considers to be "counter-sites, a kind of effectively enacted utopias in which real sites ... are simultaneously represented, contested, and inverted."[16] Maude's beauty parlor in *Plum Bun* is such a space: "A rare quality of hospitality emanated from [Maude's] presence; her little shop was always full not only of patrons but of callers, visitors from 'down home,' actresses from the current colored 'show.'" Within "this atmosphere ... there was no restriction; life in busy Harlem stopped here and yawned for a delicious moment before going on with its pressure and problems."[17] Maude's beauty parlor is a visible pause from the restrictions and dominations of black life for black women, and is a contrast to the dystopian transnational space at the end of *Comedy: American Style* where there is no alternative to US race and gender hegemony, in part because it is removed from the possibility of an enclave of black women to provide a heterotopic space. The conclusion emphasizes spatial entrapment: Olivia Blanchard Cary is isolated in a French pension and her daughter Teresa is trapped in a loveless marriage to a spiteful Frenchman. The imaginary – a "free" life across the color line as white and outside the offending nation state as expatriate – is more nightmare than fairy tale.

Fauset represents her characters as black and feminine, not as sites of reproduction or as disembodied parts (breasts, genitalia, hands) in service to others. Her representations are in conversation with Elise McDougald who identified the "shadow" over a black woman: "She is conscious that what is left of chivalry is not directed toward her. She realizes that the ideals of beauty, built up in the finer arts, have excluded her almost entirely. Instead the grotesque Aunt Jemimas of the street-car advertisements proclaim only an ability to serve without grace or loveliness."[18] Fauset's methodological and ideological concerns work against the stereotypes of black women. Her models of the feminine are not passive or objectified, but active women, club women, sorority women, shoppers, shopkeepers, salesgirls, and consumers, much like the white women in the paintings of the Fourteenth Street School, Kenneth Hayes Miller, Isabel Bishop, and Reginald Marsh. Angela Murray, an art student passing as the white Angéle Mory in *Plum Bun*, wins the John T. Stewart Scholarship to study in Fountainbleau, France, for her work "Fourteen Street Types." If Fauset reinscribes myths of femininity, and with them bourgeois consumerism, from white models into black cultural contexts, then she may have been revising the concept of femininity for racialized women.

Fauset's efforts to destabilize and dislodge the prevailing negative images of black women are evident in all of her novels. In *There Is Confusion*, Joanna triumphs in the role of "America," in "The Dance of All Nations." Once unmasked as black, her body represents a symbolic geographic inclusion of all races and ethnicities within the American nation, but it also signifies an America embodied as black. Judith Butler raises the question of how the materiality of the body can be linked to the performativity of gender.[19] Butler argues that the normative category of sex produces as well as regulates the materialization of bodies. In a broad sense, the question is especially relevant for Fauset and modernist black women writers who find it impossible to ignore the material black body, in particular the black woman's body, given the historical memory and circumstances constantly impinging upon and producing an ideality that fixes black women outside of the constitutive materiality.

Zora Neale Hurston, like Fauset, found new ways to make room for herself as a modern black woman and to make visible the conditions constricting women's lives. Focusing on material, intellectual, and cultural spaces in her work as playwright, novelist, folklorist, and anthropologist, Hurston was invested, like Fauset, in visual representations of black life, but Hurston was able to make films of what she found in her travels through a changing world.

While Hurston never lamented as did Jean Toomer that folk culture was walking in to die in the modern desert, she did contrast the old with the modern by representing changing patterns in the lives of twentieth-century blacks in the South and in Haiti. She deployed the visual as a medium to distinguish race and to identify meaning that might escape a less attuned eye. She used, for example, the language of primitivism, "primitive man" and "primitive communities," in her discourse on the "Characteristics of Negro Expression," yet within a closed space she would also separate "the Negro" from "the primitive" and overturn the hierarchy of value placed on the words of whites as opposed to blacks. Hurston concludes about language and action words in her segment on "Drama": "the white man thinks in a written language and the Negro thinks in hieroglyphics."[20] She reminds readers to see the meaning of action and gesture in the everyday drama of black life: "These little plays by strolling players are acted out daily in a dozen city streets in a thousand cities, and no one ever mistakes the meaning."[21] Her "no one" includes only black spectators, who understand with the actors in the dramas how to interpret meaning. In excluding whites from the category of knowledgeable observers, Hurston privileges action and specularity for blacks. She sets up a dichotomous space between the so-named primitive and the active black bodies moving through both her word pictures and her field films.

Raymond Williams notes that "the Left saw film, from an early stage, as an inherently popular and in that sense democratic art ... [F]ilm, like socialism itself, was seen as a harbinger of a new kind of world, the modern world: based in science and technology; fundamentally open and mobile; and thus not only a popular but a dynamic, perhaps even revolutionary medium."[22] Hurston's work participates in a comparable sense of film as an "open and mobile" medium, revolutionary in what it could capture about black lives in a democratic art form.

In 1928, Hurston traveled to the South on her second field collection trip. She had her own motor car and her own movie camera, and managed to film black life when the moving image was still in the vanguard of mechanical reproduction. The camera and car, central to her "clearing space," were provided by her patron, Charlotte Osgood Mason, a wealthy and controlling New Yorker. Hurston's trip produced approximately fifteen short 16 mm reels, of which the nine extant run about thirty minutes of raw, unedited footage preserved by the Library of Congress. Five sequences, excerpted from Hurston's footage and released on DVD, represent Hurston as anthropologist, trained by Franz Boas in the first cohort of women anthropologists with Margaret Mead and Ruth Benedict.[23] "Research," Hurston said in *Dust Tracks on a Road*, "is formalized curiosity. It is poking and prying with a purpose. It is seeking that he who wishes may know the cosmic secrets of the world and they that dwell within."[24] Her words acknowledge a spatial sense of the world she inhabits as anthropologist and filmmaker.

Hurston shot the first of the reels in January 1928 in Alabama. Her diasporic subject is Cudjo Lewis (*c.* 1847–1935) who appears in Hurston's writings as Kossula, the last survivor of *The Clotilde*, the last slave ship to reach the US at Mobile Bay in 1859. Hurston had already published an article on Lewis, "Cudjo's Own Story of the Last African Slave," in *The Journal of Negro History* based on her 1927 collection trip to the South. In 1928, she filmed Lewis on his porch and in his woodpile chopping wood. Her concern is with Cudjoe in action, rather than repose, so that he is not a relic, not a static museum-piece showcasing subjected or abject people or a remnant of enslavement, but a living transmission, an adapting survivor, and a re-animation of stolen black bodies.

The remaining footage Hurston filmed in Florida as she made her way through railroad camps, phosphate mines, and turpentine stills before heading to New Orleans. In one sequence, she filmed workers in the Everglades at the Cypress Lumber Company, where she took up residence during her filming. The logging sequence contrasts with Cudjo Lewis. On the one hand, Lewis is alone but active in manual chopping; on the other hand, the machinery of the lumber company dwarfs the men working. Hurston films Lewis at close range, but films the activities in the Everglades from a distance. One explanation may have been that the lumber workers were suspicious of a woman traveling alone in her own car, with a gun for protection and a film camera to record what she saw. Another explanation may be that Hurston is implying a social transformation from the individual working for himself to the massive machines of the lumber business removing trees from the landscape.

The most suggestive footage is of two young black women on the porch of a cabin and outside a cabin. This sequence is marked by familiarity and intimacy, with close-up shots of bodies that appear relaxed and comfortable with the camera itself, the person behind the camera, and their own black bodies. Placing women at the center of observation, Hurston focuses not on the industrial making of raw materials for the circulation of goods, or on the frenetic black body laboring in public, but on slowed, unhurried movement of faces in expressions of calm, bodies in certainty, contentment, and pleasure. She presents a visual narrative of the women's relationship as friends or relatives, of the contours of their spatial lives, of their interactions with animate and inanimate objects that constitute their homeplace, which though outdoors exudes the personal, but not necessarily the domestic.

The filmic images of the women and the porch are precursors of the fictional Janie in *Their Eyes Were Watching God* (1937). In both instances, Hurston's pictorial sense renders the individual within and against the spatial background that, given her focus on expression, cannot ultimately define the person as static or fixed. Janie redoubles the significance of the *"flâneur,"* in the sense of Hurston herself moving through the spaces of southerners, farms, towns, camps, and porches, such as those occupied by the young women she filmed, of Janie moving through scenes linked in succession by travel, and of Janie's being a spectator to her own movement through space and time and through the vocalized narrative unfolding on a porch as Janie talks to her friend. Through Janie's mobility – from rural farm community to newly incorporated all-black town to the Everglades camp – Hurston traces the potential movement of the larger community out of the exclusive patriarchal narrative and into a reciprocal pattern of developing gender awareness, agency, and subjectivity.

In a reversal of moving from print to film, Hurston goes from her recorded images of the two women to the friendship between Pheoby and Janie in *Their Eyes Were Watching God*. Interaction and familiarity form the back story that sets the narrative in motion from the perspective of a woman who migrates from the security of place to the freedom of spaces unimaginable to her opposite, the woman who remains at home, safe in the daily routine of her life, but who at the end enters into the space newly articulated as a possibility for a woman's subjective life. Pheoby, after sitting on Janie's porch and experiencing the transformative power of Janie's dramatic narrative, declares: "'Lawd! Ah done growed ten feet higher from jus' listenin' tuh you, Janie. Ah ain't satisfied wid mah self no mo'. Ah means tuh make Sam take me fishin' wid him after this.'"[25] In the content and dissemination of Janie's story, Hurston charts the fluid relationship between public and private space and public and private constructions of subjectivity.

Mary Austin in her 1922 essay "The American Form of the Novel," demonstrates that discussions of fiction in the 1920s were beginning to absorb ideas about movement central to cinema. She writes: "The novel, more than any other written thing, is an attempt to persuade, at its best to compel, men to give over for a moment the pursuit of the distant goal, and savor the color, the intensity and the solidarity of experience *while it is passing*."[26] Her emphasis is added to "*while it is passing*," so that motion or mobility from the position of a camera-like specularity becomes one way of conceiving of modern fiction.

Hurston's field films have the aspect of savoring "the intensity and the solidarity of experience *while it is passing*," which is also what she achieves in *Their Eyes Were Watching God*. Her modernism pushes against boundaries, by expanding the possibilities for seeing "real" black people within the everyday. It is a "conscious modernism," to use Tony Pickney's terminology, attendant with a recognition that "art must enact, in both theme and form, the exhilarating dynamism of a post-traditional society which is brusquely sweeping away the restrictive remnants of feudalism, liberating not just science and industry but also the experiential possibilities of the individual self."[27]

Like Hurston, Nella Larsen made determined efforts to transcend the spatial limitations imposed upon her and black people in the United States. These spatial policies, segregation and Jim Crow, reduced Larsen to the then narrow confines of a black racial identity and to limiting gender roles defined by relational identity formation. In *Quicksand* (1928) and *Passing* (1929), Larsen represented a spatial economy in fictions of the modern color line in which black Americans accommodate their lives to segregation even while pushing against the boundaries of urban, middle-class life. Both texts interrogate racial fixity using modernist stylistic techniques and innovative forms, particularly the flow of consciousness in depicting interiority and fragmented, fast-moving scenes to represent the sometimes disorienting speed of modern life. Both situate the black urban novel and its multiple emphases on streets, night life, stores, and public spaces as the province of black women as much as of black men. In reclaiming urban geography from exclusionary gender practices, Larsen expands the domain of women and the possibilities for cityscapes. She understands race as spatially and socially constructed, but she also understands fluidity and mobility as marks of all modern people, especially of city residents.

In *Quicksand*, Larsen maps the body of Helga Crane within the social spaces and institutions through which it moves, and in the process she attends to cultural phenomena and social issues related to gender, segregation, and containment. Helga performs race. Modern and restless, she acts to escape marriage and motherhood, which she links to the proscriptions of race and gender in the US and to the repressions entailed in proper middle-class black life. She seeks freedom as represented by space rather than place, and journeys through exterior and interior landscapes of dislocation in the process. Through her performances as a black body in the US and in Denmark, Helga expands the enclosed domestic or private spaces where aesthetic desires and geographic longings are repressed. In one scenario, Helga attends the Circus, a public Danish entertainment palace, "always alone, gazing intently and solemnly at the gesticulating black figures, an ironical and silent speculative spectator."[28] These Circus performances telescope her own and become the site of spectacle and desire. Helga's self-conscious gaze as a "speculative spectator" and her position alone at a public display invoke a gender freedom atypical for women and especially denied to black women. Helga is an amalgamation of New World subjectivities for people of color. Geographic moves map her consciousness of herself as a raced performative subject, which is also the strategy Larsen charts in creating Clare Kendry and Irene Redfield.

In *Passing*, Irene Redfield's mantra is safety and security in place certainty. Mired in a fixed location even when she moves between Chicago and New York, Irene has rejected movement for pause, out of which she refuses any further movement or growth, though her husband desperately wants to relocate the family including their two sons to Brazil and outside of the reaches of US racism. By mapping the geography of entrapment that is psychic as well as socio-cultural, Larsen engages racist thinking as it is enacted upon black people and leaves marks upon both the body and the psychology of an individual, who, in refusing to dislodge from stasis and move into new possibilities for living whole, ends in fracture, psychosis, and mental break-down. In representing Irene in stream-of-consciousness and narrated mono-logues, Larsen deploys an arsenal of modernist techniques and styles in one of her two powerful depictions of gender disintegration, the other being Helga Crane in the conclusion of *Quicksand*.

Clare Kendry Bellew in contrast to her friend Irene shifts attitudinally and bodily to a space not marked as black, and is linked to Helga in *Quicksand*. She understands that race is constituted and maintained out of the occupancy of space and the designations of or consignments to space. Having removed herself from race and working-class restraints, and having experienced life in the world capitals – Paris, London, Budapest – Clare occupies a cosmopolitan position of wealth and status that designates her as white. Her visible mobi-lity signifies a break with traditional conceptions of female space and a representation of flow out of racial determinants that is more in keeping with the expected freedom of modernist male subjects. In moving through social structures in which she ignores both gender and race proscriptions, Clare disrupts social meanings and avails herself of all the benefits and privileges typically accorded white men. She embodies space as freedom and Larsen's definition of passing as a simple but "hazardous business," which may also be construed as an extension of Johnson's elbow room, clearing space that is a "breaking away from all that was familiar and friendly to take one's chance in another environment, not entirely strange, perhaps, but certainly not entirely friendly."[29] Given the fluidity of modern identity and the mobility of modern people assumed in Larsen's fiction, Clare per-forms a transgressive subjectivity and reconfigures the implications of cul-tural, racial, and gender identity.

Black modernist women artists repeatedly attempted to push back against racial borders and their external signs, at the same time as they worked to locate a clearing space, elbow room, to redefine boundaries, to make visible gender expectations emanating both from the white hegemonic, dominant culture and from a black masculinist hierarchical structure within black culture and society. Perhaps more than any other contribution to modernist writing, women such as Anne Spencer, Georgia Douglas Johnson, Jessie Fauset, Zora Neale Hurston, Nella Larsen, and their sisters in the project – from Angelina Grimké and Alice Dunbar-Nelson to Helene Johnson and Dorothy West – represent a way of rethinking gender issues as spatial issues within the conditions of modern mobility and racial fixity, and in the process enter into a variety of discourses relevant to the making of modernist writing.

NOTES

1. Georgia Douglas Johnson, "Contest Spotlight," *Opportunity Magazine* (July 1927), 204.
2. Yi-Fu Tuan and Steven Hoelscher, *Space and Place: The Perspective of Experience* (Minneapolis: University of Minnesota Press, 2001), p. 3.
3. Elise Johnson McDougald, "The Task of Negro Womanhood," in *The New Negro: Voices of the Harlem Renaissance*, ed. Alain Locke (New York: Touchstone, 1999), p. 382.
4. Anne Spencer, "Introduction," in *Caroling Dusk: An Anthology of Verse by Black Poets of the Twenties*, ed. Countee Cullen (1927; New York: Citadel, 1998), p. 47.
5. Anne Spencer, "Letter to My Sister (Sybil Warns Her Sister)," in *Shadowed Dreams: Women's Poetry of the Harlem Renaissance*, ed. Maureen Honey (New Brunswick: Rutgers University Press, 2006), pp. 258–9.
6. Johnson, "The Heart of a Woman," in *Shadowed Dreams*, ed. Honey, p. 162.
7. W. E. B. Du Bois, "Foreword" to *Bronze: A Book of Verse* by Georgia Douglas Johnson (Boston: B. J. Brimmer, 1922), p. 7.
8. Johnson, "Lethe," in *Shadowed Dreams*, ed. Honey, p. 171.
9. Marita Odette Bonner, Review of *Autumn Love Cycle*, by Georgia Douglas Johnson, *Opportunity* (April 1929), 130.
10. Marita O. Bonner, "On Being Young – A Woman – and Colored," in *The Crisis* (1925), reprinted in *Double-Take: A Revisionist Harlem Anthology*, ed. Venetria Patton and Maureen Honey (New Brunswick: Rutgers University Press, 2001), p. 110.
11. Patricia Hill Collins, "Work, Family, and Black Women's Oppression," in *2001 Race Odyssey: African Americans and Sociology*, ed. Bruce R. Hare (Syracuse: Syracuse University Press, 2002), p. 117.
12. Du Bois, "The Damnation of Women," in *Darkwater: Voices from Within the Veil* (New York: Harcourt Brace and Howe, 1920), p. 181.
13. Jessie Redmon Fauset, *The Chinaberry Tree: A Novel of American Life* (New York: G. K. Hall, 1995), p. 22.
14. *Ibid.*, p. 132.
15. *Ibid.*, p. 266.
16. Michel Foucault, "Of Other Spaces," trans. Jay Miskowiec, *Diacritics* 16 (Spring 1986), 22–7, at 24.
17. Jessie Fauset, *Plum Bun: A Novel Without a Moral* (Boston: Beacon Press, 1999), p. 327.
18. McDougald, "Task of Negro Womanhood," p. 369.
19. Judith Butler, *Bodies That Matter: On the Discursive Limits of Sex* (New York: Routledge, 1993), p. 1.
20. Zora Neale Hurston, "Characteristics of Negro Expression," in *The Harlem Renaissance, 1920–1940*, ed. Cary D. Wintz (New York: Taylor and Francis, 1996), p. 175.
21. *Ibid.*
22. Raymond Williams, "Cinema and Socialism," in *The Politics of Modernity: Against the New Conformists*, ed. Tony Pickney (London: Verso, 1989), p. 107.

23. *More Treasures from the American Film Archives, 1894–1931: 50 Films*, film notes by Scot Simmon and music notes by Martin Marks (San Francisco: National Film Preservation Foundation, 2004).

24. Hurston, *Dust Tracks on a Road: An Autobiography* (Urbana: University of Illinois Press, 1984), p. 174.

25. Hurston, *Their Eyes Were Watching God* (Urbana: University of Illinois Press, 1991), p. 230.

26. Mary Austin, "The American Form of the Novel," in *The Novel of Tomorrow and the Scope of Fiction*, by Twelve American Novelists (Indianapolis: Bobbs-Merrill, 1922), p. 14.

27. Tony Pickney, "Modernism and Cultural Theory," Introduction to Williams, *The Politics of Modernity*, ed. Pickney, p. 9.

28. Nella Larsen, *Quicksand* (New York: Penguin Classics, 2002), p. 85.

29. Nella Larsen, *Passing* (New York: Penguin Classics, 2003), p. 24.

7

JEAN RADFORD

Race and ethnicity in white women's modernist literature

> The contemplation of this black presence is central to any understanding
> of our national literature and should not be permitted to hover at the
> margins of the literary imagination.[1]

As Toni Morrison and postcolonial critics have argued, the "black presence"
in America, the Jewish presence in Europe, and colonialism and empire in
Britain, are central to the literary imagination of Anglo-American modernism, "are indeed constitutive of it."[2] If modernism, broadly defined, involves
a critical relation to "Modernity," as Enlightenment, reason, and progress, it
also calls into question any simple essentialist view of identity. Racial, religious, and ethnic differences (as defined by the racialized discourses of the
period 1900–40) are thus used to represent the divisions of the modernist
subject. White women's modernist writing suggests different degrees of
ambivalence, complicity, and opposition to the dominant discourses on race
and ethnicity.

All the terms of this chapter's title deserve discussion and invite reflection,
often needing to be understood in relation to plural others rather than as
halves of binary opposites. For although nationality is a political category,
race a genetic, and ethnicity a cultural category, for modernist writing the
meanings of "race" and "ethnicity" are historically shifting and often overlapping, shaped by nineteenth-century eugenicist and social Darwinian theories and by the historical and political events of the period. In what follows,
the term "modernist" is understood in an inclusive sense. Edward Said claims
that Conrad, Forster, and others took narrative form from "the triumphalist
experience of imperialism," creating discontinuity, self-referentiality, and a
corrosive irony "whose formal patterns we have come to recognise as the
hallmarks of modernist culture."[3] Whether they feature the "Negro," the
Jew, the Indian, the Irish, or some other embodiment of the Other, those
patterns are clearly visible in the selection of women writers discussed below.

The progress and decline of the "race" were prominent issues in turn-of-the-
century Britain, not only in ethnography, anthropology, science, and religious
discourse, but in political and economic terms too. The arrival of large numbers
of Ashkenazi Jews from Eastern Europe, following pogroms in Russia, Poland,

and Romania (150,000 came to Britain, and over 2 million to the USA, between 1880 and 1914); the consequent increasing ethnic tensions, especially in London's East End and in New York's Lower East Side, over housing, sweated industries, and employment; the role of Jewish financiers in the US elections of 1896 and in the Boer War; all these factors fueled xenophobic arguments about race and ethnicity.[4] In Britain the 1905 Aliens Act effectively ended the liberal nineteenth-century policy on immigration; similar measures, already in place in the US against Asians, were only finally introduced against eastern Europeans (largely Jews) in 1924. All were underpinned by the same antisemitic discourses (which, as Bryan Cheyette has argued, inform most modernist texts[5]); while any remnant of post-Civil War tolerance toward blacks, already on the move northward to the cities, was ended by the 1896 "separate but equal" supreme court decision in *Plessy* v. *Ferguson*. These currents formed the background of the London 1911 Universal Races Congress and of the founding of the Anti-Defamation League and the NAACP.

"Aren't you glad to be English?"[6]

The fiction of Virginia Woolf (1882–1941), from *The Voyage Out* (1915) to *Between the Acts* (1941), and her seminal essays *A Room of One's Own* (1929) and *Three Guineas* (1939), set up explicit parallels between racial and gender inequality, between patriarchal and imperial power. Further, her critique of gender inequalities makes extensive use of the imagery of slavery, which, as Vron Ware has pointed out, was a part of nineteenth-century egalitarian arguments from John Stuart Mill onward.[7] Many women writers in the 1920s and 30s make similar links between patriarchy and empire, the subordination of women and the fascist "cult of masculinity."[8] Nevertheless, among white women modernists, it is Woolf's writing which triggered questions about ethnic identity, racism, and empire. Jane Marcus's essay, "Britannia Rules the Waves," and Kathy J. Phillips's *Virginia Woolf Against Empire*[9] mark a significant turn in Woolf studies, arguing that her writing continually poses the question of ethnic identity or "Englishness" in relation to British colonialism. Their readings of Woolf opened up questions of race and ethnicity for all women modernists' writing.

Marcus focuses on *The Waves* (1931), one of Woolf's most experimental fictions, but the issues she identifies are also presented, "with corrosive irony," in Woolf's earliest work, *The Voyage Out*. Clarissa Dalloway's question to Rachel Vinrace, "Aren't you glad to be English?", echoes throughout the novel as an example of chauvinism in which national identity has racial and ethnic implications. In so doing, Woolf presents an Englishness derived from Britain's imperial history which does not allow her heroine a voice or a life. Being

English does not make Rachel Vinrace "glad" and the mysterious fever which kills her in South America has its source of infection, it is implied, in the mother country. Woolf returns to Englishness in *The Years* (1937) and, in a different way, in her last novel, *Between the Acts* (1941).[10] Her writing is discussed elsewhere in this volume, but in the work of her contemporary, Dorothy Richardson (1873–1957), the theme of Englishness is also a central issue.

"I am neither English nor civilised"[11]

Pointed Roofs (1915), the first of Dorothy Richardson's thirteen-volume sequence of novels, entitled *Pilgrimage*, was published the same year as Woolf's first novel. At the start of *Pilgrimage*, Miriam Henderson experiences herself as alienated from the English femininity of her mother and sisters and in search of an imaginary community, another way of being. Her reading leads her to an anti-realist position: the recognition that language is not neutral, a simple instrument of truth:

> All that has been said and known in the world is in *language*, in words ... Everything depends upon the way a thing is put, and that is a question of some particular civilisation. (II, 99)

Her quest takes her to eugenicist tracts by Darwin, Huxley, and Schenk rather than the Gibbon read by Rachel Vinrace; she learns that women are "*inferior*, mentally morally intellectually and physically ... her development arrested in the interests of special functions ... Woman is undeveloped man" (II, 220). In the "particular civilisation" in which she lives, a woman's quest for identity leads inexorably into questions about inferiority, function, and development – and race.

Using Bunyan's *Pilgrim's Progress*, rather as Joyce uses *The Odyssey*, to provide a title and framework for her story, Richardson dramatizes this quest for identity through a series of encounters with others, at home and abroad, each of whom calls a different sense of selfhood into being.[12] The heroine-narrator is an ambivalent figure in terms of class, gender, and sexuality as the oscillation between first- and third-person narration dramatizes. She is not only "something between a man and a woman," but also "most English" and "neither English nor Civilised." Miriam's being is always Heideggerian: a "being-in-the-world" and in the different worlds through which she passes. The bourgeois and bohemian worlds of London at the turn of the century, and the Quaker stronghold to which she later retreats, call myriad selves into being. In the thirteenth, unfinished volume of *Pilgrimage*, Miriam's decision to return to London to write is a move back to the cosmopolitanism of the capital, paradoxically described as her "native heath" (IV, 656) and away from the English countryside. The move back to the metropolis gives the narrative a circular shape; the decision to write, to recall and represent the history of these different states of being, is an attempt to "realize" what is continuous or essential to her being – which can be recognized only through its difference from others.

One of the most significant others in *Pilgrimage*, introduced in the sixth volume, *Deadlock* (1921), is a young Russian called Michael Shatov, who Miriam later discovers is a Jew: "What were Jews . . .?" (III, 127). Her friendship and love affair with Shatov changes her world-view, for "even seeing England, from his point of view, was being changed; a little" (III, 151). Discussing the race scientists Renan and Taine, as well as Nordau and Spinoza, with this "intelligent foreign friend," she begins to understand the ways in which the oppostional discourses of science and religion converge around questions of "race." Shatov is an intellectual mentor ("He forced her to think"), a beloved friend who proposes marriage but, crucially, the racialized other against whom she defines herself as an individual – as the following exchange suggests:

> "I would call myself rather one who believes in the race."
> "*What* race? The race is nothing without individuals."
> "What is an individual without the race?"
> "An individual, with a consciousness; or a soul, or whatever you like to call it. The race, apart from individuals, is nothing at all."
> "You have here introduced several immense questions. There is the question as to whether a human being isolated from his fellows would retain any human characteristics. Your great Buckle considered this in relation to the problem of heredity. But aside from this, has the race not a soul and an individuality? Greater than that of its single parts?"
> "Certainly not. The biggest thing the race does is to produce a few individualities."
> "The biggest thing that the race does is that it *goes on*. Individuals perish."
>
> (III, 151)

The argument between them ends with Miriam declaring "I don't give a button for the race, and I'd rather die than serve its purposes" (III, 152). In this polarized argument, Miriam can *reverse* but not *displace* an opposition which, she feels, subordinates the individual woman to her biological functions. In terms of Michael's Jewishness, it is worth noting that the "race" he speaks for here is not a particularized (Jewish) race, but the human race; he upholds "race" over the individual in terms of survival, development, and progress. But for Miriam, his argument relegates women to their procreative functions and she reacts accordingly, linking him with a patriarchal system which would castrate or exterminate her individuality. Her consequent rejection of her Jewish lover is staged as an epiphanic moment with a different racialized other, token of the "black presence" in England, a negro sailor seen in a London dockland cafe:

> Miriam sat frozen, appalled by the presence of a negro. He sat by, huge, bent, snorting and devouring, with a huge black bottle at his side. Mr Shatov's presence was shorn of its alien quality. He was an Englishman. (III, 217)

When placed next to "a negro," "the Jew" becomes "an Englishman" but in losing his "alien" quality, Shatov also loses his "liberating" power as a catalyst, a quality which is then transferred to this newly found other:

> In the awful presence she had spoken herself out, found and recited her best, most liberating words ... Light, pouring from her speech, sent a radiance about the thick black head and its monstrous bronze face. He might have his thoughts, might even look them, from the utmost abyss of crude male life, but he had helped her, and his blind unconscious outlines shared the unknown glory.
>
> (III, 219)

The experience is claimed as a moment of "enlightenment" in Miriam's pilgrimage toward self-discovery – finding a voice of her own. It is also, as Bryan Cheyette says, a graphic demonstration of the contingent and variable nature of racial projections.[13] The fictional portrait reflects, *but is also a reflection upon*, the antisemitic discourses of the period. In the latter respect it differs from the use of Jews and Jewishness in the canonical male modernism of Eliot, Pound, and Wyndham Lewis.

"When the last comes to the last, in the woman is the race."[14]

On the question of race and "Englishness," Mary Butts (1890–1937) is in many ways closer to T. S. Eliot than Richardson. Butts shares Richardson's anti-rationalism, her redemptive notion of the feminine, and a mystical conception of English particularity, but unlike Richardson, whose heroine finally returns to the cosmopolitanism of London, the characters in Butts's fiction make a pagan-religious commitment to an ethnicity based on the land. Like Eliot, she makes use of myth and the Grail legends to re-connect the sacred past to the modern wasteland and Eliot's definition of "tradition," in *After Strange Gods* (1933), as "blood kinship of 'the same people living in the same place'" is a central theme in her two major fictions, *Armed with Madness* (1928) and *The Death of Felicity Taverner* (1932). They were, she claimed, working in parallel.

Whereas Roger Fry, Picasso, and Gertrude Stein (discussed below), look to other cultures and traditions ("primitive" in terms of Western narratives of development) for renewal and inspiration, modernists like Eliot and Butts turned to more local, and insular, primitive traditions: a pre-modern, pre-industrial England and its relation to the land and landscape. As Patrick Wright argues, this modernism is a retreat from the universalist dreams of modernity ("Liberty, Equality, and Fraternity"), so that freedom and equality are redefined in relation to a particular and contracted notion of "Fraternity."[15] In *The Death of Felicity Taverner*, the attempt to redeem and resurrect a weakened landed gentry from the threats of modernity, embodied in the Russian-Jewish Nicholas Kralin, entails the expulsion and extermination of the Jew. Kralin, whose name echoes that of Stalin, is used as a personification of all that threatens the survival of England, past, present, and future. He is a "wolf," the son of a "proletarian-idealist"[16] who believes in nothing; a "red Agent" (84) but also a capitalist whose plans to build bungalows, shops, and cinemas on the Dorset landscape for financial gain will contaminate the English heritage. He has "an abstract mind" (216), is urbanized, deracinated, and sexually depraved yet has been "psycho-analysed out of any pleasure in anything" (22).

His demonization mobilizes a wide range of incoherent, antisemitic stereo-types but, as Ian Patterson has argued, there "is nothing arbitrary about the creation of Kralin. The anti-semitism is intrinsic to the cultural critique."[17] There is arguably nothing arbitrary either, in using Boris, the dispossessed White Russian, as the instrument of what is called English "race-solidarity" (146) but which in another sense is an instance of class-solidarity. Although Kralin's death is presented as a purification ritual, one which sends his "ghost" back to meet the ghost of Felicity Taverner (260), the closing chapter is not triumphalist. It focuses on the alibis needed to defend the English family and Kralin's "executioner" (261) from detection, thus raising questions about the legitimacy of the murder.

If Kralin personifies the evils of Modernity and is described as a "devil" and a "demon," Minna Lemuel, the Jewish woman in *Summer Will Show*, a 1936 novel by Sylvia Townsend Warner (1893–1978), is more of an angel. A romantic revolutionary and artist, this is another who calls a new kind of wisdom (Sophia) into being. Sophia Willoughby, who goes to Paris in 1848 to seek her estranged husband after the death of her two children, instead falls in love with her husband's mistress, Minna; the rival becomes the beloved.

> She offered her one flower – liberty. One could love her freely … One could love her for the only sufficient reason that one chose to.[18]

The love which flowers between the two women and which liberates Sophia Willoughby from her restrictive identity – as English landowner, wife, and child-bearer – is a lesbian love. In the imperial model, homosexuality is a form of "contamination," but in Warner's novel, the celebration of lesbian love is entwined with a critique of ethnic-racial stereotypes.

For Minna is the disinterested artist, generous not greedy, a "healer" not a contaminant, a lover not a rival, and further, she is a female embodiment of the Jewish ethical tradition (of justice not charity, p. 361). The form of the novel, a mix of *Bildungsroman*, historical romance, satire, and fable, is designed as a critique of various antisemitic stereotypes, although their reversal involves a rehearsal of those same caricatures. As Freud points out, idealization is the other side of denigration. More effective than Warner's use of plot and plot resolution is her use of "the story within the story": Minna's tales of pogroms in Lithuania, in which she performs her Jewish childhood experience of persecution to a Parisian public on the brink of revolution, link a particularized history (the eastern European Jewish experience) with the more universal aspirations of June 1848, without annulling its specificity.

Summer Will Show contains one of the rare portraits of a Jewish woman in this period. Minna not only does not conform to "the Jewish male's idea of her" (Dorothy Richardson), she is an artist and the personification of love. Butts's and Warner's fictional Jews represent radically different poles of "allo-semitism,"[19] but like Michael Shatov in Richardson's *Pilgrimage* they both serve as catalysts for change. For as Sophia states after the death of her lover at the end of the novel, "I have changed my ideas. I do not think as I did" (402).

Woolf, Richardson, Butts, and Warner, despite their critical, often antagonistic, relation to English ethnic identity, write from the center, whereas Elizabeth Bowen (1899–1973) and Jean Rhys (1890–1979) write from the peripheries of empire (Ireland and Dominica respectively). Their fiction draws on the peculiar experience of a colonial elite, at home neither in the colonies nor in the metropolis, to create and valorize, in very different ways, a world of outsiders, in-betweens, and strangers. So the positive representations of Max Ebhart in Bowen's *House in Paris* and Serge Rubin in Rhys's *Good Morning, Midnight*[20] may be informed by an identification with Jews as "the foreigner of foreigners ... the permanently alien Jew," as Miriam puts it in *Pilgrimage* (III, 376). For as Helen Carr points out, colonialism and fascism reinforce each other:

> The colonial-bred Rhys's "terrified consciousness" must certainly have sensitized her to the violence and fear behind European respectability, but the paranoia she evokes is not just ... that of a "psychological type", but of an epoch.[21]

Bowen's early Irish novel *The Last September* (1929) and Rhys's late *Wide Sargasso Sea* (1966) both depict tensions between the English, the settler community, and the "natives," and both end in violent conflagrations. Divided into a three-part structure of visits and comings and goings to the Big House (Danielstown), *The Last September*, like Woolf's *The Voyage Out*, contains brilliant parodic portraits of the English but also of the hyphenated identities of the Anglo-Irish and the interaction between them. Anglo-Irish hospitality (a "neighborliness grown a bit inflated and unwieldy"[22]) of dances and tennis parties is presented as an elaborate masquerade to compensate for their distance from the metropolis and their willed ignorance of their Irish neighbors.

If the Anglo-Irish refuse to speak about the history of their occupation and the emergent nationalist forces which threaten their extinction, there is also a "resolute amnesia"[23] among the descendants of both slaves and plantation owners in Rhys's novel. Rather than Bowen's stylized comedy, or Mansfield's multi-voiced short stories,[24] Rhys uses a modernized Gothic mode to articulate the relations between the English, the white creole settlers, and the black creoles after the emancipation of slaves in 1833. Her "explicitly ethnic novel" is a compelling portrayal of the complexities of race, ethnicity, and gender on the other side of the Atlantic.

"We stared at each other, blood on my face, tears on hers. It was as if I saw myself. Like in a looking-glass." (24)

Wide Sargasso Sea has become, deservedly, a key text within critical debates on modernist, postcolonialist, and indeed postmodernist fiction.[25] Rhys's decision to use a canonical text from nineteenth-century English fiction to write back to the center is a crucial move. In Charlotte Brontë's *Jane Eyre* (1847), "Bertha" (Antoinette) Mason, the madwoman in the attic, is the white Englishwoman's colonial "Other," and within the plot, she is primarily an obstacle or impediment to the romance of the English heroine. In *Wide Sargasso Sea*, Rhys takes the madwoman out of the attic, and gives her a life and a history, to present the other side of the story. The tripartite structure of the novel gives voice not only to the creole "Bertha," alias Antoinette Cosway, but also to the Rochester figure, no longer a romantic hero but an insecure second son performing a masculine imperial role. Most significantly, the black creoles are given voice (and action) within these narratives: Tia, Daniel, and Sandi Cosway, Baptiste and Christophine. The figure of Christophine, the black slave from Martinique given to Antoinette's mother, Annette, as a wedding present, is used to voice alternative traditions of knowledge ("Read and write I don't know. Other things I know" [104]); her character is used to criticize and, where able, to mediate, the exercise of patriarchal power by the Rochester figure, and to articulate a political critique of changing forms of colonial power in the Caribbean:

> No more slavery! She had to laugh! These new ones have Letter of the Law. Same thing. They got Magistrate. They got fine. They got jail house and chain gang. They got tread machine to mash up people's feet. New ones worse than old ones – more cunning, that's all. (22–3)

The vernacular, or creole English is here used "to deride the post-emancipation rhetoric which enabled the English to condemn slavery as unjust while enriching themselves through legitimized forms of exploitation," as Benita Parry puts it.[26] The same voice is used to cast doubt about the heart of empire itself:

> "You do not believe that there is a country called England?"
> She blinked and answered quickly, "I don't say I don't *believe*, I say I don't *know*. I know what I see with my own eyes and I never see it."　　　(70)

This comment can be read in different ways: as the naïveté of the native ("this ignorant, obstinate old negro woman" as Rochester calls her [70]), or the expression of a more general epistemological skepticism. For the England that he speaks of, and to which he returns with his mad wife on a "white" ship is only a construction of England, a fantasy of "swans and roses and snow" (70). Christophine's point about the difference between belief and knowledge links to a series of binary oppositions called into question by Antoinette: dream and reality, thought and feeling, sanity and madness. If, as Judith Raiskin claims, the novel is "a deconstruction of the colonial binarisms (black/white, English/native, civilised/savage, pure/polluted),"[27] Christophine's voice makes a substantial contribution to that deconstruction – the Subaltern speaks before she is silenced.

"[F]oreignness is within us: we are our own foreigners, we are divided."[28]

The Irishman, the Jew, and the lesbian are central characters for Djuna Barnes (1892–1982) in *Nightwood* (1936), although Robin Vote, the lesbian "heroine," seldom speaks, and at the close of the novel is "barking" like a dog.[29] The major voice in the narrative is the homosexual transvestite Dr. Matthew O'Connor, himself a caricature of Irish ethnicity – a witty, loquacious drinker. *Nightwood* is a key text of modernism, not least because its lyricism, linguistic complexity, and many-voiced narrative seem to include all possible statements and their contraries. As a result, critical opinion is still divided on the text's position on race and ethnicity – and indeed on sexuality, love, and much else. Jane Marcus's essay "Laughing at Leviticus" (1991) claims that its status as "a lesbian novel or a cult text of high modernism" has obscured its function as a critique of fascism, but makes a strong case for *Nightwood* as "a kind of feminist-anarchist call for freedom from fascism."[30] Much subsequent discussion of *Nightwood*, in particular its treatment of racial themes, has been framed by Marcus's reading.

The critical problems are as difficult as the text itself. Is the self-denying Jew, Felix Volkbein, a key figure, or is he marginal? (The tattooed Nikka, "the nigger who used to fight the bear," equally important for Marcus's case, appears only in a lurid two-page description by Matthew O'Connor.) Are the expressions of antisemitism by the narrator and characters simply part of what Marcus calls its carnival of voices, and, in view of the date of publication (1936), how should these be read? Benstock points out that *Nightwood* "provides a catalogue of Hitler's intended victims and an analysis of the secret fears such outcasts instil in the larger culture"[31] – which might support Marcus's case. Other critics, contesting the carnival reading, argue that the argument of "Laughing at Leviticus" depends on a "reading back" from the Holocaust to connect the different outcasts of *Nightwood*.[32]

The very first sentence of the novel poses the question of race, introducing the Volkbeins as "that race which has the sanction of the Lord and the disapproval of the people" (3). In what follows, a series of essentialist maxims about Jews are deployed and displayed, "the sum total of what is the Jew" (4). The stories of Guido and Felix Volkbein's denial of their Jewishness can be read as a satirical portrait of the unsuccessful parvenu, whose Jewishness is representative of this type, or it may be read as a critique of the ways in which European "universalism," combined with centuries of antisemitism, forces those from different racial or ethnic backgrounds – its others, its foreigners – to assimilate. Insofar as Barnes's expressed intentions in the complex publishing history of *Nightwood* are relevant, she clearly meant to make Felix both central and sympathetic, resisting suggestions that he was expendable.[33] Her comment, in response to Simon and Schuster's editor, is significant:

> [H]ow can he say that Jews are like others, not haunted or hunted. Were they neither of these then their past has not reverberated[.] The idiot man might as well say a church has no atmosphere.
> (Letter to Emily Coleman, August 10, 1935)

For Barnes, then, Jews are "different" because of their past persecution, which Felix's memories recall. But Felix, although a Jew by birth, has no religious beliefs, belongs to no Jewish community, is a loner who seeks out marginalized aristocrats and circus players. If in the opening pages he is haunted by Jewish history, his sense of Jewishness is expressed only through his solidarity with other outsiders, not in itself a negative trait. The one feature which recalls negative stereotypes (Linett compares Barnes to Richardson on this count), is his commitment to procreation, his wish to prolong his "dynasty."[34] Clearly the debate on the implications of the text is ongoing. In what seems like a question posed to her own text, Barnes has Nora ask Felix and O'Connor: "Are you both saying what you really mean, or are you just talking?" (21). In this opaque modernist text, there may be no saying what "it really means," for either author or reader; it does however pose the question of how we talk about race and identity.

Modernism in the melting-pot

As an outsider from the world of British empire and racial hegemony, Mina Loy (1882–1966), like her close friend Djuna Barnes, occupies a special place. Anglo-Jewish by origin, she became American by adoption in 1916–18 when she was a central figure for the New York poetry magazine *Others*.[35] Her immersion in a multi-racial Greenwich Village community, and then expatriate Paris, led her to a striking identification of modernism with the voice of the immigrant as articulated in her often cited essay "Modern Poetry," published in 1925. Here she derides "God's English" as preserved by professors of Harvard and Oxford and invokes in contrast "the relationship of expression between the high browest modern poets and an adolescent Slav who has speculated in a wholesale job-lot of mandarins." America is celebrated as "a country where the mind has to put on its verbal clothes at terrific speed."[36]

Her long narrative poem "Anglo-Mongrels and the Rose: 1923–1925,"[37] makes a witty, aggressive use of ethnic stereotypes to satirize both Christian and Jewish traditions. Like Cather, Mansfield, and other women writers of the period, Loy uses her own family background to pose questions of identity and difference: a Jewish Hungarian father ("Exodus") whose mother has hair "long as the Talmud" (111), and the "English Rose" he marries – a "rose of arrested impulses / self-pruned / of the primordial attributes" (121). Each is defined by a particularist culture and their marriage is presented as a miniaturized clash of civilizations in an England of "Sundays when / England closed the eyes of every / commercial enterprise / but the church" (116). The caricatures of England and the mother's repressed English femininity are played off against a description of the father's Jewish background:

> The arid gravid
> intellect   of Jewish ancestors
> the senile juvenile
> calculating prodigies of Jehovah
> crushed by the Occident ox
> they scraped
> the gold gold golden
> muck from its hoofs   (112)

The strategy is a bold one; stereotypes of the Jewish male and the English female are deployed in sequence and their "conjugal dilemmas" ("who know not what they do / but know that what they do / is not illegal," 127) are dramatized with stark sympathy. Their "Anglo-mongrel" offspring, the speaker of the poem, is positioned between two exclusive and opposing racial/religious traditions; but contrary to racial theories on mixed marriages of the period, this is presented as creative, not degenerate: "Where Jesus of Nazareth / becomes one-piece / with Judas Iscariot / in this composite / Anglo-Israelite" (132).[38] In relation to the modernist renewal of language that Loy outlined in "Modern Poetry," the child's experience is paralleled with that of the immigrant. In a moment of linguistic illumination she sees the Jewish "ragamuffins" of Kilburn who "killed Jesus / and are bound for Hades" as desirable others:

> The common children
> have the best of her
> Though dressed in rags
> they feed on muffin   (160)

The form of the poem, its spacing and lack of punctuation, is itself a mix of concrete images and abstract propositions. The stereotypes within it are deliberately deployed, it seems to me, in the interest of a self-analysis which values hybridity – of belief systems and ethnic identities. And, in the context of discourses on the purity of the race and the dangers of "mongrelization," it can be read as a counterblast to the antisemitism which prevailed in Britain in general, and among modernists in particular.[39]

"The Negro is not. Any more than the white man."[40]

Djuna Barnes situates *Nightwood* and questions of Jewish (and lesbian) identity in the metropolis, between Paris, Vienna, and New York. Other American modernists, like Gertrude Stein (1874–1946) and Willa Cather (1873–1947), treat specifically American concerns – the importance of European immigration in building a "new population," the history and heritage of slavery – and frame these in the landscapes of "God's Chosen Country." The black presence in America is central to Stein's controversial story "Melanctha" (1909) and to Cather's final novel, *Sapphira and the Slave Girl* (1940), which I want to consider next. Blackness in these texts is used, as often in white writing, as an image for the unconscious of whites: their fears and desires, creativity, sexuality, drives as yet untamed by civilization.

In terms of modernist strategies, Gertrude Stein's novella "Melanctha,"[41] set in the black community of "Bridgepoint," has an obvious significance. In reworking her earlier lesbian fiction *Q.E.D.*, Stein produced what she considered the "first modern story," using a (heterosexual) black setting to facilitate her move away from naturalism and into a new distinctive voice. In the words of Michael North, "Modernism ... mimicked the strategies of dialect and aspired to become a dialect itself."[42] The result, although very different from *Nightwood*, resembles it in laying before the reader often crude racist stereotypes while creating a great deal of uncertainty about how to read these.

At the time of the Harlem Renaissance, many leading black writers did consider "Melanctha" to be a portrayal of the black community, and some endorsed it, notably Nella Larsen and Richard Wright. Larsen wrote to Stein that she had "caught the spirit of our race," while Wright praised "Melanctha" and its speech-rhythms in particular, claiming that she profoundly influenced his style.[43] More recently, critics have found the stereotypical descriptions of characters ("Rose Johnson was a real black, tall, well built, sullen, stupid, childlike, good looking Negress" [85]) objectionable, and point out the relation between such portraits and the essentialist theories of character held by Stein's teacher William James.[44] Formulaic as these descriptions are, they are marginal to a narrative which is largely constructed as a dialogue that is intelligent and articulate, even excessively so (in a Steinian mode). The speakers' language (which could be called "dialect") is highly stylized, and is nothing like the standard "minstrel" caricature of black speech current at the time. North claims that the constant use of synonyms, and the reiteration of words like "real," "really," "certainly," call into doubt any stable relation between language and "reality."[45] As with Rhys's use of creole dialect in *Wide Sargasso Sea*, such usage also serves to question the role of language in thinking, feeling, and knowing:

> "Don't you ever stop with your thinking long enough to have any feeling Jeff Campbell," said Melanctha a little sadly ...
> "I certainly do care for you Jeff Campbell less than you are always thinking and much more than you are ever knowing." (132)

As regards language, character, and setting, "blackness" in this text is foregrounded, yet, in the interminable discussions between the lovers Jeff and Melanctha, curiously irrelevant. It may be that the exoticism of black "Bridgepoint" plays for Stein the role which African masks played for her friend Picasso at this time, offering the possibility of a distanced, abstracted representation of forbidden desire through the agency of an imaginary, racialized "Other."[46] Indeed, Melanctha's "wandering" suggests sexual transgression at a level that would have been hard to depict in the white society in which the explicitly lesbian *QED* is situated. If it is hard to detect "irony" in its accepted sense in Stein's writing, her use of the mask approaches Said's description of it as "a form that draws attention to itself as substituting art and its creations for the once-possible synthesis of world empires."[47]

Willa Cather – race and land

About halfway through *My Ántonia* (1918), Cather's novel about memory, possession, immigration, and much else, the narrator Jim Burden reflects on the impact of immigrants on the culture of the plains:

> The girls I knew were always helping to pay for ploughs and reapers, brood-sows, or steers to fatten. One result of this family solidarity was that the foreign farmers in our county were the first to become prosperous.[48]

The comment emphasizes the economic contribution of the Bohemian settlers, their ethnic values ("family solidarity") against the shallow racism of his schoolmates in whose view "all foreigners were ignorant people who couldn't speak English."[49] Burden is less able to appreciate changes to gender roles made by "girls" like Ántonia, but the foreign newcomers to Nebraska and their right to the land is underwritten not, as with the English modernist Mary Butts, by long ancestry, but by their commitment to hard work and production. As with Barnes's use of Jewishness, the racial others of *My Ántonia*, and the reader's shifting identifications with male Jim and female Ántonia, can be read as masks for a repressed lesbian other.[50]

Born, like Jim Burden, in Virginia, Cather retained many Southern attitudes, including nostalgia for slavery, which is present in her last book. *Sapphira and the Slave Girl* is a complex and compelling study of "whiteness" in pre-bellum Virginia, and the uses and abuses of power by an aging white slaveowner. Neglected for many years, the text has re-emerged as part of a growing appreciation of Cather's modernism, and as the result of a searching analysis by the black novelist, Toni Morrison.[51] A variant of the fugitive tale, the novel presents a loyal household slave whose daughter escapes to freedom in Canada, and her mistress, Sapphira, whose abolitionist daughter aids the fugitive's escape northwards. The doubling of mother-daughter stories emphasizes the interdependence of "whiteness" and "blackness," and how, under slavery, power relationships divide families, loyalties, and selves. It includes a miniature history of another "slave-girl," the grandmother Jezebel, captured in Guinea, transported, and sold as a commodity in the market, while the epilogue, given to the white, post-bellum granddaughter, invites the reader to see the history of slavery and its legacies.

Nancy Cunard (1896–1965), like Loy, was born British; her contribution to American literature was that of a committed outsider who, inspired by the ongoing evidence of racism, tried to construct a cultural monument to the Negro people. Her persona throughout the thirties was that of a writer devoted at once to modernism and to the politics of nationalism, race, and ethnicity: the anti-fascist struggles in Spain, the liberation movements in the colonies, the fight for the Scottsboro boys. At the outset of her career, in the poem "Answer to a Reproof" (1921), she situates herself in opposition to a generalized other:

> and I
> Belong to neither, I the perfect stranger,
> Outcast and outlaw from the rules of life,
> True to one law alone, a personal logic
> That will not blend with anything, nor bow
> Down to the general rules.

The "other" of the text implicitly represents the background of class and empire ("the old bulk of centuries") against which Cunard situates herself – although the end of the poem suggests a meeting and some resolution. Throughout her life and her writings an "indomitable rebel" (as the title of Hugh Ford's biography terms her[52]), she found the defining focus of her work in her encounter, via Henry Crowder, with the black experience in the United States. This was to issue in her enduring heritage, the "anthology" *Negro* (1934). This multi-voiced text, which was to become much more than an American project, had entries by 150 contributors, of whom two-thirds were black; they included Du Bois, Langston Hughes, and Zora Neale Hurston, and also Ezra Pound, Jomo Kenyatta, George Padmore, René Char, and Paul Éluard. If its subsequent history has often been one of neglect and misunderstanding, *Negro* is now increasingly coming into its own as a monument of modernism – in a special sense. The work owed its origin to Cunard's passionate determination (she included in particular a contribution on the Scottsboro case, the current *cause célèbre*), but also to her links with disparate groups – Communist writers, Surrealists, and the black writers of Harlem in particular. Arguably, Surrealist denials of a special elevated status for the "art work" helped to shape the intricate collage of "found objects" which constitutes *Negro*. As Laura Winkiel puts it:

> reading *Negro* as a transnational modernist text . . . makes modernism look less like a radical break with the past than a disjunctive crossing of past, present and future, a crossing that expresses the condition of black modernity.[53]

Cunard herself claimed that her aim was "to throw light on the appalling way the entire colour 'question' is handled."[54] Her method, however, an assemblage of sometimes conflicting voices with her own commentaries and dissenting footnotes, carries all the hallmarks of modernist art: both autonomous and a committed work of art.

Even a brief, selective examination of white women's modernism suggests the diversity of positions on race and ethnicity, how religious, racial, and ethnic differences are used to signify both positive and negative possibilities: as catalysts for social change; as the repressed or the uncanny; the creative or destructive; as devils or angels. It also reveals ways in which literary texts always exceed, undermine, or complicate the explicit commitments of their authors. As a later modernist, or postmodernist, woman writer says, in a racialized society, "there is no escape from racially inflected language, and the work writers do to unhobble the imagination from the demands of that language is complicated, interesting and definitive."[55] For 21st-century readers, living in a post-Holocaust, postcolonial, largely globalized but still divided world, the meanings we bring to these terms and texts have changed, yet remain crucial.

NOTES

1. Toni Morrison, *Playing in the Dark: Whiteness and the Literary Imagination* (Cambridge, MA: Harvard University Press, 1992), p. 5.
2. Fredric Jameson, "Modernism and Imperialism," in *Nationalism, Colonialism, and Literature*, ed. and intro. Seamus Deane (Minneapolis: University of Minnesota Press, 1990), p. 64.
3. Edward Said, *Culture and Imperialism* (London: Chatto and Windus, 1993), pp. 227–9.
4. See David Feldman, "Was Modernity Good for the Jews?," in *Modernity, Culture and "the Jew,"* ed. Bryan Cheyette and Laura Marcus (Cambridge: Polity, 1998), pp. 171–87.
5. Bryan Cheyette, *Constructions of "the Jew" in English Literature and Society: Racial Representations, 1875–1945* (Cambridge: Cambridge University Press, 1993).
6. Virginia Woolf, *The Voyage Out* (London: Granada, 1978), p. 66.
7. Vron Ware, *Beyond the Pale: White Women, Racism and History* (London and New York: Verso, 1992).
8. Notably, Katherine Burdekin's *Swastika Night* (1937), a dystopian tale which might be said to anticipate the arguments of *Three Guineas* and *Between the Acts*.
9. Jane Marcus, "Britannia Rules the Waves," in *Hearts of Darkness: White Women Write Race* (New Brunswick, NJ: Rutgers University Press, 2004); Kathy J. Phillips, *Virginia Woolf Against Empire* (Knoxville: University of Tennessee Press, 1994).
10. See Jed Esty, *A Shrinking Island: Modernism and National Culture in England* (Princeton: Princeton University Press, 2004), and Sue Roe and Susan Sellers, eds. *The Cambridge Companion to Virginia Woolf* (Cambridge: Cambridge University Press, 2000).
11. Dorothy Richardson, *Pilgrimage*, 4 vols. (London: Virago, 1979), vol. III, p. 108. All page references in this section are to *Pilgrimage*.
12. See Jean Radford, "The Woman and the Jew: Sex and Modernity," in *Modernity*, ed. Cheyette and Marcus, pp. 91–104.
13. Bryan Cheyette, ed. *Between "Race" and Culture: Representations of "the Jew" in English and American Literature* (Stanford: Stanford University Press, 1996),

pp. 10–11. See also Jane Garrity, *Step-Daughters of England: British Women Modernists and the National Imaginary* (Manchester: Manchester University Press, 2003); Maren Linett, *Modernism, Feminism and Jewishness* (Cambridge: Cambridge University Press, 2007); Radford, "The Woman and the Jew"; Jacqueline Rose, "Dorothy Richardson and 'the Jew,'" in *Between "Race" and Culture*, ed. Cheyette, pp. 114–28.

14. Mary Butts, *The Crystal Cabinet: My Childhood at Salterns* (1937; Boston: Beacon Press, 1988), p. 171.

15. Patrick Wright, *On Living in an Old Country: The National Past in Contemporary Britain* (London: Verso, 1985), pp. 126–7.

16. Mary Butts, *The Death of Felicity Taverner* (London: Wishart, 1932), p. 21. Page references in this and the next paragraph are to this text.

17. Ian Patterson, "'The Plan Behind the Plan': Russians, Jews and Mythologies of Change: The Case of Mary Butts," in *Modernity*, ed. Cheyette and Marcus, pp. 126–40.

18. Sylvia Townsend Warner, *Summer Will Show* (London: Virago, 1987), p. 291. Subsequent page references appear parenthetically in the text.

19. For this term see Zygmunt Bauman, "Allo-Semitism: Premodern, Modern, and Postmodern," in *Modernity*, ed. Cheyette and Marcus, pp. 143–56.

20. See Jean Radford, "Face to Face with the Other: Levinas and Elizabeth Bowen's *The House in Paris*," in *Modernity, Modernism, Postmodernism*, ed. Manuel Barbeito (Santiago de Compostela: Universidade de Santiago de Compostela, 2000), pp. 93–106, and Linett, *Modernism*.

21. Helen Carr, *Jean Rhys* (Plymouth: Northcote House, 1996), p. 48.

22. Maria DiBattista, "Elizabeth Bowen's Troubled Modernism," in *Modernism and Colonialism: British and Irish Literature, 1899–1939*, ed. Richard Begam and Michael Valdez Moses (Durham, NC: Duke University Press, 2007), pp. 226–45.

23. Jean Rhys, *Wide Sargasso Sea* (London: Penguin, 2000), p. xv. Page references in the next section are to *Wide Sargasso Sea*.

24. Mansfield is not discussed here, for reasons of space, but see Angela Smith, *Katherine Mansfield and Virginia Woolf: A Public of Two* (Oxford: Clarendon Press, 1999).

25. See Delia Caparoso Konzett, *Ethnic Modernisms: Anzia Yezierska, Zora Neale Hurston, Jean Rhys, and the Aesthetics of Dislocation* (New York and Basingstoke: Palgrave Macmillan, 2002); Gayatri Chakravorty Spivak, "Three Women's Texts and a Critique of Imperialism," *Critical Inquiry* 12 (1985), 243–61; Benita Parry, *Postcolonial Studies: A Materialist Critique* (London: Routledge, 2004).

26. Benita Parry, *Postcolonial Studies*, p. 22.

27. Judith Raiskin, *Snow on the Cane Fields: Women's Writing and Creole Subjectivity* (Minneapolis: University of Minnesota Press, 1996), p. 107.

28. Julia Kristeva, *Strangers to Ourselves*, trans. Leon S. Roudiez (New York: Columbia University Press, 1991), p. 181.

29. Djuna Barnes, *Nightwood*, with a preface by Jeanette Winterson (1936; New York: New Directions, 2006), p. 179. Page references in this section are to this edition.

30. Jane Marcus, "Laughing at Leviticus: *Nightwood* as Woman's Circus Epic," in *Silence and Power: A Reevaluation of Djuna Barnes*, ed. Mary Lynn Broe

(Carbondale: Southern Illinois University Press, 1991), pp. 221–51, at pp. 222 and 221.

31. Shari Benstock, *Women of the Left Bank: Paris, 1900–1940* (London: Virago, 1987), p. 427.

32. See Linett, *Modernism*, p. 209 n. 21.

33. Cheryl Plumb, "Revising *Nightwood*: 'A Kind of Glee of Despair'," *Review of Contemporary Fiction* 13 (1993), 149–59.

34. Linett, *Modernism*, pp. 111–39.

35. See Cristanne Miller, "Tongues 'loosened in the melting pot': The Poets of *Others* and the Lower East Side," *Modernism/modernity* 14 (2007), 455–76, for the role that *Others* played in promoting an "American" modern poetic which favored the immigrant community.

36. Mina Loy, *The Lost Lunar Baedeker*, ed. Roger L. Conover (New York: Farrar Straus Giroux, 1996), p. 159.

37. Reproduced in *The Last Lunar Baedeker*, ed. Roger L. Conover (Highlands, NC: The Jargon Society, 1982). Page references in this section are to this edition.

38. For a detailed analysis of the religious themes, see Rachel Blau DuPlessis, *Genders, Races, and Religious Cultures in Modern American Poetry, 1908–1934* (Cambridge: Cambridge University Press, 2001), pp. 160–4.

39. As argued, for example, by DuPlessis, *ibid*.

40. Frantz Fanon, *Black Skin, White Masks*, intro. H. K. Bhabha (London: Pluto, 1986), p. xi.

41. Gertrude Stein, "Melanctha," in *Three Lives: The Good Anna, Melanctha and the Gentle Lena* (New York: The Grafton Press, 1909). Page references in this section are to this story.

42. Michael North, *The Dialect of Modernism: Race, Language, and Twentieth-Century Literature* (New York and Oxford: Oxford University Press, 1994), preface.

43. See Eugene E. Miller, "Richard Wright and Gertrude Stein," *Black American Literature Forum* 18 (1982), 107–12, for an attempt to explain the nature of Stein's alleged influence on Wright.

44. See Milton A. Cohen, "Black Brutes and Mulatto Saints: The Racial Hierarchy of Gertrude Stein's 'Melanctha,'" *Black American Literature Forum* 18 (1984), 119–21; and Sonia Saldívar-Hull, "Wrestling Your Ally: Stein, Racism, and Feminist Critical Practice," in *Women's Writing in Exile*, ed. Mary Lynn Broe and Angela Ingram (Chapel Hill, NC: University of North Carolina Press, 1989), pp. 181–98.

45. North, *The Dialect of Modernism*, p. 73.

46. The comparison is made in North, *The Dialect of Modernism*, p. 61.

47. Said, *Culture and Imperialism*, p. 229.

48. Willa Cather, *My Ántonia*, ed. Charles Mignon (Lincoln and London: University of Nebraska Press, 1994), p. 194.

49. *Ibid.*

50. See e.g. Katrina Irving, "Displacing Homosexuality: The Use of Ethnicity in Willa Cather's *My Ántonia*," *Modern Fiction Studies* 36 (1990), 91–102.

51. See Phyllis Rose, "Modernism: The Case of Willa Cather," in *Modernism Reconsidered*, ed. Robert Kiely and John Hildebidle (Cambridge, MA: Harvard University Press, 1983), pp. 123–45; Morrison, *Playing in the Dark*.

52. Hugh Ford, *Nancy Cunard: Brave Poet, Indomitable Rebel, 1896–1965* (Philadelphia, PA: Chilton, 1968). The full text of "Answer to a Reproof" appears on pp. 53–5.

53. Laura Winkiel, "Nancy Cunard's *Negro* and the Transnational Politics of Race," *Modernism/modernity* 13 (2006), 507–30, at 508).

54. Cunard to McKay, January 28, 1932, cited in Winkiel, "Nancy Cunard's *Negro*," 510; letter in the Nancy Cunard Collection at the Harry Ransom Humanities Research Center, University of Texas, Austin.

55. Morrison, *Playing in the Dark*, p. 13.

8

LAURA DOYLE

Geomodernism, postcoloniality, and women's writing

In his brief "Note on Modernism" in *Culture and Imperialism*, Edward Said describes canonical Anglo-European modernism as an aesthetic attempt to contain the crises of early twentieth-century imperialist capitalism. He closes his short discussion with the suggestion that modernist styles arise "as more and more regions – from India to Africa to the Caribbean – challenge the classical empires and their cultures."[1] Although later in *Culture and Imperialism* Said considers scenes of anti-colonial resistance in texts such as E. M. Forster's *Passage to India*, he never fully develops the implications of his note about the relation between anti-colonial insurgency and the appearance of modernism.

These implications are far-reaching: in fact they point toward a deep revision of the paradigm in which we read twentieth-century modernist and postcolonial literature in English. This chapter explores some of those implications, building on recent work in modernist studies.[2] I describe the ways that not only colonialism but also anti-colonialism, and not only slavery and racism but also anti-slavery, have constituted world conditions since the late eighteenth century, and I suggest that a history of insurgency and global conflict provokes what can thus be called the "geomodernist" practices of diverse artists from the late nineteenth to the twenty-first century.

To properly characterize this relation between geomodernist aesthetics and the long history of colonial conflict, and so to pursue Said's hint, we must take account of a state of being we might call "postcoloniality." We can distinguish postcoloniality from postcolonialism in the same way that Nelson Maldonado-Torres distinguishes "coloniality" from colonialism in his essay "On the Coloniality of Being."

> Coloniality is different from colonialism. Colonialism denotes a political and economic relation in which the sovereignty of a nation or a people rests on the power of another nation, which makes such nation an empire. Coloniality, instead, refers to long-standing patterns of power that emerged as a result of

colonialism, but that define culture, labor, intersubjective relations, and knowledge production well beyond the strict limits of colonial administrations. Thus, coloniality survives colonialism.[3]

Conversely, I suggest, anti-coloniality or postcolonial consciousness *precedes* the founding of a postcolonial state; this consciousness prepares the strained patterns of power within those states in the realms of culture, labor, intersubjective relations, and knowledge production – and, we should add, in the fact of battle. The record of daily negotiations and subversion of controlled labor (as narrated for instance in escaped slaves' narratives), as well as of armed rebellion and organized activism around the globe, establishes clearly that colonialism and postcoloniality are born together, in locked and often deadly embrace. Especially in the wake of the successful Haitian Revolution in the early nineteenth century, acts of resistance around the globe projected this postcoloniality for both the colonized and the Anglo-European colonizers. I shall refer, moreover, not just to postcoloniality but to post/coloniality, the slash registering the lived divide between vision and reality, the discordance between a present colonial situation (including that of slaves in the US)[4] and an envisioned postcolonial future.

In this account, instead of coming first as the pioneers, early Anglo-European and Anglo-American geomodernists grasp the world situation belatedly – as compared to the many thousands living in their nations' colonial or disenfranchised communities. Many of these Anglo writers struggle, sometimes thoughtfully, sometimes defensively, to register the insights, anger, and knowledge of those whose discontent reached a crescendo at the end of the nineteenth century. Early Anglo geomodernists had access to the means of production first – the wealth, education, and print or paint – that allowed them to express this situation in fractured forms before many anti-colonial writers. Yet the post/colonial vision was always already "known" in the colonies and simply awaited the emergence there of authors with access to print – in the Caribbean, Latin America, Ireland, Africa, India, Pakistan, Native America, and other locations.

This angle of vision freshly explains why Caribbean artists such as Kamau Brathwaite were drawn to T. S. Eliot,[5] or why Chinua Achebe has taken his titles from the poetry of W. B. Yeats: because these "third world" writers recognize and mean to signal the way that "their own" history lies at the back of canonically modernist aesthetics. They turn to the particular Anglo-European artists whose craft and consciousness led these artists to register, however partially, the global situation of post/coloniality. Thus the point is not to redeem canonical, white modernists by reading them as anti-colonial, although in some cases they were; nor to understand postcolonial writers as their aesthetic heirs. Reading within the geomodernist model, we discover how Anglo-European and postcolonial writers emerge together from a violent history and a post/colonial consciousness that pressed on all of their worlds and all of their subjectivities, however differently.

Casting modernism as geomodernism in light of this history, the second half of the chapter reconsiders the classic experimental forms of this aesthetic, with special attention to women's modernist and postcolonial fiction. I explore the meanings of two elements of modernist form – shifts in perspective and disruptions of time – as expressions of this post/colonial understanding of subjectivity and history. But first, in the next section I recall the historical record of violent invasion and active insurgency that intensified throughout the nineteenth century and was newly broadcast via radio, telegraph, photography, and newspapers, all of which created conditions for the rise of geomodernism.

"The Blackman's Burden":[6] history over here

Resistance to British colonization and to slavery is amply evident from the seventeenth century forward in, for instance, the many wars waged by American Indians in defense of their lands, the Maroon movements of the Caribbean and South America, and the revolts of both peasants and powerful elites in India beginning in the later eighteenth century and in Africa beginning in the nineteenth. Western colonialism always provoked anti-colonialism: the policies of the colonizers were continually adjusted and debated in the face of this intense resistance, as abolitionist Thomas Clarkson noted as early as 1792 and recent historians have confirmed.[7] In short, from its beginnings, European colonialism entailed wars of aggression – because there was resistance.

Most important for our purposes, the colonizing rulers and, often enough, their citizens knew about this fact of resistance. They felt the pressure of post/coloniality because they everywhere faced the vision of a time "after colonialism" among those whom they ruled. Throughout the eighteenth century, in a rising stream of travel narratives, official reports, and rumor, the news of Indian "massacres" and slave rebellions reached the ears of ordinary citizens in the Old World. Although these events seemed far away to those in comfortable middle-class homes, certainly some of the larger revolts provoked a sense of threat, such as Tacky's Rebellion in Jamaica (1760), which took six months and many British soldiers to put down.

Then, Haiti happened. That is, at the close of the eighteenth century, the successful overthrow of the French government in St. Domingue by Touissant

Louverture and the founding of Haiti in 1804 established that the Anglo-European colonial world could end and another, postcolonial one could begin. While for many whites living in slave regions, it created a "terrified consciousness," as Anthony Maingot puts it, for black and white abolitionists in Britain, France, and North America it provided proof of the instability and injustice of the colonial order.[8] Novels, histories, and plays appeared in the Americas and Europe, in effect calling all kinds of Anglo-Europeans to form a response to the possibility and righteousness of anti-colonial revolution.

Thereafter, rebellions and uprisings in European empires inevitably conjured the prospect of full revolution – a possibility that came closest to reality for the British in the 1857 Sepoy Rebellion in India. Preceded by several mid-century revolts, and fed by long-developing grievances among the "sepoy" militias of the Bengal Army (the 140,000 Indian troops who served the British in sites from Afghanistan to China), this insurrection exploded over the practice of using animal fat to grease guns, but it quickly spread to civilians and to several regions of India, culminating in a rebel government in northern India for a few months in the summer of 1857. The military response was ruthless: hundreds of thousands died – 150,000 killed in Awadh alone, two-thirds of them civilians. Although this and other insurrections, such as the Morant Bay Rebellion in Jamaica in 1865, were often cast as expressions of the "savagery" of the colonized, they inevitably heightened the British consciousness of resistance to their rule – and sometimes provoked sharp debate in England, as in the case of Governor Eyre's suppression of the Morant Bay Rebellion.

These were cataclysmic events, leaving a scent of fire and burned flesh – and an incipient atmosphere of post/coloniality. And yet the Sepoy and the Morant Bay Rebellions were only two of Britain's most defensive suppressions among dozens of colonial battles fought by their armies in the nineteenth century to secure or, more often, to expand their colonial holdings. Consider this partial list of the nineteenth-century British colonial and trade wars. These fourteen "small" wars of territorial expansion, fought outside of Europe, are only the most consequential:

> First Anglo-Burmese war, 1824–6;
> First Anglo-Afghan War, 1839–42;
> Opium Wars with China, 1839–42 and 1859–60;
> First Anglo-Maori War, 1844–7;
> First Anglo-Sikh War, 1845–6;
> Second Anglo-Sikh War, 1848–9;
> Second Anglo-Burmese War, 1852;
> Crimean War, 1854–6;

Second Anglo-Maori War and extended resistance, 1860–72;
Second Anglo-Afghan War, 1878–80;
Zulu War, 1878–81;
First Anglo-Boer War, 1881;
Second Anglo-Boer War, 1899–1902;
Third Anglo-Burmese War, 1885.

These wars were also often implicitly fought against and among European rivals jockeying to outstrip each other within the world economy. Thus as John Morrow has documented, these so-called "little" wars frequently ended by way of negotiations among Anglo-Europeans and by the same token could lead to intra-European wars, such as the First World War. The steady pressure of such wars also prompted the movement toward conscription and the increased financing of mobilization plans in Europe, all of which fed the bellicose, warring imaginary that Patrick Brantlinger and Cecil Degrotte Eby have tracked in later nineteenth-century British literature.[9]

Meanwhile, across the ocean, South American countries were fighting wars of independence from Spain (1814–26), and then soon enough were fighting trade wars among themselves (including those between Chile, Peru, and Bolivia in the 1880s), along the way violently suppressing indigenous claims to rights or lands. In the US, Anglo-Americans were assertively fighting indigenous peoples in "Indian Removal" wars throughout the later eighteenth and nineteenth centuries, and later the Mexican War, all part of a westward expansion that culminated in the invasion and annexation of the Philippines at the end of the nineteenth century. Amidst these "smaller wars" in the US, of course, there erupted the bloody Civil War, shaping racialized national memory along a fracture between north and south for generations to come – a history that deeply influenced the modernism of the young T. S. Eliot and of William Faulkner, Zora Neale Hurston, and Flannery O'Connor.

This newly embattled world was also a smaller world. By the end of the nineteenth century, railroads and shipways encircled the globe, dramatically expanding the movement of goods, as well as of the armies that could protect colonial economies. These networks also promoted the circulation of news, a circulation later supplemented by the laying of telegraph cables between the Americas and Europe in 1866, and between Britain and India in 1877. As we have seen, the news that traveled such circuits was often shocking.

These battling histories and their documentation in radio, newspapers, and photographs are the conditions we need to keep in mind when considering the relation between post/coloniality and Anglophone (geo)modernism – and when we attempt to imagine the mindset of Anglo-European writers on both sides of the ocean. It seems fair to speculate that anyone who read the newspapers would have a sense of world turbulence, of violent rebellions and suppressions. Add to this picture, too, the later nineteenth-century emergence of feminist activism in the form of demands for education as well as divorce and custody rights, leading to hunger strikes in the early twentieth century, and one begins to glimpse why the vision of a fractured world in grave upheaval might emerge, even among comfortable Anglo-Europeans. Thus did Virginia Woolf in 1927 observe that each person in London was "linked to his fellows by wires which pass overhead, by waves of sound which pour through the roof and speak aloud to him of battles and murders and strikes and revolutions all over the world."[10]

These conditions did indeed "make it new," to re-inflect the familiar modernist phrase – they shaped history as a theatre of epic, mass-murderous conflicts. In this context, no center could hold, as Yeats put it – not in Ireland or anywhere else. The "terrible beauty" born in Ireland on Easter Monday 1916 had likewise been born in Haiti in 1799 and India in 1857 and Jamaica in 1865 and Russia in 1905. The aggressive determination of several different nations to build and to *be* the center of the globe actually exposed and intensified social fractures.

At the same time, resistance and solidarity also became global, in the form of communist international congresses and pan-national or pan-ethnic congresses such as the series of Pan-African Congresses held in Europe between 1919 and 1945. Perhaps partly as a result of the epic proportions of the global aggression, and certainly fostered by new communication and travel networks, resistance also spread across borders and nations. As Frantz Fanon noted, "In spite of all that colonialism can do, its frontiers remain open to new ideas and echoes from the world outside. It discovers that violence is in the atmosphere, that it here and there bursts out, and here and there sweeps away the colonial regime."[11] Elleke Boehmer has documented the ways that independence movements in Ireland, Africa, India, and the West Indies formed coalitions, read each other's newspapers, and gained knowledge and inspiration from each other.[12] Meanwhile, in part prompted by these groups, Anglo-European ex-colonial administrators, such as Virginia Woolf's husband Leonard Woolf, began to write critiques of what Woolf called economic imperialism; women such as Emily Hobhouse in Britain helped to expose the appalling conditions of concentration camps in the Anglo-Boer Wars; and organizations were founded, such as the Anti-Imperialist League in the US (of which Mark Twain was a member and leader), to oppose, for instance, the annexation of the Philippines.

Geomodernism is an art oriented toward this global world, pressingly aware of it – among Anglophone Anglo-Europeans as well as Africans,

African Americans, subcontinent Indians, West Indians, and American indigenous Indians. This is the world in which geomodernism meets postcolonial literature, deconstructing (whether mournfully or radically) the notion of an imperial center, using literary form to register imperialism's violence and incoherence, to place its shards side by side, and sometimes to wonder about the possibilities of human transformation and global cooperation.

History inside out: geomodernist aesthetics and post/coloniality

Thinking our way into twentieth-century literature by way of this history, we freshly understand the import of those experimental forms shared by Anglo modernists and postcolonial writers. Modernist fiction has been characterized in terms of its reconfigurations of perspective and temporality. I shall follow that characterization here, recontextualizing it in light of post/colonial history and postcolonial writers. Literary critics have rightly pointed out that what counts as innovative in twentieth-century fiction has been unduly circumscribed, and that experimental form has been overly privileged in histories of early twentieth-century literature.[13] Nonetheless, it is valuable to understand why some postcolonial writers create strong experimental forms and how these experiments emerge from a certain history that is common to them and to canonical modernist writers.

By contrast with many nineteenth-century novels, much early modernist fiction abandons the objective or omniscient narrator. Narration becomes decentered, providing few objective coordinates and rendering multiple, discrepant points of view. In the earliest criticism on modernism, this feature was understood as a turn away from history and politics, while later critics have come to see it as an exploration of alienation *within* certain political histories, especially of racism and sexism. Yet this aspect of modernist form is a response not only to these histories within nations but also to a world history that is murderous, divisive, and displacing: hence *geo*modernism.

These multiple, decentered perspectives encompass a global consciousness, and more specifically a post/colonial consciousness that juxtaposes the discrepancies of here and there, us and them, margin and center, but also, and more precisely, war zone and safe zone, poor and rich, settled and uprooted. They craft a practice that I call horizon reversal, a feature that figures prominently in a range of postcolonial and modernist novels.

In Jamaican writer Michelle Cliff's novel *No Telephone to Heaven* (1987), we move between the perspectives mainly of Christopher, an orphaned, much-abused, dark-skinned Jamaican gardener who one day murders his rich, lighter-skinned Caribbean employers, and of Clare, a Jamaican-born, US-raised, college-educated, world-traveling woman. After a series of reversals in perspective in which the reader is cast between Clare's relatively easeful (if alienated) travels and Christopher's wretched state of poverty and anger, we discover finally that their paths intersect, unbeknownst to either, after she has returned to Jamaica, joined a guerilla movement, and been gunned down in the hills of Jamaica – above the movie set where the half-mad Christopher is being paid to act like a crazy native. In Kiran Desai's more recent postcolonial novel, *The Inheritance of Loss* (2006), we likewise move between two "worlds" or locations, in this case the mountains of northern India and New York City; in India we circulate among several consciousnesses, including an English-educated Indian judge, his granddaughter, and their cook, whose son Biju has emigrated to New York. Biju carries the burden of his servant-father's hopes, but he is in fact just barely surviving as an illegal immigrant. The alternations between the New York world of Biju and the cast of characters in Kalimpong throw into relief the contrast between the cook's images of his son and the son's reality at the same time that, in Kalimpong, we circulate among the discrepant perspectives of the Anglo and Indian characters.

Similarly, in Ghanian author Ama Ata Aidoo's *Our Sister Killjoy* (1977) and in many of her short stories, we follow characters as they move between Europe and Ghana, and we glimpse how their perspectives on such issues as African women wearing wigs or woman-to-woman sensuality flip-flop with their movements. Aidoo's story "For Whom Things Did Not Change" unfolds by reversals in perspective that expose the neo-colonialism of black Ghanian officials after Independence, shifting between the viewpoints of, on one hand, a black government official, Kobina, and, on the other, the poorly housed and paid servant, Zirigu and his wife Setu, who keep the small hotel in which Kobina stays (and for whom Kobina is at first just a darker-skinned white "massa"). In Andrea Levy's *Small Island* (2004), we travel between Jamaica and England and among the perspectives of four characters – two of them black Jamaican and two white British – whose lives, loves, and losses intersect before, during, and after the Second World War. In Sandra Cisneros's *Woman Hollering Creek* as we journey back and forth across the Mexican/American border we also shift between Mexican and Mexican-American subjectivities.

These postcolonial fictions are all practicing what has traditionally been called multi-perspective narration and typically deemed modernist. Yet, to indicate the post/coloniality embedded in these texts and so to clarify their geomodernist character, this feature might more helpfully be called a structure of "horizon reversal." That is, in all of them, as we move from one perspective to another, we also see the story from its "other side," within an altered backdrop. As the characters travel and points of view shift, "her" becomes "me," and "over there" becomes "here" – so that all at once the incommensurability, the tragic complementarity, and the potential collapse or exchangeability of these locales becomes manifest. These stories confirm Sai's conclusion at the end of *Inheritance of Loss*, "Never again could she think there was but one narrative."[14] Yet this novel and others also reveal that these contrasting narratives meet in an imperial, economic matrix through which all of the characters travel. The narratives track the characters' failed attempts to cross or combine worlds, while signaling, through horizon reversals, the need to acknowledge the fact and the unsustainability of this uneven, global, and post/colonial state of things.

Many postcolonial and US minority women's novels craft such reversals to dramatize, in particular, the gender investments and sexual crimes that intensify this collision of worlds. Toni Morrison sets her first novel, *The Bluest Eye* (1970), in one black neighborhood, but she practices a form of horizon reversal that registers the larger violent environment. Her novel traces the misguided need for intimacy expressed in Cholly Breedlove's rape of his daughter Pecola, while also establishing this event within the history of racist sexual violence – which, for Cholly, begins with his sexual humiliation as a teenager by a pair of white men. The third-person narration that tells this backstory alternates with the first-person narration of Claudia MacTeer, child of a neighboring black working-class family, who looks on at Pecola's impoverished family and bleak fate. Capturing the subterranean, cruel commerce between black and white worlds that gets repeated within one black neighborhood in Ohio, Claudia confesses that her own and the neighborhood's families "cleaned ourselves on her," fashioning themselves as the upright black families in contrast to Pecola's family's degradation.[15] Likewise in Ama Ata Aidoo's "For Whom Things Do Not Change," the white massa's buying of young black girls from their families gets repeated in the new order of things where the big men leading the country do the same – a repetition that Aidoo reveals and yet quietly counters in the honest dialogues between Zirigu and Setu as they labor to grasp the surprisingly respectful behavior of their current "big man" guest at the hotel. Indeed, the wife Setu's questions and active influence within the "servant's" side of this story form an important part of its transformative post/coloniality.

If we describe these narratives' multiple perspectives as horizon reversal, we more aptly name their postcolonial and feminist thrust and, accordingly, we grasp the ways that a feminist post/coloniality shapes canonical modernist novels that were written earlier. The geomodernist fiction of Phyllis Shand Allfrey wryly alerts us to this shared post/coloniality of consciousness. Allfrey, a mid-twentieth-century white West Indian writer and activist, focused on white characters haunted by a sense of the post/colonial "over-there" or in other words by the presence of the colored peoples whose labor supports their relative comfort.

Allfrey's story "O Stay and Hear," for instance, can be read as a witty allegory of the way a questioning white consciousness "borrows" its newly ironic sensibility from darker-skinned servants. It is told mainly from the perspective of the white mistress or "madame-là" of a home on a Caribbean island, and it records the woman's keen awareness of her brown-skinned servants, specifically her cook Ariadne and maid Melta, two close friends who laugh and sing as they work. At key moments the story fleetingly shifts "over there" into Ariadne's and Melta's points of view as they tease Madame-là ("It is giving them great pleasure to satisfy her curiosity tormentingly, bit by bit" as she asks them questions "sounding lost").[16] Madame-là "notices how pretty both girls are," and also "that Ariadne is the one with the crisp, scornful upper lip" (18). Later, as she and her husband watch the girls ironing their hair, she asks him "why they should want to have their hair straight as ours when they mock at us so!" (21).

The madame-là is clearly sensing a point of view on herself that she cannot understand; she is baffled by her servants' combination of imitation and mockery of whites – or in other words their enactment of "colonial mimicry" in Homi Bhabha's sense. And yet all the while, as the story finally reveals, she herself is being transformed by them as she begins to imitate *them*. The story ends with a small dinner party in which the madame-là shows high spirits, her questions to her guest "borrowing," as the narrators says, "an inflection of mockery from somewhere" (232). At this moment Melta enters with a fruit jelly dessert, which looks, as we learn in the final line of the story, "as if it is shaking – shaking with secret laughter" (23). In these circumstances, knowledge originates in the kitchen and travels from there to the dining room, where hostesses "borrow" from the scornfully curled lips and secret knowledge of servants, subalterns, and slaves. In this final scene, we also learn that the knowledge is sexual, for her male guest has told a story that, unbeknownst to him, reveals to the mistress that a friend of his is the likely father of her servants' light-skinned children. Allfrey's own writing likewise embodies this borrowing of a sense of irony even as it reveals a slowly dawning knowledge – all of which quietly conveys to her white readers that what she and they know is issuing from somewhere "over there."

In the light of Allfrey's insights we can see afresh the ways that many Anglo geomodernist novels are organized around or against a post/colonial "over-there." Several of Virginia Woolf's novels fit this description to complicated effect, as Woolf works to render her characters' sexual as well as post/colonial stories. In her first novel *The Voyage Out* (1915), her white English heroine Rachel boards a boat to South America, from which perspective she suddenly sees England as "a very small island . . . a shrinking island"; in South America she takes a trip up-river in which she simultaneously falls in love with a young Englishman and encounters, in native village women, "the motionless inexpressive gaze of those removed from each other far, far beyond the plunge of speech," so that Rachel and her lover suddenly feel "very cold and melancholy."[17] Shortly thereafter, Rachel dies of a fever from "over there" that has somehow infected the English woman and her promising new world of love.

Woolf's later novels are set mostly in England, but the white world of her characters is presented as absorbing the violence of imperialism. That violence registers in the warring imaginations of fathers like Mr. Ramsay and the deaths of sons in the First World War, in both *Jacob's Room* and *To the Lighthouse*; in the return of colonial administrators to London whose habits of fondling knives in their pockets is juxtaposed, in *Mrs. Dalloway*, against the suicidal feelings of war veterans like Septimus Smith; and in the death of sahibs like Percival in *The Waves*, a character ironically presented as a hero stationed "over there" in India who, tellingly, never speaks but around whom the other six characters are oriented – a British community whose center collapses when Percival dies. It is in *Mrs. Dalloway* that Woolf most critically signals the post/colonial thrust of her writing, first of all and implicitly through the title character Clarissa Dalloway, who senses that her London milieu is shaped by "spectres who stand astride us and suck up half our lifeblood, dominators and tyrants," so that she, too, feels "stirring about in her this brutal monster, . . . this hatred . . . making her delightful home rock, quiver, and bend as if indeed there were a monster grubbing at the roots."[18] The novel links this tyranny at home to tyranny abroad in its portrait of the psychologist, Dr. Bradshaw, who wishes to put the suicidal Septimus in an institution. Woolf casts Bradshaw as a man working under the false principles of "Proportion and Conversion," in particular conversion, a "Goddess" who "offers help but desires power" and so "feasts on the wills of the weakly, loving to impress, to impose, adoring her own features stamped on the face of the populace" and "even now engaged – in the heat and sands of India, the mud and swamp of Africa, the purlieus of London" (100).

As this last line indicates, Woolf's groundbreaking novelistic form and sense of political irony emerge, like the Madame-là's knowledge in Allfrey's story, at least partly from her sense of what's happening "over there." Woolf's famously rapid movement from one point of view to another occurs under the pressure of this post/colonial world, presenting discrepant subjectivities as it moves in the course of a paragraph, for instance, from the anguished Septimus's hallucinatory perception of the colonial administrator Peter Walsh as "the dead man in a grey suit" to Peter's shallow view of Septimus and his desperate wife merely as "lovers squabbling" (70–1). As noted, Woolf was acutely aware of the "battles and murders and strikes and revolutions all over the world," and of the time-and-space-collapsing technology by which she knew of these: just so do the continual horizon reversals of her novels capture this strange global circuitry. Even while focusing only on white British characters, she thus conveyed her own involvement in and consciousness of a violent milieu of post/coloniality.

Other early Anglo modernists similarly tell stories mainly from the perspectives of their white characters, but they nonetheless embed these perspectives within a larger post/colonial history. Jean Rhys's novels probably do so the most fully. Herself a white West Indian from Dominica who migrated to London and Paris, Rhys's early novels include Caribbean characters as well as others who are displaced in a warring world. Such is the case in *Good Morning Midnight*, set in the interwar-world of 1938. One key scene of the novel stages a Russian Jewish émigré's recounting of his encounter with a desperate mulatto woman from Martinique who is neglected in Paris by her white husband and despised by her neighbors; the text implicitly juxtaposes her against the female protagonist, Sasha Jansen, herself alone and desperate, and later betrayed by an unidentified foreigner who wins her sympathy by showing her his war wounds. Rhys's novel is a meeting ground of displaced nationalities and races, tossed here and there by waves of war, all of whom encounter each other under the sign, so to speak, of the post/colonial mulatto woman.

Rhys's later novel *Wide Sargasso Sea*, set just after emancipation in nineteenth-century Jamaica, more explicitly tells the story of post/coloniality in the intertwined lives of Antoinette Cosway, her disoriented husband newly arrived from England, and their servants. Written as the backstory of Bertha, the first wife of Charlotte Brontë's Rochester who becomes the creole madwoman in the attic in her novel *Jane Eyre*, this novel rewrites Brontë's text in form as well as in content – a choice on Rhys's part that is itself a kind of literary-historical horizon reversal. *Wide Sargasso Sea* experiments with reversals of perspective in a way that later postcolonial writers would master, placing us on both sides of the Atlantic, with characters looking back at the other island, and switching us dizzyingly between the consciousnesses of Antoinette and Rochester as well as that of the English servant, Grace Poole. Notably, although this novel never enters the consciousness of Christophine, Antoinette's black servant in Jamaica, Rhys establishes through lengthy dialogue that Christophine is a main character with a crucial if disturbingly unclear role in the breakdown of relations between Antoinette and her husband. This, Rhys hints, is the hidden post/colonial world that (temporarily) disrupts the romance of Rochester and Jane Eyre, and by extension underlies the appearance of settled order in Brontë's England.

Thus do these canonical geomodernist narratives register the post/colonial or post/slavery surround. The authors let us know that the histories of racism, colonialism, and world wars include counter-voices and non-white subjectivities, and that the fractured nature of their forms are precipitated by these disavowed presences – these "returns" from the colony in the form of Peter Walshes or isolated mulatto women in run-down hotels. With more regularity and more starkness, postcolonial novels take horizon reversals to their radical conclusion. They tear us away from material security and set us down amid murder and abjection; they catapult us out of a community into friendless exile; they slip us out of sanity into desperation or madness. And, as they move us between locales, they expose the false appearance of security on the "safe" side of the line.

Post/colonial time

Geomodernist authors telling the tale of post/coloniality rearrange our sense of time as well as of space and perspective. In Arundhati Roy's *God of Small Things*, we continually approach the moment of the English girl Sophie Mol's arrival and death in India. The novel's looping temporal structure, wherein we move forward up to a penultimate moment before this crisis and then circle back in time to approach it again from another perspective, has led readers to compare Roy's method to Faulkner's, although Roy had not read Faulkner when she wrote the novel and she discounts this comparison.

This looping form, however, may be understood as the structure of a geopolitical history they share. Traditionally, the non-chronological representation of time in modernism has been understood, again, to be a function of modernism's turn inward. Critics have often described modernists such as Woolf or Joyce as shedding "clock time" and representing subjective time, especially its currents of memory. Attention to memory and subjective time can indeed illuminate Roy's and other postcolonial authors' work, especially when considered in relation to personal and historical traumas. But the looping forms of temporality in geomodernist fiction also reconstruct time for the reader.

Approached from this angle, repetitions of event in these novels are not only a compulsive return to a traumatic legacy. Through these returns and repetitions, we are also made to feel that certain events have "already happened" insofar as they are decreed by a social logic or ideology; lives are driven by the barreling locomotive of colonial or racist and sexist world history – so that Faulkner's Joe Christmas is fated to kill Joanna Burden and Roy's Veluthi (an "untouchable") is fated to die for loving Ammu. In the latter novel, Ammu's children Rahel and Esthappen are jolted from sleep to witness "history's henchmen" beating Velutha nearly to death – an event the novel has been approaching and retreating from as part of the crisis of Sophie Mol's visit. As the narrator remarks, "There was nothing accidental about what happened that morning. Nothing *incidental*. It was no stray mugging or personal settling of scores. This was an era imprinting itself on those who lived in it. History in live performance."[19] Thus the future can seem to be always already created, a fate toward which everyone is involuntarily moving, or being moved. The repetitive temporal returns in these works thus capture the material force of ideologies and beliefs that make lives unfold according to a plan that protects some and sacrifices others.

Michelle Cliff's *No Telephone to Heaven* follows this pattern of overdetermined temporality to powerful effect while also narrating its complement, the counter-history of resistance. Set during the upheaval of the 1970s in Jamaica, the scene that the novel opens with and continually returns to is that of an old truck lumbering steeply uphill on a muddy, broken road, hauling guns and people in khakis to the site (although we don't know it yet) of their insurrectionary attack. From this opening scene, we fall back in Chapter 1 to the previous years of planning on the farm of "Miss Mattie's granddaughter" that led them to this moment, although we don't know yet who Miss Mattie's granddaughter is. In the next chapter, we start up the hill again, and then fall back again to a time just before the plans begin in earnest – the night that Christopher murders his employers, a night on which, quite apart from the murder scene, we briefly meet a woman named Clare Savage. In the middle of this same long chapter we fall back further, to Christopher's childhood, to the shantytown of the Dungle where he grew up, a world of begging, foraging, disease, and hunger ringed round by the contempt of others, and then in the same chapter we move forward again to the movements that lead him to kill his light-skinned disrespecting employers one night.

Then a swerve. In the next section, Chapter 3, we leap across the sea and back in time again, to our other protagonist Clare Savage at age seven in a car in Florida, traveling with her newly emigrated family. We learn the story of her parents' decision to pass for white in the US, her mother's increasing alienation under this lie, her mother's departure from the father and return to Jamaica with the younger daughter, Clare's sister, and Clare's lonely childhood with her father. At the start of the next chapter we find ourselves back on the truck, where we learn that Clare is Miss Mattie's granddaughter and that she, now thirty-six years old, is on this truck. In the rest of the novel we shuttle between this truck ride and scenes of Clare's life before the truck ride.

Although this looping structure with its struggling movement uphill ends, like so many geomodernist and post/colonial novels, in death and loss (here, the murder of Clare and the other guerillas), the action to which we continually return is an action of resistance to the determinations of imperial history. In other words, Cliff is recording the "other" side of imperialism's history: counter-imperialism. This, too, this uphill work of resistance, is a driving, returning world-historical force, undertaken by characters who wearily, fearfully, yet persistently revive that resistance, even sometimes against their own wishes, against their dreams of another life, another set of choices. Cliff's novel emphasizes that this counter-history, too, keeps arriving within this looping structure that holds the future hostage to a colonial past.

In short, this kind of temporality in Cliff and other female geomodernists recreates history's progress as history's questions and breaks (other such authors would include Anita Desai, Nadine Gordimer, and Zadie Smith as well as earlier canonical writers like Rhys, Woolf, and Djuna Barnes – and among the men, Nuruddin Farah, J. M. Coetzee, Ralph Ellison, Joyce, and Faulkner). These authors fashion their narratives to capture the experience of living within a long history of coercive ideologies and refusals or disavowals of that coercion.

And at the same time, to the extent that these narratives are always stepping back from the overdetermined moments of crisis, they give us an opening in which to imagine, and hope, that the crises might not (have) happen(ed). They offer us a consciousness of post/coloniality that might change the direction of history. It is in this gap, for example, that the friendship between the twins and Sophie Mol in *God of Small Things* develops – against our (and the twins') early expectations before we meet her that she will be just another basis for negative colonialist judgments and frowning looks from the adults. In this way, the looping structures work to represent the potential for divergence from ideological and historical determinism, challenged not only by armed resistance but also by mere contingency and by unexpected love or tenderness. The narratives register a desire to step back from a world in which the fatedness of violent coercion is so tightly coupled with the fatedness of violent resistance. By foreshadowing the event – the violence – and then whisking us back to a better moment and an alternative current of interactions, they gesture toward a path not determined and a future that is neither post nor colonial, in which the meanings of those words suddenly dissolves within another, alternative language, like the one Rahel and Esthappen keep creating together beyond the hearing of adults. All of this constitutes what we can think of as their formal rendering of a post/colonial temporality.

In these interrelated dimensions of place and time, geomodernist authors express a global post/coloniality. To describe the relation among such authors as borrowing or influence overlooks their co-rootedness in this global world. Instead, working from opposite directions along the post/colonial continuum of modern history, Anglo-European and postcolonial geomodernists together rework our fundamental modes of orientation within time and space. They place us within the fracture that divides here from there and they force us to feel our caughtness within the forces of history as well as to acknowledge the possibilities and alternative commitments lurking within the unpredictable time-lags of everyday life.

NOTES

1. Edward Said, *Culture and Imperialism* (New York: Vintage, 1994), p. 190.
2. See Simon Gikandi, *Maps of Englishness* (New York: Columbia University Press, 1996); J. Ramazani, *The Hybrid Muse: Postcolonial Poetry in English* (Chicago: University of Chicago Press, 2001); Elleke Boehmer, *Empire, the National, and the Postcolonial, 1890–1920: Resistance in Interaction* (New York: Oxford University Press, 2002); Laura Winkiel and Laura Doyle, eds., *Geomodernisms: Race, Modernism, Modernity* (Bloomington: Indiana University Press, 2005); R. Begum and M. V. Moses, *Modernism and Colonialism: British and Irish Literature 1899–1939* (Durham, NC: Duke University Press, 2007); and Mary Ann Gillies, Helen Sword, and Steven Yao, eds., *Pacific Rim Modernisms* (Toronto: University of Toronto Press, 2009).
3. Nelson Maldonado-Torres, "On the Coloniality of Being: Contributions to the Development of a Concept," *Cultural Studies* 21.2/3 (March/May 2007), 240–70, at 243.
4. I use the term post/coloniality to encompass the African diaspora in the Americas. Although it fits less neatly in the US, since after 1776 the problem is slavery more than colonization per se, post/coloniality appropriately recalls the colonial origins of slavery and names the conflicted consciousness and struggle that has accompanied resistance to this initially colonial institution.
5. Brathwaite mentions the recordings of Eliot that he and other Caribbean writers of the 1930s and 40s listened to. He explains that what "turned us on" was Eliot's "dry, deadpan delivery, the 'riddims' of St. Louis," which resonated for them with "the dislocations of Bird, Dizzy, and Klook." See E. Kamau Brathwaite, *Roots* (Ann Arbor: University of Michigan Press, 1993), p. 286. Simon Gikandi connects this sense of dislocation to the "crisis of late colonialism" which, he says, was also "the crisis denoted by modernism" (*Maps of Englishness*, p. 158). My own point expands on Gikandi's to highlight the longer history of dislocation and war that encompassed both Eliot and Caribbean writers.
6. "The Blackman's Burden" is the title of a poem by Adjua Mensah, published in the "Women's Column" *Accra Evening News*, Ghana, August 2, 1949. See *Women Writing Africa: West Africa and the Sahel*, ed. Esi Sutherland-Addy and Aminata Diaw (Paris: Karthala, 2001), p. 209.
7. See T. Clarkson, "The True State of the Case, respecting the Insurrection at St. Domingo," reprinted in *Slave Revolution in the Caribbean, 1789–1804: A Brief History with Documents*, ed. L. Dubois and J. D. Garrigus (New York: St. Martin's Press, 2006), pp. 113–15. Also see P. J. N. Tuck, *Warfare, Expansion, and Resistance* (London: Routledge, 2002), p. 212. For other important, wide-ranging histories of resistance, see R. Blackburn, *The Overthrow of Colonial Slavery*,

1776–1848 (London and New York: Verso, 1988), and P. Linebaugh and M. Rediker, *The Many-headed Hydra: Sailors, Slaves, Commoners, and the Hidden History of the Revolutionary Atlantic* (Boston, MA: Beacon, 2000).

8. Anthony P. Maingot, "Haiti and the Terrified Consciousness of the Caribbean," in *Ethnicity in the Caribbean*, ed. Gert Ootindie (London: Macmillan, 1996), pp. 53–80. Also see Blackburn, who remarks that "The overturn in St. Domingue and the consolidation of black power in Haiti had a terrible message for the slave order throughout the Americas. Black rebels in Cuba in 1812, in the United States in 1820, in Jamaica and Brazil in the 1920's, found inspiration in Haiti" (*The Overthrow of Colonial Slavery*, p. 257).

9. Patrick Brantlinger, *Rule of Darkness: British Literature and Imperialism 1830–1914* (Ithaca, NY: Cornell University Press, 1988), and Cecil Degrotte Eby, *Road to Armageddon: The Martial Spirit in English Popular Literature, 1870–1914* (Durham, NC: Duke University Press, 1987).

10. Virginia Woolf, "The Narrow Bridge of Art," in *Collected Essays* (New York: Harcourt Brace Jovanovich, 1967), vol. II, p. 222.

11. Frantz Fanon, *The Wretched of the Earth*, trans. Constance Farrington (1961; Harmondsworth: Penguin, 1986), ch. 1, "Concerning Violence," pp. 54–5.

12. See Boehmer, *Empire, the National, and the Postcolonial*.

13. For instance, see Rita Felski, *Doing Time: Feminist Theory and Postmodern Culture* (New York: New York University Press, 2000).

14. Kiran Desai, *Inheritance of Loss* (New York: Atlantic Monthly, 2006), p. 355.

15. Toni Morrison, *The Bluest Eye* (New York: Penguin, 2005), p. 205.

16. Phyllis Shand Allfrey, in *It Falls into Place*, ed. Lizbeth Paravisini-Gebert (London: Papillote Press, 2004), p. 18. Further references will appear in the text. Allfrey's story "O Stay and Hear" was first published in September 1954 in *Argosy* 15.9.

17. Virginia Woolf, *The Voyage Out* (New York: Harcourt Brace, 1948), pp. 32 and 284–5.

18. Virginia Woolf, *Mrs. Dalloway* (New York: Harcourt, 2002), p. 12. Further references will appear in the text.

19. Arundhati Roy, *The God of Small Things* (New York: Harper Perennial, 1998), p. 293.

9

MAGGIE HUMM

Women modernists and visual culture

Introduction

As Ann Ardis argues, the New Woman is *the* key figure in turn-of-the-twentieth-century debates about gender, visual cultures, and modernity.[1] Changes in gender relations, from 1882 – the year of Virginia Woolf's birth – to the 1920s, interact with the development of modernism. Women were central players in new city spaces as suffragettes and in novelists' newly imagined public modernities, for example in Dorothy Richardson's *Pilgrimage*. Women's experiences of urban modernity included the spheres of art galleries and cinemas which offered new modes of collective seeing. Women artists and art critics were highly visible in, and major contributors to, London journals. By the turn of the century, there were over thirty women critics contributing signed articles with some, for example the writer Alice Meynell, earning over £400 a year. In turn, twentieth-century women's modernism is obsessed with issues of visuality.

Women modernists, including Virginia Woolf and her sister the artist Vanessa Bell, were also the first generation of women to be active photographers and cinema-goers from childhood. Like Bell, many women painters were photographers. For example, the American artist Susan Sears began photography at the same time as she was exhibiting paintings, and she joined Alfred Stieglitz's Photo-Secession in 1904. Women contributed to other modernist photographic movements including the Bauhaus, and were active domestic photographers with "vest-pocket Kodaks." Visual culture, then, had a profound influence on modernist women's lives, art, and writing. For example, women modernists, more than men, incorporated everyday and maternal experiences into their aesthetics and were devotees of cinema, reflecting a modern world in which women were 87 percent of film audiences by the 1920s. However, when analyzing gender issues in relation to visual modernism, it is difficult to hold to a firm dichotomy between feminine and masculine modernisms. Yet we need to examine modernist women's continuous attention to domestic photography, cinema, and the arts in the context of the everyday with attention to the links between gender and modernist visual cultures. And despite differences of education, location, and sexual orientation, there are similarities in the ways women modernists "see differently" issues of identity and spectatorship.

In general, modernists learned a great deal from cinema techniques, for example film's use of a continuous present. Cinema offered modernism new ways of thinking about space, time, and identity in relation to mass culture. The writers Colette, H. D., Bryher, Dorothy Richardson, and Virginia Woolf all wrote about cinema in an accessible, autobiographical, often experimental idiom attentive to issues of gendered spectatorship. Modernist women explore the cinema worlds of women and children and cinema's aesthetics and technologies, understanding film to involve gendered as well as scopic processes. Rather than dismissing popular audiences, they create what could be termed a psycho-social aesthetics with gendered representations at its core. One good example is the way in which Dorothy Richardson's first article in the film journal Close Up describes the new audience of Monday morning women viewers tired of washdays,[2] but also utilizes the image of a wave, drawing on the new physics of relativity, to describe cinema's dynamic qualities. In the pages of Close Up and other journals, modernist women constructed themselves as modern women of letters making sense of cinema for a modern and gendered public. The cinema writing of modernist women makes an important contribution to visual culture, not only by exposing the ideological power of the visual, but also by addressing women's ways of looking.

Colette

The French writer Colette contributed to this modern aesthetic world. From 1914 onward, Colette indefatigably wrote film reviews, film scripts, and subtitled the important German film Mädchen in Uniform, and many of her novels were adapted for the screen. In her vivacious, anecdotal reviews, Colette envisaged a cinema with women and children as active viewers enjoying the performances of powerful women stars like Mae West. Colette was intensely interested in the impact of film on audiences, and how spectators experience particular films. Rather than crafting a universalizing criticism, her reviews dramatize her own reactions to films, together with the reactions of fellow viewers and actresses. In her first article "Le Ciné," published in Le Matin, she refuses the stance of a distancing critic by ethnographically inventing the gossip of women extras waiting to perform. "Say something! We look as if we're waiting for the Metro."[3] In later reviews Colette deliberately "staged" dialogue sketches of knowledgeable women with children sharing a viewing of the films *The Cheat* and *L'Outre*. In "Bel Gazou and the Cinema," a daughter's apparently innocent eye enables Colette to ironically attack inadequately inter-titled silent films.

Colette was also very aware of the historical context and the material nature of cinema. As early as 1910, she warned that American cinema's commercial domination of European markets would follow on from the American institution of "conservatories solely for cinema."[4] Colette's film reviews describe cinema as if it were women's public space in modernity, and she created a specifically feminine style for this audience. For example, her work abounds in domestic metaphors. In a 1917 review of *Maciste Alpin*, soldiers carry captured men back to camp "a little like a housewife bringing home the leeks."[5] A newly heroic feminine subject emerges in Colette's reviews. In her essay "Les Cinéacteurs," Colette praises Mae West as an auteur like Balzac, "the principal interpreter of her films."[6] Colette admires the way in which West escapes women's stereotypical roles, "does not get married at the end of the film, does not die, does not take the road to exile."[7] Colette's construction of herself as a specifically female viewer in her writing, identifying with West as a woman, is also a key feature of other modernist women's film writing.

CLOSE UP

H. D. (Hilda Doolittle)

A leading Imagist poet by 1914, H. D. arrived at a turning point in her career when she gave birth to her daughter Perdita in 1919 and began her relationship with Bryher.[8] H. D.'s poetry ranges from Imagist poems like "Sea Garden" to the modernist long poems *Trilogy* and *Helen in Egypt*. One major feature of H. D.'s cinema essays is the way in which H. D. deploys autobiographical viewing experiences and describes everyday audiences as knowledgeable viewers. The first issue of *Close Up*, the film journal edited by H. D., Bryher, and Kenneth Macpherson, in July 1927 contains H. D.'s first essay inaugurating a series of twelve substantial pieces grouped as "The Cinema and the Classics." The essays bring together her ideas about cinema montage and Imagism in critiques of directors Carl Dreyer and G. W. Pabst and of Russian cinema, and interviews with film-makers and actresses. Working with Bryher and Kenneth Macpherson, H. D. helped to script, edit, and possibly co-direct the film *Borderline*, as well as the now vanished film *Wing Beat*. In H. D.'s essay *The Borderline Pamphlet*, issued to support the film, she describes the "unrelenting" work of cinematography in which "the cinema-camera is a Renaissance miracle or a Greek incarnation."[9]

H. D.'s film essays are much the longest and most carefully structured of any contribution to *Close Up*. The scale of the series enabled her to combine a detailed analysis of films with discussions about cinema as an institution, including her own spectating experiences and observations of cinema audiences. Where her poems and fiction, for example *Nights*, were often first published in limited editions for a specialist readership, H. D.'s cinema writing aims at a much broader audience. Her weaving of autobiography into critical narrative is at its most potent and persuasive in those essays directly about women stars like Garbo and about films with female protagonists like Carl Dreyer's *Joan of Arc*. To H. D. Garbo signifies beauty, a Helen of Troy, a silver goddess whose photographs H. D. mounted in a special scrapbook. "Greta Garbo, as I first saw her, gave me a clue, a new angle and a new sense of elation."[10] Garbo, H. D. believes, offers a new, feminine acting style, an intensity of representation too powerful to be dominated by a male gaze. H. D. performed her character Astrid in the film *Borderline* in "heavy, Garbo-like make-up," with "dark intensity."[11] H. D. also identified with Louise Brooks's performance in *Pandora's Box* and felt "a personal right to *Pandora*, that it personally was partly of my making."[12] H. D. positions herself as a woman spectator. The director Pabst is "almost a magician" precisely because he "brings out the vital and vivid forces in women as the sun in flowers."[13] H. D. immediately responded to the shock-like attraction of Russian cinema. Her essay "Russian Films" grandiloquently associates Russian films with the Bible because ideas in both, according to H. D., were "carved in lightning on the rock of Sinai."[14] Describing herself as a paradigmatic female viewer is a crucial theme in H. D.'s cinema essays. In "Conrad Veidt" for example, she first carefully describes her own experiences before describing the film itself.[15] H. D. creates a gendered film spectator because she is looking at her own image.

Rather than insisting on a distancing and analytic critical style, H. D.'s gaze is social and collective. Her cinema writing contains fascinating phenomenological accounts of her film-viewing experiences which somewhat resemble the tableaux passages in her fiction in which characters "perform" events and emotions. For example, in H. D.'s novel *Bid Me to Live* the character Julia comes to understand her life, and the lives of those around her, through the visual. "They seemed to be superimposed on one another like a stack of photographic negatives. Hold them up to the light and you get in reverse light-and-shade. Julia and Bela seated on that same chintz-covered couch, a composite."[16] Visual language provides H. D., as it did Virginia Woolf, with ways of describing relationships in modernity. H. D., like other modernist women, addresses a popular audience speaking in an engaging personal voice which is always gendered. This blurring of boundaries between the autobiographical and the social, and between the critic and the common viewer, is a major theme of women's modernism.

Bryher

As well as co-founding *Close Up*, together with H. D. and Kenneth Macpherson, Bryher took on many of the journal's editorial functions, coordinating articles, correspondence, and printing. In Bryher's twenty-two *Close Up* articles, her autobiography *The Heart to Artemis*, and two film books *Film Problems of Soviet Russia* (1929) and *Cinema Survey* (1937), she addresses issues of gender, politics, education, and avant-garde aesthetics in a style that is always accessible. Born Annie Winifred Ellerman, Bryher took her pseudonym from a favorite Isle of Scilly and, with her father's wealth, could found and support *Close Up*. Although in *The Heart to Artemis* Bryher claimed "it never occurred to me that I should ever take movies seriously," and "my own interest, however, was in education rather than film," her film writing shares other modernist women's exuberant, self-reflexive attention to popular audiences and gender issues.[17]

The Heart to Artemis describes Bryher's percipient interest in psychoanalysis (she was one of the first subscribers to the *British Journal of Psychoanalysis*), her friendships with women, and her understanding of modernism. In addition to H. D., with whom she had a lifelong relationship, Bryher's friends included Colette, Adrienne Monnier, Sylvia Beach, and the community of Paris-based modernist women writers. Women are at the center of Bryher's work. In "Defence of Hollywood," for example, she makes the intriguing suggestion that the "excellent" actress Clara Bow should be directed by Dorothy Arzner so that Bow could "be herself."[18] Like H. D., Bryher identifies with women film stars. Bryher describes meeting the actress Anita Loos in a hotel like a typical woman cinema-goer's dream moment, like "the ceaseless shooting of movie scenes."[19]

Dorothy Richardson

Throughout her twenty-three film essays in *Close Up*, Dorothy Richardson shares her sister modernists' concern with an autobiographical, feminine standpoint. Her themes are visibly "feminine": supporting women's need to identify with stars; refusing to separate life from art; frequently addressing an everyday woman spectator; and describing a feminine language of film. Under the rubric title "Continuous Performance," Richardson's essays contain extensive reviews of cinema practices, of cinema architecture, and the roles of music and sound, as well as critiques of particular films. In her first contribution to *Close Up*, Richardson immediately personalizes the essay form. She describes how she gave up theatre-going, "all too high pitched," in favor of cinema because her first sight of the screen – "the balm of that tide" – and "the shining eyes and rested faces" of women viewers had such an impact on her.[20] She democratically positions herself as an ordinary cinema-goer sharing the experience of other women in the cinema, on "a washday" Monday, "tired women, their faces sheened with toil, and small children."[21]

In Richardson's major essay "The Film Gone Male," she genders silent film as feminine and the talkies as masculine.

> And the film, regarded as a medium of communication, in the day of its innocence, in its quality of being nowhere and everywhere, nowhere in the sense of having more intention than direction and more purpose than plan, everywhere by reason of its power to evoke, suggest, reflect, express from within its moving parts and in their totality of movement, something of the changeless being at the heart of all becoming, was essentially feminine.[22]

When speech is added to film, Richardson argues, film becomes "a medium of propaganda ... it is a masculine destiny."[23] Here she reverses a gendered binary opposition in which the symbolic is privileged and instead praises *silent* film as feminine because it is antilinear, not directive, continually "becoming."[24] It is silent cinema which captures the feminine: our memories, our time, our fluidity, and our language. The feminine is primarily affective rather than logical because, Richardson argues, the feminine can "suggest, reflect, express."[25] She describes women's spectatorship as active, not passive, and as rapidly feminizing the cultural space of cinema. Rather than a masculine "mere glance over the shoulder," women share "universal, unchanging, unevolving verities."[26]

"The Film Gone Male" is remarkably prescient of current feminist themes. Richardson argues that spectators are not passive consumers and cinema is not a social narcotic. Women spectators who identify with women stars are not simply identifying with total artifice, with impossible fantasy, but engaging in a form of cultural appropriation, investing their own lives with some glamour. For example, in "Animal Impudens," she claims that women stars place "the frail edifice of my faith in woman at last upon a secure foundation."[27] Richardson's fluid syntax, which uses the plural first person and the present tense, makes her essays open and collective. Audiences might be "life-educated" but their artistic judgments are not inferior to those of film critics. For example, women audiences do enjoy happy endings, but this desire Richardson celebrates as "a tribute to their unconscious certainty that life is ultimately good."[28] Richardson's celebration of women's cinema experiences, women's identification with stars, and their desire for happy endings allows films to be assessed in terms of women's situated knowledges rather than only through a high-art aesthetic.

Gertrude Stein

Gertrude Stein was one of the first women modernists to own and appreciate avant-garde art. An émigré writer in Paris, together with her brother, Stein was a patron of Picasso and Braque. Stein's writings closely respond to modernist art. For example, *Three Lives* was stimulated by Cezanne's paintings.

Close Up published two essays by Stein in 1927, "Mrs Emerson" and "Three Sitting Here." The essays do not directly describe film. Like all Stein's work, they are not directly referential, but some passages indicate her interest in cinema and are highly visual and abstract, drawing on her knowledge of the paintings of Matisse and Picasso. Stein's use of repeated single moments placed in sequence resembles film stills and she herself compared her use of the continuous present to the sequential nature of film. The narrator's hesitancy, giving more space to the views of others than her own – "they say" – matches other modernist women's attention to spectators. In "Three Sitting Here" Stein focuses on surface detail, and the essay is more visibly modernist. Not only had cinema offered Stein "a solution of this thing" (how to create portraits in a continuous present), but, she believed, cinema was the defining feature of her moment of modernity: "our period was undoubtedly the period of the cinema."[29]

Marianne Moore

Ironically, in 1933, just as *Close Up* was devoting more space to modernist women's writing, it ceased publication. In that last year the American poet Marianne Moore contributed two reviews, and Nancy Cunard dramatically publicized the Scottsboro case in which black hobos were wrongfully sentenced for the rape of a white girl. It was Bryher who had helped to publish Marianne Moore's *Poems* (1921), and H. D.'s first literary criticism in August 1916 was an appreciation of Moore's work. Moore's "Fiction or Nature" in the September 1933 issue of *Close Up* describes the first American showing of *Mädchen in Uniform*, and her "Lot in Sodom" in December 1933 is an imagistic review of that film. Her well-known opposition to self-revelation in her poetry, and her famous constant revisions and rhetorical conciseness, are in fact not a marked feature of her cinema writing. Like other women modernist cinema critics, Moore autobiographically takes the standpoint of a common viewer: "As I was coming out of the playhouse I overheard an incorrigible movie unenthusiast say, 'It has richness of imagination enough to last you a year and makes you want to see a film every week.' I agree."[30]

Vanessa Bell

Like other modernist women, including Gertrude Stein and Dorothy Richardson, the artist Vanessa Bell has an interest in the everyday. In a sense, Bell's artistic eclecticism provides a key to answering questions about gender and modernism. What we witness in the writing of Dorothy Richardson and Virginia Woolf and the art of Vanessa Bell are the tensions of gendered modernism: the ways in which everyday reality is a necessarily more contingent force in the thinking of women artists and writers, and the ways in which this contingency might be represented artistically in repetitive, as well as eclectic forms, particularly in visual culture. Bell was a major designer as well as a modernist painter. She designed for the Omega Workshops; rooms for her brother Adrian Stephen; fireplaces for Virginia Woolf; furniture for her husband Clive Bell; carpets for friends; a complete Music Room for the Lefevre Gallery; carpets and panels for the cruise ship the Queen Mary; a dinner set for the art historian Kenneth Clark; and she was continuously decorating her own homes. Cyril Connolly's incisive comment about Bell's Music Room, "a rare union of intellect and imagination," points to Bell's lifelong attempt to reconcile formalism with expression.[31] Bell's dust-jacket designs for the Woolfs' Hogarth Press books, including *Kew Gardens*, *The Waves*, *Flush*, and *To the Lighthouse*, similarly experiment with the tension between structural forms and expressive details. Bell's book designs would, Virginia claimed, "be a tremendous draw."[32] As Diane Gillespie points out, Bell's book-jacket designs are formally consistent in their "justified left margins" but have "uneven right ones" and "all sorts of variations from diagonals to curves."[33] Simon Watney claims that Bell's designs for her own home at 46 Gordon Square, London, were similarly "at once descriptive and starkly abstract."[34]

Taking photographs and making photo albums were central activities in Bell's creative life, as they were for other modernists. Bell's photographs employ various conventions and genres and are frequently mobile and expressive, ranging from monumental portraits and tableaux to erotic portraits of her children. Her photographs owe much to the influence of her great-aunt Julia Margaret Cameron, the famous Victorian photographer. There are also clear analogies between Bell's paintings and her photographs. For example, her most significant paintings, *Studland Beach* and *The Tub*, were painted at the same time her most interesting photographs were taken. In the 1890s Sarah Sears, similarly influenced by Cameron, frequently photographed her daughter Helen nude as well as in elaborate costumes. But, as Erica Hirschler points out, although women artists were encouraged to portray their children this was "both a trap and an opportunity. Children were seldom the subject of important public commissions."[35] Yet the physical and mental well-being of children were key issues of concern to educationists at the beginning of the twentieth century. Bell was herself interested in early childhood development and attempted to set up and teach a nursery school at her country house, Charleston. Together with Clive Bell, Vanessa painted a nursery at 33 Fitzroy Square, exhibited in December 1913, which incorporated large Matisse-like animal reliefs flowing across the ceiling and walls.

In short, Vanessa Bell's photographs function as creative prequels to paintings, providing a testing space for her to judge "significant form"; as formal artistic representations in themselves; and as autobiographical and emotive expressions. Bell's photo albums are marginal to conventional art history but are a particularly pertinent site of the struggles between the public and the private, between the formally expressive and the everyday moment, which also occur in other modernist women's work.

Virginia Woolf

The production of new ways of seeing and knowing the world was the project of the modernist writer Virginia Woolf as well as modernist artists, for example Picasso and Braque. Virginia Woolf continually experiments with features of vision, radically reframing the visible world in her writing. Woolf's long involvement with visual culture over many decades is striking in its wide range of formal means, subject matter, and genres, including reviews of art and cinema and domestic photography. These share major themes: the importance of a common viewer, gender differences, and anti-institutionalism, all coalescing in a commitment to an artistic ethics. In Woolf's writings visual images play a constitutive role in creating a surface aesthetic, while at the same time images are often clues to multiple and repressed femininities.

From the age of fifteen, photographs framed Woolf's world. She was familiar with family photography, for example the photographs taken by her father, her brothers, her sister, and her great-aunt Julia Margaret Cameron. She wrote about photography in her diaries, letters, and essays, and used photographic terms descriptively in her fiction. Before her marriage, and then together with Leonard, she took, developed, and preserved over a thousand photographs in albums. She skillfully transformed friends and moments into artful tableaux and she was surrounded by female friends who were also energetic photographers.[36] Lady Ottoline Morrell's photographs "come out so much better than the professionals"; and the writer Vita Sackville-West and artist Dora Carrington all exchanged photographs with Virginia.[37] Woolf needed photographs in order to write. For example, she asked Vita, in 1931, for "a photograph of Henry" (Vita's cocker spaniel): "I ask for a special reason, connected with a little escapade" which became Woolf's book *Flush*.[38] The use of photographs in *Flush*, *Three Guineas*, and *Orlando* parallels the multiple references to photographs in many of Woolf's novels, such as *Jacob's Room*, as well as in her diaries and letters. In *Night and Day*, for instance, Woolf judges characters by the photographs they display in their houses. The whole tonal quality of *To the Lighthouse*, Hermione Lee claims, is inflected by Woolf's memory of Cameron's photographs and, I would add, Woolf's own photography.[39] In *To the Lighthouse* much of the narrative weight of the novel is sustained in images which act as visual analogues to plot developments.

But even in her eight short fictions "Portraits," Woolf uses a specifically photographic vocabulary like a camera negotiating vertical and horizontal frames of portrait and landscape. Although she does not divest "Portraits" of sounds (trains, markets) and smells (urine, petrol), it is the visual surface that frames unrevealed information. This enables the urban spaces of modernity in these stories to become places of relationships rather than sites of a dominating male gaze. Woolf's continuous attention to photography throughout her life impacts on "Portraits," with women characters looking at the modern world. Each story has a different focus, takes a different photograph of what Walter Benjamin calls the unconscious optics of modernity, or the ways in which photographs can register moments outside immediate perception. Photography arrests moments in time, capturing non-linear gestures and invisible feelings. Photography graphically highlights personally significant details such as favorite objects, as Woolf does so often in her writing. In addition photography's composition by field mirrors Woolf's juxtaposition of the everyday with deep philosophical ideas.

Virginia Woolf was intermittently a novelist but continually a critic. She wrote over 500 critical reviews and essays, which often interweave autobiographical asides together with conjectures about art, literature, and life. Woolf's essays of the 1920s specifically about modernism, "Modern Fiction" (1925), the revised version of "Modern Novels" (1919), "The Narrow Bridge of Art" (1927), and "Phases of Fiction" (1929), share a concern with visual cultures. Like snapshots, the essays' momentary reflections often connect by focusing on objects. Woolf's "The Narrow Bridge of Art" evokes differing perspectives and filmic views. Woolf suggests that the future novel will contain "the stimulus of sight, the effect on us of the shape of trees or the play of colour," like a series of impressions from an avant-garde film.[40]

"The Cinema"

Woolf's "The Cinema" is one of the first British essays about avant-garde cinema. The essay was triggered by her interest in *The Cabinet of Dr Caligari*, directed by Robert Wiene in Germany in 1919. The film depicts a story told by a madman about a psychopathic murder, and weaves together nightmare and reality. Woolf's essay is only tangentially about the film itself and focuses more on issues of the psychoanalytic and film spectatorship in general. "The Cinema" addresses the central concerns of other women modernist film critics: how "common viewers" experience film and film's psychic power; the relationship between film and the arts; and film's status and future. Woolf's account of the unconscious optics of film and film's future is based on a clear premise that film is a new dynamic, psychic, and cognitive process. Woolf suggests that when the eye and the brain together "look at the King, the boat, the horse, ... the brain sees at once that they have taken on a quality which does not belong to the simple photograph of real life. They have become not more beautiful, in the sense in which pictures are beautiful, but shall we call it (our vocabulary is miserably insufficient) more real, or real with a different reality from that which we perceive in daily life."[41] Woolf's image of the eye and the brain, which appears also in her essay "Walter Sickert," in *Three Guineas*, and elsewhere in her work, matches Freud's model of the unconscious.

Woolf argues that cinema should refuse mimeticism, especially the direct representation of literary texts, because "the results have been disastrous to both."[42] "The Cinema" is a sophisticated analysis of how cinematic processes, in particular film's use of dialectical montage, interpellate spectators. Like her sister modernists, Woolf is engagingly self-reflexive, placing her own experiences into her writing for a common reader. Reader and narrator are "we," as in "we have time to open the whole of our mind wide to beauty."[43] Woolf's exploratory exposition moves at a reader's speed from point to point, juxtaposing the avant-garde *The Cabinet of Dr Caligari* with a popular newsreel of the Grand National to engage common viewers – a vivid feature of women modernists' writing.

Three Guineas

Contemporaneously, and still today, Woolf's *Three Guineas* is a radical, anti-patriarchal, anti-fascist, and pacifist work. Woolf's argument is that war can only be prevented with gendered changes in education, employment, and intellectual life. She connects fascist military oppressions with the marginalization of women in general and creates the Outsiders' Society, the disenchanted daughters of educated men. Virginia Woolf's *Three Guineas* shares in a gendered modernist visual culture with its use of published and "narrated" photographs. The published photographs – of lawyers, Church leaders, academics, and the army – Woolf counters with the narrator's memories of photographs of the dead bodies of Spanish women and children. Paradoxically, the public photographs become timeless dead icons of patriarchy, while the narrator's repeated mnemonic of the absent photographs of the Spanish dead becomes a lively vehicle, enabling Woolf to develop her attack on patriarchy. The "narrated" Spanish photographs show experiences unacknowledged by patriarchal culture. While these photographs are not gendered in essence, although they do feature domestic houses and children's games, the narrator's memory and her bodily responses to the photographs are marked by gender difference.

Woolf emblematizes the contrast between the published photographs, which are a visual history of institutionalized patriarchy, and her memories of absent photographs in two very different narrative modes. In her account of the public photographs, the narrator's body is largely absent. Indeed the narrator frequently comments on the difficulties posed by that absence. Woolf makes her sexual politics very clear not only by deconstructing the public photographs in the text but also by physically displacing the narrator's body from the world she observes. The masculine "body" is openly diseased. Patriarchy's infantile fixation is "an egg we called it; a germ. We smelt it in the atmosphere."[44] Similarly "fathers in public, massed together in societies, in professions, were even more subject to the fatal disease."[45] Yet the narrative of the absent photographs is close both to the narrator and to the arguments Woolf makes about women's bodies and wartime atrocities. The dominant histories in the visible photographs, to which the narrator has no physical access in the text and which are icons of masculine ideologies, are a convex mirror of Woolf's memories of women's bodily, social, and economic inequalities matched by the violence in the absent photographs.

Three Guineas is a dense, composite image/text which exposes and resists dominant histories with Woolf's active, alternative forms of memory. Woolf shows how a long history of patriarchal controls over women's bodies leads to military fascism, and the two kinds of photograph highlight this argument. Her deep knowledge of photography – her constant photographic practice and photo-album construction, and the continued experience of being photographed throughout her life – inspired Woolf to choose photography as a generative medium in *Three Guineas*. As Woolf incisively concludes, "we can best help you to prevent war not by repeating your words and following your methods but by finding new words and creating new methods."[46]

Woolf's modernism, like the modernism of H. D. and Dorothy Richardson, is in urgent dialogue with the technologies of modernity.

Conclusion

Modern visual cultures – photography and cinema – provided modernist women writers and artists with a medium for border crossings between literature and the arts. Virginia Woolf's imagistic short fictions and *Three Guineas*, as well as the cinema writing of modernist women and the art of Vanessa Bell, reveal gendered features of memory and identity. Women's cinema writing explores a far wider range of visual experiences in dialogue with spectators and cinema practice. Without reifying an essentialist gender binary, it does seem to be the case that it is modernist women writers, in the main, who identify with feminine desires: identifying with stars, using film as therapy, and describing audiences as socially constituted and gendered. Modernist women writers often address gendered constituencies in their work and explore forms of representation outside of masculine modernism.

NOTES

Parts of this chapter appeared in Maggie Humm, *Modernist Women and Visual Cultures: Virginia Woolf, Vanessa Bell, Photography and Cinema* (©Edinburgh University Press, 2002). All rights reserved; reprinted by permission.

1. A. L. Ardis, "The Gender of Modernity," in *The Cambridge History of Twentieth-Century English Literature*, ed. Laura Marcus and Peter Nicholls (Cambridge: Cambridge University Press, 2004), p. 70.
2. Dorothy Richardson, "Continuous Performance," *Close Up* 1 (1927), 34–7.
3. Colette, *Colette at the Movies: Criticism and Screenplays*, ed. A. Virmaux and O. Virmaux, trans. S. W. R. Smith (New York: Frederick Ungar, 1980), p. 13.
4. *Ibid.*, p. 20.
5. *Ibid.*, p. 28.
6. *Ibid.*, p. 62.
7. *Ibid.*
8. D. Boebel, "The Sun Born in a Woman: H. D.'s Transformations of a Masculinist Icon in 'The Dancer,'" in *Unmanning Modernism: Gendered Re-Readings*, ed. E. J. Harrison and S. Peterson (Knoxville: University of Tennessee Press, 1997).
9. H. D., "The Borderline Pamphlet," in *The Gender of Modernism*, ed. Bonnie Kime Scott (Bloomington: Indiana University Press, 1990), p. 114.
10. *Ibid.*, p. 28.
11. Cassandra Laity, *H. D. and the Victorian Fin de Siècle* (Cambridge: Cambridge University Press, 1996), p. 145.
12. H. D., "An Appreciation," *Close Up* 4.3 (1929), 56–68, at 56.
13. *Ibid.*, 64–5.
14. H. D., "Russian Films," *Close Up* 3.3 (1928), 18–29, at 18.
15. H. D., "Conrad Veidt," *Close Up* 3 (1927), 34–44.

16. H. D., *Bid Me to Live* (London: Virago, 1984), p. 89.
17. Bryher, *The Heart to Artemis* (London: Collins, 1963), pp. 202 and 261.
18. Bryher, "Defence of Hollywood," *Close Up* 2.2 (1928), 41–51, at 47.
19. Bryher, "An Interview With Anita Loos," *Close Up* 2.4 (1928), 12–15, at 12.
20. Dorothy Richardson, "Continuous Performance," *Close Up* (1927), 34–7, at 36.
21. *Ibid.*, 35.
22. Dorothy Richardson, "Continuous Performance – The Film Gone Male," *Close Up* 9.1 (1932), 36–8, at 37.
23. *Ibid.*, 38.
24. *Ibid.*, 37.
25. *Ibid.*, 37.
26. *Ibid.*, 36.
27. Dorothy Richardson, "Continuous Performance VIII – [*Animal Impudens* . . .]," *Close Up* 2.3 (1928), 51–5, at 52.
28. Dorothy Richardson, "Continuous Performance IX – The Thoroughly Popular Film," *Close Up* 2.4 (1928), 44–50, at 50.
29. Gertrude Stein, *Writings and Lectures 1911–1945*, ed. P. Meyerowitz (London: Peter Owen, 1967), p. 105.
30. Marianne Moore, "Lot in Sodom," *Close Up* 10.4 (December 1933), 318–19, at 318.
31. R. Shone, *Bloomsbury Portraits* (Oxford: Phaidon, 1976), p. 239.
32. Virginia Woolf, *Letters of Virginia Woolf*, ed. N. Nicolson and J. Trautmann, 6 vols. (London: Hogarth Press, 1976–84), vol. IV, p. 298.
33. D. F. Gillespie, *The Sisters' Arts: The Writing and Painting of Virginia Woolf and Vanessa Bell* (New York: Syracuse University Press, 1988), p. 125.
34. Simon Watney, *English Post-Impressionism* (London: Studio Vista, 1980), p. 40.
35. E. F. Hirschler, *A Studio of Their Own: Women Artists in Boston 1870–1940* (Boston, MA: Museum of Fine Art Publications, 2001), p. 110.
36. See Maggie Humm, *Snapshots of Bloomsbury* (London: Tate Publishing, 2006).
37. Woolf, *Letters of Virginia Woolf*, ed. Nicolson and Trautmann, vol. III, p. 46.
38. Woolf, *Letters of Virginia Woolf*, ed. Nicolson and Trautmann, vol. IV, p. 380.
39. Hermione Lee, *Virginia Woolf* (London: Chatto and Windus, 1996), p. 90.
40. Virginia Woolf, "The Narrow Bridge of Art", in *Granite and Rainbow: Essays by Virginia Woolf*, ed. L. Woolf (London: Hogarth Press, 1958), p. 23.
41. Virginia Woolf, "The Cinema," in *The Essays of Virginia Woolf*, vol. IV, *1925–1928*, ed. A. McNeillie (London: Hogarth Press, 1994), p. 349.
42. *Ibid.*, p. 350.
43. *Ibid.*, p. 349.
44. Virginia Woolf, *Three Guineas*, in *A Room of One's Own and Three Guineas*, ed. M. Barrett (Harmondsworth: Penguin, 1993), p. 266.
45. *Ibid.*
46. *Ibid.*, p. 272.

10

SUZETTE A. HENKE

Modernism and trauma

The Greek word "trauma" literally refers to a physical wound and, until the last century, alluded strictly to bodily injury. As Jill Matus reminds us, both trauma and its iteration as combat fatigue syndrome, described in the twentieth century as post-traumatic stress disorder or PTSD, are "historically produced categories" whose foundations pre-date Freudian psychoanalysis in hypotheses formulated by nineteenth-century writers.[1] A British military psychiatrist, Charles Samuel Myers, first coined the term "shell shock" in 1915, but it was not until the mid-1970s that therapists began to make "critical linkages between the trauma of war and the traumas of civilian life."[2]

Contemporary theorists seem to agree on a definition of trauma in terms of overwhelming life experiences that shatter the social and psychological sense of self and precipitate existential crisis, characterized by "flashbacks, nightmares and other reexperiences, emotional numbing, depression, guilt, autonomic arousal, explosive violence or a tendency to hypervigilance."[3] The American Psychiatric Association, in the fourth edition of its *Diagnostic and Statistical Manual of Mental Disorders*, identifies the following symptoms: "recurrent and intrusive recollections of the [traumatic] event, ... 'psychic numbing' or 'emotional anesthesia,'" and feelings of alienation characterized by a "markedly reduced ability to feel emotions."[4] PTSD symptoms are generally categorized under three principal headings: flashbacks, including nightmares and relentless intrusions of traumatic memories; hypervigilance and arousal by sudden acoustical noises; and emotional constriction, numbing, and anhedonia (the inability to feel). Freud made an important distinction between the passive state of *melancholia*, with its sense of paralysis and "worthlessness caused by overidentification with the lost object," and the active "working through" of feelings of loss and bereavement.[5]

As Judith Herman observes, traumatic memories, obtrusive and haunting, tend to be "wordless and static" impressions, manifest in the form of "vivid sensations and images."[6] Trauma stories often remain stereotyped, repetitious, and devoid of emotional content, even as the confessional narrative that evolves is compulsively repeated. The twentieth century has seen the "transformation of witness as victim to witness as survivor, and to witness as performer, telling the tale of survival as a form of self-therapy."[7] Such stories share "the idea that narrative testimony, in the form of an active remembering and telling can enable a move from the state of helpless victimage to a mode of action and even potential self renewal."[8] Clearly, the historical trauma of the First World War ushered in a pervasive chord of cultural upheaval that would dominate twentieth-century women's fiction – from novels by Rebecca West and Virginia Woolf focused on shell-shocked British veterans; to H. D.'s expatriate representation of wartime repercussions on the home front in London; to bleak, nihilistic interwar fiction by the American writer Djuna Barnes. Female modernist novels exhibit the powerful influence of post-traumatic testimony in works that attempt to represent a range of quotidian traumas suffered not only by soldiers in battle and war veterans haunted by military flashbacks, but by noncombatants who, in domestic isolation, endure an overwhelming sense of loss, bereavement, anxiety, and emotional rupture.

Rebecca West's *Return of the Soldier*: shell shock and erotic obsession

Shortly after Myers inaugurated the term "shell shock" to identify combat fatigue in soldiers fighting on the front during the First World War, Rebecca West wrote *The Return of the Soldier*, the "first English novel about shell shock."[9] The protagonist Chris Baldry has repressed a large segment of his past – from the dissolution of an idealized passion for Margaret Allington in 1901 to his current manifestation of combat fatigue syndrome.[10] *The Return of the Soldier* portrays a curious devotion on the part of its self-deceived narrator, Jenny Baldry, Chris's female cousin, who functions as champion, go-between, and envious rival to both Kitty, Chris's wife, and Margaret, the erstwhile lover. Chris and Kitty have apparently "walled off" the death of their two-year-old son Oliver, whose filial ghost abides as a melancholic fantasy associated with denial and "impacted grief."[11] A shell-shocked Chris not only denies the loss of this child, but retreats even further back into youthful reverie, fixated on an unattainable love object emblematic of consuming but insatiable passion. He continues to feel a post-adolescent infatuation for Margaret, a sanctified figure once enshrined in a "niche above the altar" of a faux Greek temple on Monkey Island.[12]

For West's traumatized veteran, shell shock triggers an amnesia that obliterates faith in British public-school ideals and conjugal commitment. His inaugural traumatic experience was, ironically, not that of war, but the wound embedded in erotic frustration when he lost Margaret in an explosive outburst of rage and jealousy. Trapped in a loveless marriage, Chris later reacts to his son's death with intractable melancholia. Unable to mourn, he resembles Charcot's hysterical patients paralyzed in a posture of impotence and denial. When Margaret finally confronts Chris with the reality of filial loss, she magically restores his spirit to the spousal and military obligations that once defined, and will henceforth circumscribe, an upper-class lifestyle based on duty and privilege.

West clearly schematizes the Freudian notion of *catharsis* that originally "conceived recovery ... as a purgation" of forbidden Eros.[13] The Freudian analyst Dr. Anderson cannot make Chris happy; he can only make him "ordinary" (*RS* 81). Paradoxically, Chris Baldry recuperates from so-called "shell shock" in order to face a failed marriage and the likelihood of death or injury in military service. His reward will be a tragic re-enactment of the age-old story of aristocratic and patriotic self-sacrifice for the sake of the British Empire.

H. D.'s private war: trauma in *Asphodel* and *Bid Me to Live*

A devastating series of personal and cultural traumas circulated around the American poet Hilda Doolittle's expatriate maturation during the First World War: an unexpected pregnancy in 1914, during her marriage to Richard Aldington, and a shattering stillbirth in 1915; the death of her brother Gilbert in combat at Thiacourt in 1918; her father's death from stroke soon afterward; a second unplanned (and "illegitimate") pregnancy; a life-threatening bout with influenza; and desertion by Aldington after the birth of Perdita, Cecil Gray's child, in 1919. Only the impact of severe trauma could explain H. D.'s lifelong efforts to revise, reiterate, and reinterpret her First World War experiences. As late as the 1950s, she continued to work with Erich Heydt at Kusnacht Klinik to disinter the "repressed emotion centered on the birth of her stillborn child."[14] The loss of her first baby, followed by spousal abandonment, provoked protracted symptoms of post-traumatic stress disorder. It was Freud who prescribed autobiography as "scriptotherapy" (writing as healing) when, overwhelmed by a "flood of war memories" in the 1930s, H. D. confessed in a letter to her lesbian partner Bryher: "Evidently I blocked the whole of the 'period' and if I can skeleton-in a vol. about it it will break the clutch ... the 'cure' will be, I fear me, writing that damn vol. straight, as history, no frills."[15]

In *Bid Me to Live*, shock waves echo through two entirely different arenas – the male world of military conflict and the female world of wartime vigilance, isolation, impotence, and fear. In writing through the gaps of historical trauma, H. D. deliberately leaves holes in her narrative to create a palimpsest that shows signs of erasure – a smooth surface rubbed clean of pain, with a text doubling back on itself in a gesture of radical repression. What H. D. envisages so poignantly in *Bid Me to Live* and *Asphodel* is the implicit analogy between the text of a woman's body, scarred and mutilated by the stress of childbearing, and military heroism: "Men were dying as she had almost died."[16]

Julia Ashton, the H. D. figure in *Bid Me to Live*, has been traumatized by a stillbirth that leaves her shell-shocked and grieving. Her own battle will be with physiological forces that make love a perilous expression of intimacy and sex a dangerous battleground. Stillbirth has gouged a "gap in her consciousness" suggestive of psychic numbing: "A door had shuttered it in."[17] At the beginning of the novel, Julia is suffering from post-traumatic dysphoria, a symptom of PTSD characterized by "confusion, agitation, emptiness, and utter aloneness ... Depersonalization, derealization, and anesthesia ... accompanied by a feeling of unbearable agitation."[18] Hysterically, she identifies with the "horror of a flayed saint" pictured in the Louvre (*B* 37). Maternal loss and mourning over her baby's death are part of a "deadly crucifixion" (*A* 113) characterized by post-traumatic symptoms of hyperarousal and anhedonia.

In *Bid Me to Live*, trauma elicits obsessional anger displaced and redirected against Richard Aldington/Rafe Ashton, who returns from France belching "poisonous gas and flayed carcasses" (*B* 39). Julia composes her memoirs to compensate for an object loss interpreted by the psyche as an ego loss. During the war, she creates a collage of memories to ease her melancholic bereavement over the failure of both marriage and maternity. Her writing functions as an exercise in scriptotherapy, to reformulate tormenting flashbacks in the shape of coherent narrative. This "agony in the Garden," she insists, "had no words" (*B* 46). Scorning Rafe as a "great, over-sexed officer on leave" (*B* 47), a failed Orpheus with bronze head and late-Roman physique, Julia/Eurydice, "paralysed" with fear (*B* 133), relinquishes her testosterone-driven lover to the voluptuous Bella Carter. How can amorous desire flourish when every act of lovemaking might engender a life that potentially threatens one's own? Richard Aldington's love affair with Dorothy "Arabella" Yorke was evidently inaugurated with H. D.'s tacit consent and consummated "in the Aldingtons' own bed curtained off at one end of H. D.'s large room."[19] Bella Carter emerges in the novel as a caricature of Yorke, portrayed as the seductive siren of Rafe's libidinal imagination and an illusory anodyne to trench warfare.

Sequestered in the landscape of Cornwall, Julia Ashton, H. D.'s alter ego, begins to identify with ancient Druidic priests of nature. Idealizing her fellow artist Frederico (based on D. H. Lawrence), she rewrites the Camelot myth by choosing a Sir Galahad figure, Cyril Vane (based on Cecil Gray), in lieu of the legendary King Arthur. In dialogue with an absent Father/God, she chooses creative independence over phoenix immolation to Rico's voracious ego. Julia embraces his ideal *gloire* (*B* 177) as a symbol of an ineffable future. *Bid Me to Live* ends on an amorphous note of hope and resurrection, though H. D.'s daughter Perdita has been conceptually erased from the text. Not until *Asphodel* did H. D. feel free to depict the dilemmatic choices surrounding her daughter's birth. The protagonist, Hermione Gart, awaits a sign from the gods: "If a swallow flies straight in," she tells herself, "I'll have it [the child]" (*A* 154). The *gloire* erupts with salvific force, filling the black hole at the center of consciousness with ecstatic light/life. Hermione identifies with Mother Mary, who "had a baby with God," and reminds herself that she is risking her life "like any soldier" (*A* 170).

As H. D. explained in a 1929 letter to her former fiancé Ezra Pound, she felt deeply wounded by Richard Aldington's 1919 rejection. When he appeared at Hilda's flat and threatened her with arrest if Perdita were assigned his sacred patronymic, H. D. felt as if she were "literally 'dying.' I mean, anything in the way of a shock brings that back and I go to pieces."[20] Shortly after Aldington's divorce petition in 1937, H. D. insisted: "I have lived with a subterranean terror, an octopus eating out my strength and vitality for almost eighteen years ... I was frozen ... as a deer in a forest or a rabbit or hare is frozen ... I was dead. Richard did not injure me or hound me ... He killed me."[21] H. D. eventually recovered from the most deleterious effects of post-traumatic stress disorder through scriptotherapy, whereby she wrote and wrote again the narrative of life-shattering events that led to her breakdown in 1919. In *Bid Me to Live* and *Asphodel*, veiled autobiography implements therapeutic recovery from the haunting resonances of wartime trauma.

Virginia Woolf, Septimus Smith, and post-traumatic stress disorder

In "A Sketch of the Past," Woolf recalls the moment when her half-brother Gerald Duckworth lifted her onto a "slab outside the dining room door" and "began to explore [her] body ... [W]hat is the word for so dumb and mixed a feeling?"[22] Shortly thereafter, she describes nocturnal hauntings by the face of a savage animal leering at her from a looking-glass. Anatomizing this memory in "A Sketch of the Past," she speculates that it must have been her acute sensitivity to pain, her "shock-receiving capacity," that spurred her to become a writer. By reformulating trauma, she could exorcize its debilitating effects. "It is only by putting it [trauma] into words that I make it whole," she proclaims, while triumphantly concluding that, by virtue of scriptotherapy, the psychological wound "has lost its power to hurt me" (*MOB* 72). Childhood sexual abuse was one of several factors that affected Woolf's sporadic episodes of psychological distress. I should like to suggest that traumatic personal losses, including the death of her mother in 1895, of her half-sister Stella in 1897, of her father Sir Leslie Stephen in 1904, and of her brother Thoby in 1906, also affected her so-called breakdowns, possibly misdiagnosed as mania, depression, or bipolar malady. What seems extraordinary is the fact that from 1915 until 1941 – a period of twenty-six years – Woolf endured chronic physical and psychological illnesses while continuing an impressive reading program, extensive travel, numerous social engagements, and prolific literary creation.

Without question, Virginia Woolf drew on her own experience of mental distress and psychic dissociation as a model for Septimus Smith in *Mrs. Dalloway*. In her manuscript notes, she wonders if his figure will be "founded on R [Rupert Brooke?]," with "eyes far apart," and neither "degenerate" nor "wholly an intellectual. Had been in the war."[23] Or should this troubled character be "founded on me"? His personality is to "be left vague – as a mad person is," so he "can be partly R.; partly me."[24] Smith clearly shows symptoms of PTSD when he confesses his "inability to feel" as a nameless war crime. During periods of hyperactivity, he exhibits a radical swing between self-hatred and megalomania. One moment, he feels despicable; the next, he proclaims himself a martyred messiah, "the Lord who had come to renew society."[25]

In Woolf's holograph of "The Prime Minister," a draft of the early scenes of *Mrs. Dalloway*, Septimus emerges as a deviant and idiosyncratic figure. Tormented by flashbacks, he imagines himself a sacrificial scapegoat: "One might give one's body to be eaten by the starving, and then ... be a martyr, and then, as I am going to die, I will kill the Prime Minister."[26] Woolf's shell-shocked veteran articulates a death wish associated with memories of the First World War. He plans to sacrifice himself for the redemption of starving refugees by offering his body in eucharistic communion. Envisaging himself as the man-god slain to expiate the sins of a guilty community, he becomes a self-appointed judge and avenging angel.

A psychiatric casualty of war, Smith suffers from the symptoms of combat fatigue identified by Solomon, Laor, and McFarlane in an essay on "Acute Posttraumatic Reactions in Soldiers and Civilians": (1) "Distancing," including "reports of psychic numbing." (2) "Anxiety," sometimes "paralyzing," along with "thoughts of death." (3) "Fatigue and guilt about poor performance in combat." (4) "Loneliness and vulnerability," especially in the wake of battlefield deaths. (5) "Loss of self-control ... and a range of impulsive behaviors." The veteran's "psychic numbing becomes so pervasive that it blocks not only pain, horror, and grief, but also the perceptions needed to make realistic judgments."[27]

Smith's megalomanic self-image has become porous, and he experiences his body as "macerated until only the nerve fibres were left" (MD 102–3). Uplifted by a sense of mystical identification with the universe, he feels united with the leaves and trees of Regent's Park, with roses painted on the wall of his room, with cynanthropic canines, and with birds twittering messages in Greek. Before the war, Smith had been incapable of adopting a socially constructed masculine persona. Like West's protagonist, he fostered a narcissistic ego-ideal romantically projected onto an inappropriate love object, Miss Isabel Pole. In order to handle the death of his commanding officer Evans, he adopted a façade of stoicism that eventually drove him mad. Unable to conform to society's expectations regarding gender and class, he withdrew into a world of megalomania and terror. According to Karen DeMeester, "traumatic war experiences shattered the cohesion of his consciousness and left it fragmented, a stream of incongruous and disconnected images."[28]

This troubled young man succumbs, in panic, to feelings of estrangement and despair, alienation and existential dread. But his suicidal leap from a Bloomsbury window, so obviously a defeat for the maimed historical subject, might nonetheless be interpreted as an act of romantic heroism that saves him from joining the "maimed file of lunatics" (MD 98) he once saw being herded in a queue along Tottenham Court Road. He has, like Shelley's Adonais, preserved his identity from the corruption of the world's slow stain. Smith's melodramatic performance of suicide effects a "mimetic-contagious transmission of psychic suffering" to Clarissa Dalloway, a middle-aged society hostess whom he has never met.[29] His death proves to be the final symbolic act whereby he attempts to incorporate meaning and value into overwhelming personal and historical trauma.

Traumatic resonance in Djuna Barnes's *Nightwood*

There is some evidence that Djuna Barnes, like Virginia Woolf, experienced the trauma of childhood sexual abuse. She may have been molested by her grandmother, Zadel Barnes; and she may have endured an adolescent rape either perpetrated or orchestrated by her father, Wald Barnes. Djuna loved her grandmother passionately and shared Zadel's bed for more than a decade, but Phillip Herring fails to descry traumatic resonance in her "thoughts on sleeping for fifteen years beside Zadel and playing with her breasts."[30] Barnes made a shocking confession to George Barker when she attributed her lesbianism to "her father raping her when she was a very young girl"; but she "told James Scott a rather different story," charging that, at the age of sixteen, "she was raped by an Englishman three times her age with her father's knowledge and consent."[31] Shortly before her eighteenth birthday, Djuna was coerced into an ill-fated marriage to the 52-year-old Percy Faulkner, with whom she cohabited for less than two months.

To a large extent, *Nightwood* unfolds as a confessional narrative of post-traumatic stress and manic-depressive mood swings, with Robin Vote (based on Barnes's lesbian lover Thelma Wood) incorporated into this enigmatic text as an absent presence. *Nightwood* suggests subtle evocations of an original traumatic moment, a Lacanian lack-in-being (*manque-à-être*) analogous to the Catholic doctrine of original sin. According to Alan Williamson, Barnes focuses on "a myth which bears a close kinship to the Christian myth of the Fall," but draws on "Hermetic tradition, according to which man was created, in the union of conscious mind and animal matter, as a single hermaphroditic being, whose fragmentation into separate sexes occurred at the time of the Fall," when "animal vitality took on rational consciousness," and the human individual suffered a fatal bifurcation "between its need for love and its intrinsic isolation."[32]

Barnes imbues *Nightwood* with post-traumatic resonance without offering a convincing objective correlative for the psychic fragmentation, intrusion, constriction, or incipient hysteria that haunts the text. She constructs a polyphonic chorus of dramatic soliloquies mediated by a prophetic voice that spews forth irresoluble riddles. The novel is a mosaic of epigrams on the part of Doctor Matthew O'Connor, whose utterances are punctuated by the lyrical lamentations of Felix Volkbein and Nora Flood. Both feel traumatized by Robin's rejection and approach the Doctor in search of ethical absolution for "slapping" Robin awake and alienating her affections.

All the characters in *Nightwood* are convinced that their lives take meaning from the relational structures that they impose on the drama of existence. All are shackled to a compulsive belief in a coherent ego and the illusion of unitary selfhood. They obsessively generate post-traumatic narratives exuded from their entrails like verbal spiderwebs. Emulating Nikka, a black man "tattooed from head to heel with all the *ameublement* of depravity,"[33] each emblazons allegories of identity over every square inch of his or her sexual/textual body. Barnes insists that one can never capture a true, holistic picture of the self because the dream of psychological coherence is a Lacanian fantasy, a misty collection of images fused in "that priceless galaxy of misinformation called the mind" (*N* 212).

Romance, too, proves deceptive because no stable ego exists to love or be loved. One merely cobbles together an idealized image from a collection of mental impressions soldered together in aesthetic fantasy. Clinging to myths of prelapsarian wholeness, the fragmented ego strives for "at-onement" with its legendary other half. The very naïveté of this project prophesies its futility. All too often, the "lover has committed the unpardonable error of not being able to exist" (N 136). Robin is, in fact, the only character in *Nightwood* who eschews obsessive autobiographical reformulation. Amalgamating the roles "of child and desperado" (N 56), she enjoys a dream-like self-sufficiency contingent on post-traumatic constriction. Androgynous wife and lover to herself, she exhibits not a mask, but a crystalline surface whose dissociated passivity might suggest symptoms evoked by a repressed history of childhood sexual abuse.[34]

Robin's companions (re)construct her image as an autonomous figure, the "mirage of an eternal wedding cast on the racial memory" (N 59). Trapped in Felix's narcissistic historical project, Robin is raped into maternal connection with an(other), "like a child who has walked into the commencement of a horror" (N 74). A melancholic *Stabat Mater*, she plays the sacrificial role of female Christ. When Felix exploits her body for the perpetuation of his false aristocratic lineage, he forces her, "by pain and violence, into an awareness of another being, in a kind of psychological rape."[35]

The traumatized Robin, in a state of radical dissociation, cannot envisage a place of emotional sanctuary. In a relationship of introverted self-mirroring, she accepts Nora's offer of womblike refuge. As mother/lover/other, Nora centers the beloved in a blameless innocence prior to the moment of splitting that signals ruptured subjectivity. When Robin sees her own fragmented ego reflected in Nora's stabilizing gaze, she suffers an uncanny sense of post-traumatic anxiety. Sealed in a dream of hermetic isolation, she searches – through crime, betrayal, and sexual abjection – for the lost bedrock of infantile psychic immunity.

Doctor Matthew-Mighty-grain-of-salt-Dante-O'Connor plays the role of father (or mother) confessor to all the actors in Barnes's melodrama. An unlicensed physician, he dons a golden-curled wig in mock imitation of "the other woman that God forgot" (N 143). Like a magician or shaman, he speaks in riddles, weaving therapeutic tales from stories of ineffable anguish, as his analysands seek solace in a form of practical "talk therapy." O'Connor is simultaneously lauded as a wise counselor and skewered as a holy fool. Barnes withholds the satisfactions of narrative closure in an open-ended text that concludes with a puzzle or rebus, a Gordian knot that cannot be untangled.

The book's final chapter, "The Possessed," depicts a curious ritual that might be interpreted as the mimesis of bestial transgression and sodomous perversion. Robin apparently transfers her love for Nora, an erstwhile savior and madonna, to a canine object of sexual seduction. What seems like a frustrated attempt at animal copulation suggests an obsessive-compulsive traumatic rupture in the staging of erotic desire. In symbolic abjection, free-floating drives are neither consummated nor exorcized. Robin, trying to retrieve the shattered illusion of prelapsarian wholeness, engages in a strange, barking vocalization that, in its utter ambiguity, leaves readers suspended over an abyss of stylized futility. As woman and dog re-enact Dionysiac mysteries, Robin emerges as a modern Cassandra torn between damnation and prophecy: "Cannot a beastly thing be analogous to a fine thing, if both are apprehensions?" (N 178).

Who can judge whether such folly be diabolical or divine? For Barnes, life is little more than a "permission to know death," a long lamentation over the bittersweet taste of a world not conscious of our consciousness. In a nihilistic cosmos characterized by "nothing, but wrath and weeping" (N 233), who would not welcome the somnambulist's trance? Sanctioned by her madonna-lover, in a gaze of "fixed dismay," Robin crawls into the "space between the human and the holy head, the arena of the 'indecent eternal'" (N 222). Solemnizing her degradation, she retrieves the wholeness, world-inwardness, and animal innocence traditionally reserved for saints, fools, "infants, angels, priests, [and] the dead" (N 118).

Conclusion

In *Trauma and Recovery*, Judith Herman proposed that the "most common post-traumatic disorders are those not of men in war," but of the effects of overwhelming psychological experiences on ordinary citizens in everyday life.[36] For women in particular, severe crises associated with gender, sexuality, and female reproduction can precipitate powerful and enduring emotional upheavals. Resonant shocks that shatter an individual's sense of agency in the world include rape and incest; conjugal battery or abuse; pregnancy compromised by miscarriage or by the dilemmatic choice of surgical abortion; and the loss of a child through stillbirth or neonatal death. Both Freudian talk therapy and the analogous practice of scriptotherapy can offer a degree of psychological palliation by enabling survivors to reformulate traumatic memories and post-traumatic flashbacks through controlled, coherent, and cathartic testimony.

Many of the women authors examined in this chapter were writing for their lives in autobiographical narratives that enabled them to exorcize and eventually come to terms with emotional traumas that left them figuratively bloodied but spiritually unbowed. Through the testimonial reconfiguration of overwhelming life experiences, female modernists were able to assert heroic agency through artistic projects that enabled them to master life-shattering events and marshal their creative resources in the interests of bold, experimental, often healing works of fiction.

NOTES

1. Jill Matus, "Emergent Theories of Victorian Mind Shock: From War and Railway Accident to Nerves, Electricity, and Emotion," in *Neurology and Literature, 1860–1920*, ed. Anne Stiles (London: Palgrave Macmillan, 2007), p. 166. Nineteenth-century pre-trauma theorists include Herbert Spencer, Alexander Bain, and George Henry Lewes. In their essay on the "History of Trauma in Psychiatry," Bessel van der Kolk, Lars Weisaeth, and Onno van der Hart describe contributions by Charcot, Janet, Freud, and Ferenczi to the field of trauma studies, in *Traumatic Stress: The Effects of Overwhelming Experience on Mind, Body, and Society*, ed. Bessel A. van der Kolk, Alexander C. McFarlane, and Lars Weisaeth (New York: Guilford Press, 2007), p. 56.

2. Van der Kolk *et al.*, "History of Trauma in Psychiatry," p. 62 and *passim*. The American psychiatrist Abram Kardiner, after training with Freud, formulated a theoretical model of PTSD in *The Traumatic Neuroses of War* (1941).

3. Ruth Leys, *Trauma: A Genealogy* (Chicago: University of Chicago Press, 2000), p. 2.

4. American Psychiatric Association, *Diagnostic and Statistical Manual of Mental Health Disorders*, 4th edn., rev. (Washington, DC: American Psychiatric Association, 1994), pp. 424–5.

5. Ana Douglass and Thomas A. Vogler, *Witness and Memory: The Discourse of Trauma* (New York: Routledge, 2003), p. 42.

6. Judith Lewis Herman, *Trauma and Recovery* (New York: HarperCollins, 1992), pp. 175, 38.

7. Douglass and Vogler, *Witness and Memory*, p. 41.

8. *Ibid.*

9. Elaine Showalter, *The Female Malady: Women, Madness, and English Culture, 1830–1980* (New York: Viking Penguin, 1987), p. 190.

10. Despite protestations to the contrary, West seems to have projected a good bit of herself into Margaret, with Chris serving as a stand-in for West's lover H. G. Wells, and his wife Jane the prototype for the ice-maiden Kitty. West's emotional frustration is evident in a 1913 letter she wrote to Wells while she was pregnant with their son Anthony: "During the next few days I shall either put a bullet through my head or commit something more shattering to myself than death . . . I always knew that you would hurt me to death some day . . . You've literally ruined me. I'm burned down to my foundations" (*Selected Letters of Rebecca West*, ed. Bonnie Kime Scott [New Haven: Yale University Press, 2000], pp. 20–1).

11. Herman, *Trauma and Recovery*, p. 69.

12. Rebecca West, *The Return of the Soldier* (1918; rpt. New York: Penguin, 1998), p. 40. Hereafter cited as *RS*.

13. Rebecca Saunders, *Lamentation and Modernity in Literature, Philosophy, and Culture* (New York: Palgrave Macmillan, 2007), p. 16.

14. Susan Stanford Friedman, *Psyche Reborn: The Emergence of H. D.* (Bloomington: Indiana University Press, 1981), p. 21.
15. Susan Stanford Friedman, ed. *Analyzing Freud: Letters of H. D., Bryher, and Their Circle* (New York: New Directions, 2002), p. 264.
16. Hilda Doolittle (H. D.), *Asphodel*, ed. Robert Spoo (Durham, NC: Duke University Press, 1992), p. 192. Hereafter cited as *A*.
17. Hilda Doolittle (H. D.), *Bid Me to Live* (1960; rpt. London: Virago Press, 1984), p. 15. Hereafter cited as *B*.
18. Herman, *Trauma and Recovery*, pp. 108–9.
19. Caroline Zilboorg, ed. *Richard Aldington & H. D.: The Early Years in Letters* (Bloomington: Indiana University Press, 1992), p. 38.
20. Quoted in Friedman, *Psyche*, p. 17.
21. Caroline Zilboorg, ed. *Richard Aldington & H. D.: The Later Years in Letters* (Manchester: Manchester University Press, 1995), p. 63.
22. Virginia Woolf, "A Sketch of the Past," in *Moments of Being*, 2nd edn., ed. Jeanne Schulkind (New York: Harcourt Brace, 1985), p. 69. Hereafter cited as *MOB*. On trauma and Woolf's writing, see David Eberly and Suzette Henke, "Introduction," in *Virginia Woolf and Trauma*, ed. Henke and Eberly (New York: Pace University Press, 2007), pp. 1–17.
23. Helen Wussow, *The Hours: The British Museum Manuscript of* Mrs. Dalloway, transcribed and edited by Helen Wussow (New York: Pace University Press, 1997), p. 418.
24. *Ibid.*
25. Virginia Woolf, *Mrs. Dalloway* (1925; rpt. New York: Harcourt Brace Jovanovich, 1990), p. 25. Hereafter cited as *MD*.
26. Virginia Woolf, "The Prime Minister," *Jacob's Room Holograph Notebook, Part III*, New York: Henry W. and Albert A. Berg Collection, New York Public Library, Astor, Lenox and Tilden Foundations, transcribed by Suzette A. Henke, in *Gender in Modernism: New Geographies, Complex Intersections*, ed. Bonnie Kime Scott (Urbana: University of Illinois Press, 2007), p. 586.
27. Zahava Solomon, Nathaniel Laor, and Alexander C. McFarlane, "Acute Posttraumatic Reactions in Soldiers and Civilians," in *Traumatic Stress*, ed. Van der Kolk *et al.*, pp. 106–7.
28. Karen DeMeester, "Trauma, Post-Traumatic Stress Disorder, and Obstacles to Postwar Recovery in *Mrs. Dalloway*," in *Virginia Woolf and Trauma*, ed. Henke and Eberly, p. 80.
29. Leys, *Trauma*, p. 17.
30. Phillip Herring, *Djuna: The Life and Work of Djuna Barnes* (New York: Penguin Books, 1995), p. 55.
31. *Ibid.*, p. 53.
32. Alan Williamson, "The Divided Image: The Quest for Identity in the Work of Djuna Barnes," *Critique: Studies in Contemporary Fiction* 7 (1964), pp. 60–1.
33. Djuna Barnes, *Nightwood* (London: Faber, 1937), p. 31. Hereafter cited as *N*.
34. The possibility of childhood sexual abuse was suggested to me by Wilhelmina Healy in English 654 at the University of Louisville, Spring 2008.
35. Williamson, "The Divided Image," 69.
36. Herman, *Trauma*, p. 28.

11

SOWON S. PARK

Political activism and women's modernism

Politics and aesthetics

Within one tradition of Western thought, politics and the arts have been categorized as distinct and separate entities. So when aesthetics is under discussion, political concern is often dismissed as dogmatic, ephemeral, or partial, and when politics is of chief interest, aesthetics is swept aside as immaterial, insubstantial, or obscure. The way literature has been defined and categorized in the West has been shaped by such binary formulations. Consequently, there has been a long and deep conflict between the model that regards art as representing eternal ideas that are antecedent to human thinking and the model that understands art as a form of concrete communication or social interaction that is historically situated. The two models are predicated on radically different kinds of relationship between the writer and the world: the former requires the writer to have an aesthetic knowledge of the world that comes from detachment whereas the latter demands the writer to possess and to actively use cognitive knowledge.

Such categorical division based on mutual exclusivity has been rejected by the Frankfurt school of Marxist critics between the 1930s and the 1950s, either by claiming that every literary practice mediates a socio-political content, or conversely, by seeing political discourse as a form of literature.[1] This alternative view, that literature and politics are inevitably bound together, mutually entailed and so inseparable, has become almost as familiar as the traditional view in the postmodern era.

When it comes to women's politics and literature, the problem of this categorical division and mutual exclusivity does not quite follow the same historical trajectory. This is because women's writing and political engagement have always been evidently mutually dependent. Between 1890 and 1920, for example, the first-wave feminist movement ignited a veritable explosion of literature written about, by, and for women. In the form of poetry, sketches, plays, burlesques, polemical essays, tracts, articles, short stories, and novels, feminist activism generated an unprecedented amount and range of literature. Furthermore, feminist politics transformed the institutionalization and production of women's writing through newly created suffrage and popular presses, creating new socio-cultural conditions. So, important shifts in the literary field of British women's writing were the direct consequences of women's political activism. This, in turn, was made possible by the power of the written word to formulate, disseminate, and consolidate ideas of selfhood and to construct a sense of unified gender identity.

This interdependence between politics and literature as exemplified by the first-wave women's movement provides a great counter-example to the mutually exclusive formulations of politics and aesthetics, but it was, for most of the last century, largely dismissed by literary critics, including feminists. There are two reasons. First, there is the adoption of modernism as a normative ideal in much of the literary criticism of the twentieth century. As the scope of modernist literature, in the early stages of the development of its field, was predominantly masculine, feminist modernist critics made huge interventions and succeeded in reinscribing women writers into the canon. But as a corollary, there existed a tendency in literary criticism to divide women modernists who revolutionized form in literature from the "conventional" writers, including those who produced campaign literature with a view to revolutionizing the world. The ascendancy of modernism also meant that the realist mode of writing has often been relegated to an inferior status. This division not only created false, or overstated, differences and very important ellipses, but also established a hierarchy so that texts that exhibited certain kinds of modernist experimentation were focused upon, analyzed, evaluated, and validated at the expense of the realist writers. Even the texts that are remarkable in their reflections of, as well as interventions in, the advent of modernity have been occluded by modernist works of this period that exhibit textual experimentation of a particular kind. But the history of women's literature is not identical to canonical literary history, and attempts to illuminate women's contributions to existing literary movements, such as modernism, are often inadequate to bring to light the significant and fundamental points in women's literary development.

Second, feminist theory itself has contributed to the neglect of the interface between women's aesthetics and politics. Toril Moi's championing of Virginia Woolf as a *political* writer in her landmark study *Sexual/Textual Politics* in 1985, and her implacable ideological denunciation of "anglo-american" literary criticism, set the stage for the series of interconnected developments that associate modernist stylistic traits like frequent ellipses, open-ended sentences, multiple climaxes, and non-linear narratives with the "feminine" or the politically feminist. Moi's polemic in which she extolled Woolf as a revolutionary feminist writer because she rejected the "metaphysical essentialism underlying patriarchal ideology, which hails God, the Father or the Phallus as its transcendental signified," was followed by important studies such as Ellen Friedman and Miriam Fuchs's *Breaking the Sequence*. They asserted:

> In exploding dominant forms, women experimental writers not only assail the social structure, but also produce an alternative fictional space, a space in which the feminine, marginalized in traditional fiction and patriarchal culture, can be expressed. Thus the rupturing of traditional forms becomes a political act, the feminine narrative resulting from such a rupture is allied with the feminist project.[2]

Readings based on French feminist theory dominated literary criticism in the 1980s and 1990s and resulted in brilliant excavations of women modernists to complement the narrow masculinist models. But equating experimental poetics with feminist politics gave rise to an inadequate account of the historicity of both. The postulation of a vigorous opposition between politically naïve "realist" literature and truly subversive semiotic "modernist" literature not only silences the vast quantity and array of writing prompted by the first-wave women's movement but also mystifies and rarefies feminist aesthetics, producing the stark alternative between agitational didacticism and a minority elite modernism in which our thinking about feminist political aesthetics is too often locked.

The avant-garde aesthetics of suffragette politics

Militant in action and militaristic in spirit, the British suffragettes created and sustained a mass political movement which, in both dimension and kind, was unprecedented. Though various feminist political issues – access to higher education and the professions, prostitution, venereal disease, married women's property, divorce, children, and suffrage – had been pledged causes in the more progressive circles for the preceding half-century, the modern suffragettes succeeded in heralding a new stage in the public perception of women as agents of political change through their radical agitation for the vote.[3] The rapidity with which they became entrenched in British culture was remarkable. Within five years of its inception, the National Women's Social and Political Union (WSPU, 1903–17) had branches and representatives all over the country and held some 60,000 public meetings, and its weekly paper *Votes for Women* had reached sales of 30,000. The WSPU's expansion also rapidly fostered a revival of "constitutional" suffrage activism which had slumped for twenty years after the defeat of the 1889 women's suffrage bill. The number of branches for the constitutionalist suffragists who campaigned under the umbrella organization of the National Union of Women's Suffrage Societies (NUWSS, 1897–1919) increased sharply from 33 in October 1907 to 474 in February 1914. In addition, the suffragettes provoked tremendous reaction among thousands of anti-suffragists who banded together in national organizations. A slice of militant history gives some idea as to the extent of the suffragettes' operation. The cases of suffragette arson or attempted arson recorded between April 1913 and May 1914 in England alone include 19 churches destroyed or damaged, 100 houses and buildings burnt, 13 stations burnt, 6 trains fired, 11 golf links or bowling greens damaged, 27 bombs found, and 29 cases of attempted arson. The militants' agitations were not always unlawful or violent. The act of standing up and heckling during speeches and in theatre performances, for example, was regarded as militant as it was something that ladies simply did not do. In addition to arson, hunger strikes, and public displays, one group lowered a suffragette on a rope outside the building where the Prime Minister, Mr. Asquith, was having dinner, and another carved "Votes before Sports" on his golf green.

Though their illegal and semi-illegal activism was frequent, often extreme, and wide-ranging, the suffragettes took great care to project an image of virtuous gentility. As Cicely Hamilton (1872–1952), feminist activist, theorist, novelist, and playwright, noted, "A curious characteristic of the militant suffrage movement" was "the importance it attached to dress and appearance and its insistence on the feminine note."[4] Suffrage leaders – such as Charlotte Despard, the President of the Women's Freedom League (WFL, 1907–61); Emmeline and Christabel Pankhurst, the leaders of the WSPU; Flora Annie Steele, the Second President of the Women Writers' Suffrage League (WWSL, 1908–19) – were all exceptionally feminine in dress and all took particular care to appear so in public. The WSPU meetings were stage-managed so as to have younger and feminine girls sitting in the first row on the platform. Official dress code dictated frilly dresses and not coats and skirts. Editorials in *Votes for Women* stressed the importance of visual presentation and for their group in the Women's Coronation Procession of June 1911 the WSPU chose twenty-one girls dressed in long white frocks with elbow sleeves presenting an image of gentle, innocent purity. Image-control was regarded as a fundamental political strategy. As Joel H. Kaplan and Sheila Stowell have noted in their study of the production and consumption of images of women in the early twentieth century:

Suffrage supporters embraced *haute couture* as a means of combating anti-suffrage propaganda. Dressing well, as a retort to caricatures of the dowdy spinsters or "would-be man," became, under the circumstances, a political act, as women fought for their rights *as women* to occupy space previously occupied by men alone.[5]

To produce the desired effect, the suffragettes felt obliged to obliterate every trace of unfemininity so that they could not be belittled by the hierarchy of heterosexual economy. But while taking pains to employ the set of signifiers which denote femininity, and thus, on the surface, the dominant social norms constructed around patriarchal structures and ideologies, they radically broke away from the denoted implications through their violence, creating a discourse constructed around ambivalence. The effect was continual "estrangement" – because the force of the suffragettes came from the fact that their acts of militancy were committed, not from the outer fringes of society, but from its very heart. Some of the central tenets of gender and class were destabilized by window-smashers dressed in identical fashion to the ladies pouring tea in middle-class drawing rooms. "Agitation by Symbol" was what the suffragettes called this strategy and its force came from a semiology that juxtaposed femininity – an emblem of Victorian gentility – with violence, its antithesis, generating what is now called subversive mimesis. Since the overall effect of this procedure on the public was to be one of shock, one had to wrench elements of everyday life from their original contexts, denuding them of their familiarity and thereby stirring the beholder from a state of passivity into an active and critical posture. This method is, in essence, identical to the artistic technique developed more self-consciously by other contemporaries now grouped under the umbrella of "modernists." In literary terms, it is the method called estrangement effect (Verfremdungseffekt) that Brecht and the Russian Formalists developed and which the Surrealists were to perfect in the ensuing years.

Artistic estrangement was carried over to larger cultural formations in suffrage politics.[6] An example is their refusal to separate art and other forms of social life. Just as the avant-gardists of the Weimar Republic and the early Soviet Union revolted against the elitism of high modernism with their slogans, "Art in the service of the revolution" and "the Artist as a humble functionary and social engineer," suffragettes believed art should be integrated with revolutionary social practice. A typical example was on March 10, 1914, when Mary Richardson slashed Diego Velázquez's *The Toilet of Venus* (known as "The Rokeby Venus") in the National Gallery. The reason she gave afterward was as follows: "I have tried to destroy the picture of the most beautiful woman in mythological history as a protest against the government for destroying Mrs. Pankhurst who is the most beautiful character in modern history."[7] Richardson's destructive act is in fact a creative bid to re-shape the way of looking at female nudes as well as to question the validity of their cultural location. Like the Vorticists and the Futurists whose masculinist "blasting and bombardiering" have been extensively discussed in the context of the gender of modernism, the suffragettes were equally committed to wiping the slate of tradition clean and "making it new." The revolutionary music in Baku made by factory hooters in the open air in 1922 can be seen in the same frame with the suffragette marching songs sung in Holloway conducted by Ethel Smyth with a toothbrush.[8]

Some feminists had deep reservations about the avant-garde strategy of the suffragettes. For example, Teresa Billington-Grieg (1877–1964), a "non-violent militant" suffragette leader and the author of *The Militant Suffrage Movement* (1911) criticized this form of feminist strategy as inauthentic:

> I do not condemn the present day militancy because it has gone too far. I fear that it will never rise to the heights to which it originally showed potential aim. What I condemn in militant tactics is ... the playing for effects and not for results – in short, the exploitation of revolutionary forces and enthusiastic women for the purposes of advertisement ... The crime of the militant suffrage movement in my eyes is that it is not real.[9]

Playing for effects and privileging the appearance of things over the "real" strongly prefigure the culture of postmodernism, including the detractors it attracts. The mainstream histories, on the whole, view the militancy of the WSPU and the WFL as an obstruction rather than a service to equal franchise.[10] Furthermore, the distinction between the constitutionalist suffragists and militant suffragettes is by no means sustainable when examined in depth, so permeable are the boundaries which circumscribe the two positions. But the significance of the suffragettes is much broader than the issue of suffrage and therefore suffrage should not be the foremost criterion in assessing them. As they themselves continually asserted, their campaign was for "Not the Vote only but what the Vote means." As Lady Rhondda (1883–1958), a suffragette, journalist, editor of *Time and Tide*, and co-founder of the Six Point Group, argued, "The vote was really a symbol. And the militant fight itself did more to change the status of women – because it did more to alter our own opinion of ourselves – than ever the vote did."[11] The suffragettes' theatrical and sensational avant-garde strategies, mediated by images through mass print, re-negotiated the idea of Woman in the public arena and produced new relations within gender politics.

Textual strategies

If the suffragettes used aestheticization as a primary means of their political campaign, the literature of the period was no less affected by politics. For one thing, feminist politics was crucial in the shaping of modernism, in both form and content.[12] But modernism was just one part of the large-scale transformation that took place in the literary marketplace as a result of the women's political negotiations. Feminist politics also created the conditions for a new culture of women's literary output.

The spectacle of woman that the suffragettes staged through their sophisticated, large-scale, and frequent public marches was sensationalized in the newly formed daily newspapers. Photography and reportage went hand in hand with the suffragette displays. The synergy of mass print and the suffragette spectacle was made possible by the tremendous increase in the scale of the production and distribution of newspapers.[13] Indeed the suffragette spectacle was shaped and to an extent created by the needs of the newspapers, which in turn were driven by the necessity to meet their readers' appetite for sensational spectacles and stories. Before the militancy, reports of feminist issues in the established papers were minimal, with the exception of the *Manchester Guardian*. Women's suffrage, for example, was discussed within the confines of periodicals with a small circulation like the *Contemporary Review* or the *Westminster Review*. Then spectacle exploded the mass print media and revived the interest in the cause, which in turn dramatically increased the number of suffrage and feminist journals. *Jus Suffragi* (1906–29), *Women's Franchise* (1907–11), *Votes for Women* (1907–18), *The Vote* (1909–33), *Common Cause* (1909–20), *The Suffragette* (1912–15), *Women's Dreadnought* (1914–24), *Independent Suffragette* (1916–17), *Freewoman* (1911–12), *Time and Tide* (1920–77), and *Woman's Leader* (1920–32) were sites in which women identified and affirmed their private experiences and consolidated them into collective, public, political knowledge, and were repositories of a wide range of polemics, plays, short stories, mini-biographies, and news.[14] Some of the national newspapers began to take a pro-suffrage stance: the *Daily Mail*, the *Daily Herald*, *Pall Mall Gazette*, and the *Standard* (which had a page devoted to suffrage called "The Woman's Platform") gave substantial space for feminist discourse and even anti-suffrage papers like the *Times* carried debates surrounding the issue. Journals like the *Contemporary Review*, *Clarion*, *Examiner*, *Fortnightly Review*, *Nineteenth Century*, and *Westminster Review* all regularly published feminist articles and literature.

So not only did the politicization of women impel them to write, many for the first time, and bring disparate women writers together, but it also drove them to take an active role in publishing and distribution. The Woman's Press and their iconic shop in 156 Charing Cross Road were not only fundamental to the political campaign of the WSPU but also formed a landmark as an independent publisher of women's literature, prompting a new degree of professionalism in all aspects of literary production. Organizations like the WWSL and the Actresses' Franchise League provided a cohesive and potent base from which the writers and the actresses produced a steady stream of political literature and performances; and this further enabled women to experiment as a group with the possibilities of a discourse of political dissent and political aesthetics.[15]

If politics raised women's literary production to a new scale, literature was a formative force in the politicization of women. Suffragettes of all classes professed that texts had been crucial in the shaping of their political identity.[16] The world of the written word, as any political leader cannot fail to be aware, overlaps considerably with the world of action. Elizabeth Robins (1862–1952), the first President of the WWSL and an Ibsenite actress, playwright, novelist, and feminist activist, vigorously belabored the political importance of words. Like other suffrage leaders, Robins stressed that the world was changing so fast that people had a tendency to see it in language that had been left behind by events. She also observed that it was represented according to male and class interests. This outmoded, mistaken way of seeing or thinking about the world caused women to act in ways inappropriate to their situation and hence was a practical political problem. "One of the most important, most indispensable services to Social Reform would have to be undertaken by the writers," Robins stated to the WWSL, because it was the writers' role to discern what an insidious influence the language in which we think exerts on the way we act.[17]

Just a cursory inspection of the correlation between the world of ideas and the world of action around this period evinces that, concomitant with feminist politics, a new articulation of terms such as "feminist," "new woman," "suffragist," "suffragette," "free woman," and "androcentricity" came into circulation, embodying a different way of looking at gender and a resistance to categories and concepts constructed around dominant patriarchal norms. The writers of the league, who included Olive Schreiner, May Sinclair, Evelyn Sharp, Violet Hunt, and Ivy Compton-Burnett, had, of course, a more profound commitment to this project: they were to forge a new language to correspond to the realities of modernity and to resist inequality, as women's lives did not correspond to the vocabulary they had for describing them. The new language they had in mind was not that of syntactical dislocations and formal disruptions now more habitually associated with radical dissent, but one that represented truth as it was politically, philosophically, and socially lived.

The clear-sighted strictures of Elizabeth Robins on the misuse of language emphasize the need to correct the overwhelming misrepresentation of women's lives that was paraded as reality. Indeed, a large proportion of suffrage periodicals was devoted to the repudiation of "androcentrism" that was too naturalized for most people to see: well-known songs, sections from plays, novels, and familiar narratives such as fairy tales, and conventional myths were parodied and revised. In addition to feminist rereadings, the task of the woman writer was to penetrate deeper into the structure of reality and provide an authentic account of the world as it was actually experienced by women, for that was a crucial step in the bigger project of instructing, persuading, and inciting. To give the air of authenticity, the methodology adopted by women writers was often documentary realism. Some sections in Robins's play *Votes for Women* and its novel counterpart, *The Convert*, for example, are almost verbatim reports of the meetings and speeches at the Huddersfield by-election in 1906, aimed to cut through the tremendous misrepresentations of political dealings in the established press and to communicate to the reader who did not have access to the political world. An affirmation of this world would enable both men and women to see the "real" world hidden from view by the fog of patriarchal ideology, and this cognition would set people free. "There she stands – the Real Girl! – waiting for you to do her justice," Robins exhorted her fellow members of the WWSL.[18]

Doing justice to the "real" girl and the "real" world and discovering truthful social reality are attendant upon the idea of the writer uncovering her own eyes and discovering her own sense of self through that process. "Let us open our eyes, and we shall also find the fog of illusion lifting," urged Charlotte Despard.[19]

Consequently this period is rich in women's narratives that focus heavily on the twin process of political and individual awakening. But the *bildungsromanae*, memoirs, biographies, and autobiographies are often overshadowed by studies of those narratives of the same period that foreground the instability of the "I," made by feminist postmodernists eager to sanction poststructural ideas of unstable subjectivities. But to assert that for the woman writer, the position of "I" is necessarily displaced or never at one with itself because the subjectivity in language is positioned as male, is to ignore that women writers not only fought to achieve unified subject positions in contemporary and historical dialogues but also enacted them socio-politically.

The predominance of the first-person point of view in political literature is closely related to another of the distinctive methodological emphases of suffrage literature: interpellation of the reader as a subject. The process of reader-identification governed by a female point of view through woman-centered narratives is a powerful component made stronger by the lines of women's publishing that extended themselves forcefully through the political process. The interpellation worked particularly powerfully in narratives that created symbolic identification with the protagonist. So biographies of the "pioneers" constituted a particularly strong sub-genre of suffrage periodicals. In the frequent biographical sketches in suffrage magazines and newspapers and in suffrage pageants and plays, women intellectuals, writers, artists, spiritual leaders, and warriors were enthusiastically celebrated, ranging from Boadicea to Queen Victoria to St. Hilda to Madame Curie. But the figure most often used was the virtuous virgin soldier, as embodied by Joan of Arc. The ideal ego provided by St. Joan constituted the female subject as an enabling and empowering source of agency against the patriarchal order and is reflected widely in the literature: Emily Wilding Davison's "L'Envoi" (1912), Ethel Smyth's *Female Pipings in Eden* (1934), and Evelyn Sharp's "The Women at the Gate" (1910) all equate the saint with the suffragette by making into spiritual causes what were essentially political struggles. Likewise, Constance Lytton's *Prisons and Prisoners: The Stirring Testimony of a Suffragette* (1914), Annie Kenney's *Memoirs of a Militant* (1924), Helena Swanwick's *I Have Been Young* (1935), and Hannah Mitchell's *The Hard Way Up: The Autobiography of Hannah Mitchell, Suffragette and Rebel* (1968) are some of the autobiographies that focus heavily on the process of political awakening, as do the novels *Suffragette Sally* (1911) by Gertrude Colmore, *The Soul of a Suffragette* (1913) by W. L. Courteney, and *The Cost of a Promise* (1914), by Mrs. Bailey Reynolds.[20] If the reader's interpellation and symbolic identification were prominent devices employed by suffrage writers, it was because they were both instrumental in creating, encouraging, and sustaining the goal of personal political agency.

This was in great contrast to modernist writers who often sought forces beyond the individual, tended toward the "impersonal" in their literary ideals, and put great stake in the "autonomy" of their art. Among the high modernist circles, there were also growing tendencies to believe that art is not an expression of the individual but a medium of a higher tradition. Paradoxically, elitist notions of cultural aristocracy were burgeoning at this point in history and the idea of a supremely achieved individual also became prevalent. Terry Eagleton has pointed to this contradiction and has argued that it is at this moment in history that the "impersonality" of art and the "uniquely particular" became the aesthetic aim of many writers – T. S. Eliot, D. H. Lawrence, W. B. Yeats.[21] At the same time, the market value of art was becoming more dependent upon the signature – the authenticity of the producer – than on the work itself. Thus while high literary ideals were gravitating toward the notion of the impersonal, literary pieces were becoming firmly located under the individual signature. By contrast, political writers had little interest in social distinction and prestige while being intransigently committed to constructing a sense of personal agency – literature was less of an "emotive" or "poetic" act than a "conative" one. The political writers' concern that society should appropriate its texts helps explain the writers' relative indifference about the socio-legal ownership of them. As Robins noted in 1911, "a vast amount of the most effective work done by the Writers has been anonymous."[22] That anonymous, collective art was not only possible but actually thrived under the same conditions that are habitually regarded as the inevitable causes for human isolation serves as a valuable corrective, providing an outlet from the dead end of alienation in which so much thinking about high art remains confined. The political solidarity, community, and friendship found in the very texture of suffrage literature – in both content and form – puts a welcome perspective on the fragmented and solipsistic modernist protagonist, locked in his or her own private world. If, for the suffrage writer, the negotiations with modernity were given collective direction by political faith, that direction led them to a position diametrically opposite to the developments in high modernist aesthetics.

The tension between the elitist literary culture and the populist political culture is summed up in a scene in Christopher St. John's suffrage play, *A Defence of the Fighting Spirit* (1909). Two girls are discussing the Woman question. Gertrude, the protagonist, enumerates at length a list of what is unjust in the relationship between the sexes. "Then become a suffragette!" suggests Diana, her friend. "The word offends my literary taste!" flinches Gertrude unequivocally. This send-up of the attitudes of the upper classes toward the popular political movement of suffrage re-affirms the now familiar view that literature or art, by the early twentieth century, was constituted as more or less the opposite of political engagement. Art, as the aestheticists would have it, starts to exist for its own sake by the end of the nineteenth century, turning its back on drab utility, announcing autonomy from social functions. Though the contempt of the elite for the masses is, of course, not unique to the early twentieth century, the hierarchy becomes more pronounced then. Indeed, the "great divide" thesis that modernist "high" art constituted itself through a "strategy of exclusion by an anxiety of contamination by its Other: an increasingly consuming and engulfing mass culture" is now widely accepted.[23] The dynamic between the elitist literary culture of the early twentieth century and the popular political culture of women's suffrage goes some way toward explaining why it was that many distinguished writers were ambivalent about women's suffrage.

The difficult relationship between political activism and literary expression is illustrated by the general pattern followed by many prominent modernist writers' involvement with suffrage politics: initial sympathetic involvement, passing to disillusionment and varying degrees of rejection. One of the more common reasons for the writers' renunciation stemmed from the feeling that feminist politics was just bad art. Rebecca West captured this typical disaffection in her novel *The Judge*. Ellen, the protagonist, is magnetically drawn to suffrage politics but finds herself antagonized by the unaesthetic features of the speech at a suffrage rally:

> Here was a cause so beautiful in its affirmation of freedom that it should have been served only by the bravery of dignified women and speeches lucent with reason and untremulously spoken, by things that would require no change of quality but only rearrangement to be instantly commemorable by art; yet this Scotch woman, moving with that stiffness of the mental joints which nations which suffer from it call conscientiousness, had managed to turn a sacramental gathering of the faithful into a steamy short-tempered activity, like washing day.[24]

Ellen feels estranged because the speaker does not have "something of the dignity of nature and art."[25] Virginia Woolf's enthusiasm waned for reasons not dissimilar. Like Ellen, Woolf was, in principle, an eager supporter of women's suffrage, but the realities of political engagement conflicted with her taste; after attending a suffrage rally in Kingsway, London, she lamented:

> I get one satisfactory thrill from the sense of multitude; then become disillusioned, finally bored and unable to hear a word ... I watched Mrs Pethick-Lawrence rising and falling on her toes, as if half her legs were made of rubber, throwing out her arms, opening her hands, and thought very badly of this form of art.[26]

It is an aesthetic objection that increasingly alienates her and there is a clear dissociation of herself from the suffragists which keeps her from direct political engagement. After this, Woolf stopped attending the suffrage rallies, though she continued to organize and run meetings of the local Women's Cooperative Guild in Hogarth House in Richmond until 1920 and continued to go to the annual conferences of the Guild until 1922.

It is edifying to remember that the mainstays of the opposition to women's suffrage were educated literary women such as Mrs. Humphry Ward, "Ouida," Beatrice Webb, and Elinor Glyn. Their attitudes do not seem so peculiar when it is remembered that Charlotte Brontë, Elizabeth Gaskell, Elizabeth Barrett Browning, George Eliot, and Mrs. Oliphant had, for different reasons, at different times, all opposed women's suffrage. Anti-suffragism among middle- and upper-class literary women was so prevalent that Brian Harrison in his study of anti-suffragism concluded, "Anti-suffragism was the obvious destination for well-to-do late Victorian literary women."[27] As one prominent anti-suffragist, Violet Markham, who later converted to suffragism, confessed in her autobiography, "if I erred, I erred in good company."[28]

Another reason behind the ambivalence or antipathy was the belief that political reform was futile – that the vote, for example, was of little value to women. Underlying this belief is the assumption that liberation and development rely on sheer individual will, rather than originating from social structures. It is, therefore, no surprise to find that these opinions came from the section of society that could overcome barriers to educational and social opportunities by virtue of birth. As Dorothy Richardson explained:

> In principle much had been gained. The exclusively sexual estimate of women had received its death-blow. But it soon became apparent that academic education and the successful pursuit of a profession implied a renunciation of domesticity. The open heaven of "emancipation" narrowed to the sad and sterile vista – feminism for spinsters. From that moment public opinion see-sawed between the alternatives of discrediting domesticity and of dividing women into two types – "ordinary" women, who married, and "superior" women who did not . . . This feminism was, therefore, in practice, a class feminism – feminism for ladies.[29]

Those who gained the first fruits of feminism based on the higher-education road to emancipation and equality were alienated from the less fortunate, and the model of feminism worked, in this sense, to reinforce the sense of division among women as a group. Conversely, in feminist politics, unity arose from strengthening the category of women as a victimized group, and hence the reluctance of women who did not feel victimized to identify with political causes. Beatrice Webb succinctly stated in 1926, "At the root of my anti-feminism lay the fact that I had never myself suffered the disabilities assumed to arise from my sex."[30] It was for these reasons that Elizabeth Robins declared that "the exceptional woman is one of our biggest obstacles."[31]

It is a critical commonplace to note that, by the end of the nineteenth century, the waning of religious faith brought about the collapse of fundamental assumptions and certainties; and that modernism is, among other things, an expression of the anxieties of personal and cultural displacement, and of attempts to come to terms with the "relative" spirit of the times. If, for the modernist writer, a "uniquely particular" aesthetic became an expression of these anxieties, then the modernist aesthetic precluded the kind of collective faith that drove political art.

Oscar Wilde observed that, "[modern] art finds her own perfection within, and not outside of, herself," and recent methods of construing the narrative text as a free play of signifiers are agreeable to that idea. But no text is entirely free-floating, which is not to imply it is securely tethered either. If feminist literature of the early twentieth century sought to find perfection outside itself and not within, it is because its practitioners could neither afford to assert, nor believe in asserting, the autonomy of the work from life; thus they made it possible for us to create some full account of texts wherein their roots in historically specific human practices are a very part of their aesthetics.

NOTES

1. See Ronald Taylor, ed., *Aesthetics and Politics* (London: Verso, 1977).
2. Ellen G. Friedman and Miriam Fuchs, eds., *Breaking the Sequence: Women's Experimental Fiction* (Princeton, NJ: Princeton University Press, 1989), p. 4.
3. The suffrage movement refers to the period from 1867, when suffrage societies were becoming organized, to 1918, when British women were given limited franchise. The suffragette movement is more specifically associated with the activities of the Women's Social and Political Union and the Women's Freedom League.
4. Cicely Hamilton, *Life Errant* (London: Dent, 1935), p. 75.
5. Joel H. Kaplan and Sheila Stowell, *Theatre and Fashion: Oscar Wilde to the Suffragettes* (Cambridge: Cambridge University Press, 1994), p. 7.
6. See Richard Wolin, *Walter Benjamin: An Aesthetic of Redemption* (Berkeley: University of California Press, 1994), p. 125.
7. Mary Richardson, *Laugh a Defiance* (London: Weidenfeld & Nicolson, 1953). Richardson stood (unsuccessfully) three times as a socialist parliamentary candidate and joined Mosely's British Union of Fascists as its women's organizer in 1934. Mrs. Pankhurst, the president of the WSPU, was moved in and out of prison nineteen times between April 1913 and July 1914 under the Temporary Discharge for Ill Health Act (April 1913), dubbed "The Cat and Mouse Act" by the suffragettes. Mrs. Pankhurst had been on numerous hunger strikes and was forcibly fed and was often on the verge of death.
8. See John Willett, *The New Sobriety 1917–1933: Art and Politics in the Weimar Period* (London: Thames and Hudson, 1978).
9. Teresa Billington-Greig, *The Militant Suffrage Movement: Emancipation in a Hurry* (London: Franklin Palmer, 1911), p. 138.
10. See Martin Pugh, *Women and the Women's Movement in Britain* (London: Macmillan, 1992) and Brian Harrison, "Women's Suffrage at Westminster 1866–1928," in *High and Low Politics in Modern Britain*, ed. John Stevenson and Michael Bentley (Oxford: Clarendon Press, 1983) for historical readings that downgrade the suffragettes for their inability to win favours from the political establishment.
11. Margaret Haig, Viscountess Rhondda, *This Was My World* (London: Macmillan, 1933), p. 299.
12. See Marianne DeKoven, "Modernism and Gender," in *The Cambridge Companion to Modernism*, ed. Michael Levenson (Cambridge: Cambridge University Press, 1999), pp. 174–93.
13. The *Daily Mirror* was launched in November 1903 as a newspaper for women with a woman editor and women staff, reflecting the growing female readership in

the market. It was not a success and the editor Mary Howarth was succeeded by Hamilton Fyfe.

14. There were also important antecedents: see pro-suffrage/feminist periodicals and newspapers such as *Englishwoman's Review* (1866–1910), *Women's Suffrage Journal* (1870–90), *Shafts* (1892–1900), *Woman's Opinion* (1874), *Woman* (1887), *Women's Gazette* (1888–91), *Women's Penny Paper* (1888–90), *Woman's Herald* (1891–3), and *Woman's Signal* (1894–9).

15. See Katharine Cockin, Glenda Norquay, and Sowon S. Park, eds., *Women's Suffrage Literature*, 6 vols. (London: Routledge, 2007), for a range of literature prompted by the suffrage movement.

16. See, for example, Emmeline Pethick-Lawrence, "Why I Went to Prison," WSPU pamphlet in the Museum of London Suffragette Files, and Cicely Hamilton, *Life Errant*.

17. Elizabeth Robins, "To the Women Writers," in *Way Stations* (London: Hodder & Stoughton, 1913), p. 110 (a speech given to the members of the WWSL at the Waldorf Hotel, May 14, 1909).

18. Elizabeth Robins, "The Women Writers," in *Way Stations*, p. 236 (a speech given to the members of the WWSL at the Criterion, May 23, 1911).

19. *Vote* (January 27, 1912).

20. For a list of suffrage novels, see Elizabeth Crawford, *The Women's Suffrage Movement: A Reference Guide 1866–1928* (London: UCL Press, 1999), pp. 467–71.

21. Terry Eagleton, *The Ideology of the Aesthetic* (London: Basil Blackwell, 1990), pp. 374–5.

22. Elizabeth Robins, *Way Stations*, p. 225.

23. See Andreas Huyssen, *After the Great Divide* (Bloomington: Indiana University Press, 1986).

24. Rebecca West, *The Judge* (1922; reprinted London: Virago, 1980), p. 52.

25. *Ibid.*, p. 58.

26. Diary entry, Saturday March 9, 1918, in *The Diary of Virginia Woolf*, ed. Anne Olivier Bell, vol. I, *1915–1919* (New York: Harcourt Brace Jovanovich, 1977), p. 125.

27. Brian Harrison, *Separate Spheres* (London: Croom Helm, 1978), p. 22.

28. Violet Markham, *Return Passage* (London: Oxford University Press, 1953), p. 96.

29. Dorothy Richardson, "The Reality of Feminism," *Ploughshare* (1917), 241.

30. Beatrice Webb, *My Apprenticeship* (1926; reprinted Cambridge: Cambridge University Press, 1979), p. 355.

31. Elizabeth Robins, "The Suffrage Camp Revisited," in *Way Stations*, p. 66.

12

HEATHER INGMAN

Religion and the occult in women's modernism

In 1887, Madame Blavatsky arrived in London to publicize her occult philosophy, a heady mix of Neo-Platonism, Buddhism, and Kabbalistic mysticism. Despite accusations of fraud from the Society for Psychical Research, Helena Blavatsky's Theosophical Society flourished, reflecting the renewed interest in spiritualism in the 1880s. Reacting against the rise of Darwinism and a society increasingly devoted to scientific and technological progress, spiritualism developed as a counter-cultural movement in which women were dominant as teachers and mediums. Annie Besant, lampooned by Virginia Woolf in *The Waves* (1931), is just one example of someone who combined campaigning for women's rights with active involvement in the Theosophical Society.

The alliance of spirituality and feminism was empowering, as is evidenced in the work of New Woman writers at the turn of the century, when writers like Sarah Grand and George Egerton took up the theme of women's superior spiritual powers in fiction that foreshadows the modernist aesthetic with its emphasis on dreams, the subconscious, and formal stylistic experimentation. Egerton's short stories in *Keynotes* (1893) and *Discords* (1894) resist social constructs of femininity, allying women instead with nature, the primitive, and the spiritual in a way that anticipates the work of female modernists. Her writing reveals distaste for organized religion, particularly the Irish Catholicism of her youth, and her argument that women's maternity privileges them over men anticipates Jane Harrison's influential work on early matriarchal civilizations.

In 1920 the Anglican Lambeth Conference issued a statement that "the Church must frankly acknowledge that it has undervalued and neglected the gifts of women." The statement came rather late: the number of women exploring their spirituality outside the established churches was one factor behind the decline in Church of England attendance during the inter-war period which, by 1937, saw the Archbishop of Canterbury abstaining in a vote on divorce on the grounds that he no longer found it possible to impose the full Christian standard in law on a largely non-Christian population.[1]

Rose Macaulay's difficulties with institutional religion are recorded in her correspondence with Father Hamilton Johnson at the time of her return to the Anglican church, and hostility to institutional religion is a marked feature of writing by female modernists.[2]

Institutional religion

In *The Voyage Out* (1915), Woolf satirises unthinking adherence to religious orthodoxy in the comical sermon Rachel hears during matins and she highlights Christianity's imperialistic overtones in the figure of the evangelical Miss Kilman in *Mrs. Dalloway* (1925) and the would-be missionaries, Edgar and Eleanor, in the pageant of *Between the Acts* (1941). Sylvia Townsend Warner, too, explores the links between Christianity and colonialism in *Mr. Fortune's Maggot* (1927) where the Reverend Fortune comes to realize that his mission to convert the Polynesian islanders is based on little more than an urge to dominate. Warner, brought up in Harrow public school, where her father was house master, was exposed in her youth to a great deal of institutional Anglicanism. Her diaries and letters reveal that she later became fiercely anti-clerical. Ivy Compton-Burnett's loathing of Christianity is palpable in her novels where God is portrayed as a patriarchal bully (*Daughters and Sons* [1937]) and mothers are hampered in their mothering by Christian idealizations of motherhood (*Men and Wives* [1931], *Elders and Betters* [1944]).

If in *Pilgrimage* Dorothy Richardson uses her alter ego, Miriam Henderson, to criticize the Church of England's refusal to ordain women, she also displays reservations about the role of women in Orthodox Judaism, represented in *Deadlock* (1921) by Michael Shatov. Though initially attracted to Shatov, Miriam is doubtful about marrying him and a meeting with Mrs. Bergstein, a Jewish convert, convinces her that adopting Shatov's religion would end her individual life as a woman. Richardson draws on the antisemitic discourse of supersessionism to proclaim Christianity's superiority in this regard over Judaism.[3] The final volumes of *Pilgrimage*, *Dimple Hill* (1938) and *March Moonlight* (1967), chart Miriam's growing attraction to the Society of Friends. Time spent with a Quaker family leads Miriam to conclude that, unlike Orthodox Judaism and Anglicanism, the Friends do not institutionalize a patriarchal God but allow space for feminization of the divine. In the end, however, in a trajectory that reflects Richardson's own attraction to Quakerism in the years between 1907 and 1911 and her later repudiation of it, Miriam's commitment to her art wins out over membership of the Society of Friends (though not over Christianity more broadly).

Anzia Yezierska's writing, like Richardson's, criticizes Orthodox Judaism for the restrictions it placed on women's lives. Born in a Russian-Polish village outside Warsaw to a Jewish family who fled to the U.S. in 1890, Yezierska, in her autobiographical novel *Bread Givers* (1925), depicts Sara Smolinsky's efforts to free herself from her father's Orthodox Judaism. Though Sara is in many ways a pioneer, the emotional cost of her struggle is made clear as she remains torn, like her creator, between the Old World and the New.

Like Yezierska, Antonia White was never able to disentangle herself entirely from the religious values imposed on her by her father, an adult convert to Roman Catholicism. White's autobiographical novel, *Frost in May* (1933), is an indictment of pre-Vatican II Roman Catholicism and of the convent schools associated with it. Nanda's artistic temperament clashes with an authoritarian school where the humility of the Virgin Mary is upheld as an ideal in order to suppress female ambition. The fate of White's tortured and self-blaming heroine in the remaining three novels of her quartet prolongs this conflict between faith and art until, in *Beyond the Glass* (1954), her heroine ends up in an asylum, unable to free herself from her father's influence and from the literal interpretations of Catholic doctrine and the belief in female inferiority inculcated by the nuns.

More positive accounts of convent schools feature in the novels of Kate O'Brien, an Irish writer who is starting to be claimed for modernism. *The Land of Spices* (1941) juxtaposes unsatisfactory families with the all-female community of a convent school that is empowering for staff and pupils alike. Although she described herself as a "Catholic-agnostic," O'Brien remained colored by her Irish Catholic upbringing, her novels portraying convent schools as enabling Irish girls to develop their potential for leadership and creativity and to transcend the gender roles ascribed to them by Irish nationalism. In works like *The Land of Spices* and *That Lady* (1946), O'Brien associates her heroines' Catholicism with their stance against political tyranny, whether in de Valera's Ireland, Philip II's Spain, or Franco's republic. Her novels underline the appeal of the Catholic church for sexual dissidents: in *Mary Lavelle* (1936), Agatha, a lesbian, takes refuge in the Catholic church in a way that has parallels with Radclyffe Hall who found in the Catholic church protection against the homophobic world outside. In Hall's novel *The Well of Loneliness* (1928), Stephen regards her inversion as God-given and is prepared to suffer martyrdom.

Writers like O'Brien and Hall are useful reminders that not all female modernists were automatically hostile to institutional religion. Elizabeth Bowen regularly attended Church of Ireland services and its influence shows in the three parts of *The Death of the Heart* (1938), which are structured around the litany. Similarly, three successive feast days in the Catholic calendar provide the structure of Kate O'Brien's novel, *The Ante-Room* (1934), where Agnes's Catholicism enables her to resist the romance plot and side with her sister over her lover. In a revealing statement, Dorothy Richardson confessed that she believed that an artist's link with religion was nearly entirely aesthetic,[4] while Sylvia Townsend Warner's partner, Valentine Ackland, remarked that Townsend Warner's interest in her own excursions into different faiths was prompted by her interest in the aesthetics of the different religions and their links with creativity.[5] In her letters and diaries, Virginia Woolf expressed attraction to the aesthetics of the religion she saw practised abroad, such as an Easter procession she watched in Madrid in 1923. Biblical influences and Christian symbolism have been discerned in the patterning of her novels, in the references to the Eucharist in *Mrs. Dalloway*, to *Genesis* and the Last Supper in *The Waves*, and to the Edenic fall in *To the Lighthouse* and *The Waves*, though used in a way that marks Woolf's break from Christian values.[6] In the Society of Outsiders outlined in *Three Guineas* (1938), Woolf envisages women attending church services and reading the New Testament in a spirit of critical inquiry that might eventually, she argues, result in a new kind of religion altogether. By continuing to wrestle with the problem of Christianity, Woolf was attempting to formulate her own ideas and resist unthinking adherence to her parents' agnosticism.

Mysticism

Mystical visions have always been one way of challenging orthodox religious discourse and for this reason the mystical experiences of figures like Catherine of Siena and Teresa of Avila, lending them the spiritual authority to bypass the masculinist structures of the Catholic church, attracted the attention of women writers in the modernist era. Earlier writers like William James in *The Varieties of Religious Experience* (1902) had explored the psychological basis for mystical experiences. As investigations into the influence of the mind on physical health developed, medicine and mysticism grew closer. In 1922, G. I. Gurdjieff, an Armenian Greek mystic who promoted the interrelationship between the mind, the body, and the emotions, founded his Institute for the Harmonious Development of Man at Fontainebleau, where Katherine Mansfield stayed during the last few months of her life in the hope of a cure. Gurdjieff's disciple, P. D. Ouspensky, published his best-seller, *Tertium Organum*, about different levels of consciousness in 1912. It was translated into English in 1923 and Ouspensky gave lectures and séances in London in 1921.

Evelyn Underhill's writings made her one of the chief exponents of mysticism in the modernist era. In *Practical Mysticism* (1914), Underhill argues that, far from being an esoteric pastime for an elite, mysticism is potentially within everyone's reach and in simple, non-technical language she outlines ways of training one's consciousness to reach new levels of awareness. Like James, she emphasizes that though mystical states cannot be sustained for long, some memory of their content remains and influences the conscious life of the subject. After Underhill's return to the Church of England in 1921, she wrote a study of Christian mysticism, *Mystics of the Church* (1925), in which she stresses that authentic mystics use their visions, not to withdraw from life, but as a practical motivating force for action.

In her biography of Joan of Arc, published in 1938, Vita Sackville-West likewise emphasizes the practical outcome of Joan's mystical trances which, she argues, never inclined Joan to hysteria or ecstasy but were accepted by her as part of her everyday life, inspiring her to practical action on behalf of the Dauphin and France. Sackville-West's portrait of Teresa of Avila, published in 1943, similarly dwells on Teresa's practicality and administrative ability, and it has been argued that Sackville-West turned to these lives of female mystics in an effort to find a private faith outside the traditional religious structures that dissatisfied her.[7] The idea of mysticism as a practical motivating force in daily life is present in the fiction of two contemporaries of Underhill and Sackville-West, namely Virginia Woolf and May Sinclair, without, however, these visionary experiences being set in a Christian, or even specifically religious, context.

Woolf's "moments of being," described in "A Sketch of the Past," were momentary insights she had experienced from early childhood, secular, even aesthetic experiences, producing feelings akin to those of the mystics, but without their corresponding religious revelation. In this context, she became interested in her aunt, Caroline Stephen, who wrote several highly influential works on Quaker mysticism in which she argues for the authority of the individual's visionary experiences.[8] For Woolf, though, her "moments of being" were linked to her vocation as a writer and were shorn of any link to a transcendental being. She lends such moments to characters like Mrs. Ramsay in *To the Lighthouse* (1927) and Eleanor in *The Years* (1937), who both experience trance-like feelings of oneness with the world without believing in a creator God.

Yet, daughter of agnostics, married to a lapsed Jew, and surrounded by Bloomsbury skeptics, Woolf could not entirely trust the moments of vision so crucial to her vocation as a writer, not least because she feared the link between visions and mental illness. She needed authorization for her mystical experiences from people whose intellect she could trust and her meeting with W. B. Yeats in 1930 has been cited as pivotal in this regard, encouraging Woolf to treat her mystical side seriously.[9] Woolf's reading of works by Arthur Eddington and James Jeans popularizing the findings of quantum physics that were breaking down the old dualism between mind and matter also gave her confidence in her moments of vision, and she set out to explore them in the book that was first called *The Moths* and later became *The Waves*, explaining in her diary: "now, if I write *The Moths* I must come to terms with those mystical feelings."[10] *The Waves* is filled with moments when the characters become conscious of some underlying pattern to life. Such moments are never associated with religious orthodoxy but are primarily motivated by an aesthetic appreciation of life and linked to an individual's psychology. They transcend gender, being scattered among male and female characters.

If Woolf's moments of being were primarily instinctive and aesthetic, May Sinclair, exploring similar moments of visionary insight in her novels, sought to evolve a philosophy to explain them, influencing in this regard T. S. Eliot.[11] Receiving little formal schooling, Sinclair read psychology and philosophy at home for many years, studying William James, Henri Bergson's work on the interpenetration of mind and matter (*Mind-Energy* [1920]), and the Eastern philosophy that began to filter into the West in the early decades of the twentieth century. Her philosophical work, *A Defence of Idealism* (1917), demonstrates familiarity with Buddhism, the Upanishads, and the Vedanta, as well as with the work of the Bengali poet and mystic, Rabindranath Tagore, whom she had met during his lecture trips to England between the years 1912 and 1920. As a result of her reading, Sinclair evolved her own brand of mysticism, calling it the New Mysticism to distinguish it from the Christian variety. Like her friend Underhill, Sinclair saw mysticism as part of, rather than an escape from, everyday life, but she disagreed with Underhill over the relative merits of Christian and Eastern mysticism. Underhill regarded the latter as life-denying in comparison with Christianity, whereas for Sinclair Eastern mysticism was the highest form, doing away with the mind-body dualism she believed bedevilled Western Christianity.

Sinclair fictionalized the ideas expressed in *A Defence of Idealism* in her autobiographical novel *Mary Olivier* (1919), in which she portrays the eponymous heroine's lifelong quest to discover what she can believe to be true about God. Exposed to Victorian Christianity in her childhood when God becomes confused in her mind with her tyrannical and unpredictable father, Mary Olivier starts to deconstruct this religion as she grows up, noting its illogicalities and preferring Spinoza's God to the Christian. In the course of this spiritual journey, she has to resist her beloved mother who relies on orthodox Christianity to socialize her daughter into femininity. In this Mary is helped by moments of "ecstasy" that give her confidence to explore the divine and establish her identity in the face of opposition from her mother, the church, and Victorian society in general. These moments of insight are associated by Mary with intimations of the divine, but are carefully distinguished from the Christianity in which she finds it impossible to believe. From 1913 Sinclair was involved in the Medico-Psychological Clinic, and the ending of *Mary Olivier* intertwines mysticism with her interest in psychoanalysis as Mary both sublimates her love for Richard and paradoxically finds fulfillment through trusting her mystic insights of a reality beyond the self. As in Woolf, mysticism in Sinclair transcends gender: in *Arnold Waterlow* (1924), the eponymous hero experiences moments of insight akin to Mary's and pursues a similar spiritual journey toward selfhood. For both Woolf and Sinclair, mystic intuitions were a means of affirming their artistic vocation and breaking with the orthodoxies of the past without denying the need for an interior spiritual life.

The female divine

If female modernists drew on mysticism to convey the personal and private visions underpinning their artistic vocations, those searching for a way for women to celebrate their subjectivity and creativity by embodying the divine principle in themselves, without need for a male mediator, tended to think in terms of society as a whole and were led back into history, or even pre-history.

The work of anthropologists like Ruth Benedict (*Patterns of Culture* [1935]), highlighting the fact that many beliefs Western society held to be innate were in fact culturally constructed, opened up the possibility that the patriarchal order of that society, built around worship of a male God, was not inevitable. Jane Harrison's studies of Greek mythology led her to trace the way in which in Greek religion the Mother Goddess came to be robbed of her power: Demeter and Kore, Mother and Maid, were not, she explained, two women originally, but aspects of one Goddess, representing woman before and after maturity. In *Mythology* (1924) and in the earlier *Prolegomena to the Study of Greek Religion* (1903), Harrison links the decline of the Mother Goddess with the thwarting of women's creativity in the patriarchy and argues that retrieving her power would liberate women's creativity and spirituality.

In *Mythology*, Harrison depicts matriarchal societies as communal, cooperative, and life-giving, encouraging women's independence and creativity and fostering egalitarian relationships between women and men. The American writer Charlotte Perkins Gilman depicts the matriarchy in a similar light in *The Man-Made World: Or, Our Androcentric Culture* (1911) where she argues that though we cannot know for certain what these ancient matriarchies were like, we may be sure they involved what Gilman terms "loving service," rejection of hierarchical power structures, and a female experience of the divine. She too presents the Goddess's original power dwindling away in an androcentric culture to a male-pleasing daughter figure and calls for the necessity of recovering the maternal. For writers such as Harrison and Gilman, retrieving ancient matriarchal societies was not a historical exercise, but part of their search for female empowerment and for different ways of living in the future.

Woolf met Harrison on several occasions and her work confirmed for Woolf certain ideas she had been groping towards for years centering on the connection between the retrieval of the buried mother in Western society, the daughter's sense of empowerment, and female creativity. Harrison's project of uncovering an earlier matriarchal civilization fitted in with Woolf's need as an artist and a woman to retrieve a female artistic heritage. Her writing may be read as an attempt to recover the buried mother's world from *To the Lighthouse*, where Lily's vision of Mrs. Ramsay inspires her to complete her painting, to *The Waves* where the opening paragraph revisions *Genesis* as a woman brings light to the world.

The connection between female embodiment of the divine and female empowerment and creativity is apparent in Emily Coleman's autobiographical novel, *The Shutter of Snow* (1930), where Marthe Gail's claim to be Christ returned to earth in the form of a woman becomes a way of retrieving her creativity and gaining control over a life dominated by male authority figures in the shape of her father, her husband, her doctors, and a masculinist God. Much of H. D.'s work may be interpreted as a quest for the female divine. *HERmione*, an autobiographical prose work written in 1927, portrays Her finding her identity through being mirrored in her female other, Fayne Rabb, positioned in the text not only as Her's friend but also as a nature goddess and prophetess who awakens Her's sexuality and creativity. These themes of female spirituality, sexuality, and creativity are evoked in the powerful poem "The Dancer," part of a triad composed after H. D.'s psychoanalysis by Freud gave her renewed confidence in her art and her sexuality.

H. D.'s mystical vision of "writing on the wall," which she associated with the ancient prophetic traditions, had been interpreted by Freud as desire for union with the suppressed mother ("Writing on the Wall" [1944]) and a combination of the energies released by psychoanalysis and anxiety occasioned by living through the war in London prompted her to explore her maternal spiritual inheritance of Moravianism in *The Gift*. *The Gift* recounts the ceremonies and rituals of H. D.'s childhood.[12] Mamalie, H. D.'s maternal grandmother, enlightens her as to women's central role in the Moravian church and, in associating herself with the hermetic mystical traditions of the Moravians and their wish to harmonize ancient European wisdom with native American spirituality, H. D. locates her artistic creativity in a spiritual inheritance that includes not only Mamalie, but also her musician-artist mother who buried her talents in domesticity.

H. D.'s poetic *Trilogy* (*The Walls Do Not Fall* [1944], *Tribute to the Angels* [1945], *The Flowering of the Rod* [1946]), likewise written in London against the backdrop of the war, envisages the regeneration of the world through a female divinity, presenting the bombing of London in terms of the ancient ruins at Karnac, which H. D. visited with Bryher in 1923. In a London now ruined, as the ancient Egyptian temples were ruined, the writer will be the preserver of sacred traditions and values, aided in this, not by Christ, but by the Holy Spirit, "go-between interpreter" who explains the "symbols of the past / in to-day's imagery."[13] *Tribute to the Angels* invokes Mary, "the Lady," not as Christ's mother but as a goddess linked to pre-Christian figures such as Venus. It is she who blesses the sacred quest of writers amidst the devastations of war and, like Woolf's "moments of being" and Sinclair's ecstasies, confirms H. D.'s belief in her artistic vocation.

After the war, H. D. continued reworking ancient female deities, turning them into modern-day prophetesses who bring a new aesthetic and spiritual vision to redeem the world: in *Helen in Egypt*, H. D. frees Helen from Homer's portrayal, transforming her into a goddess of love urging reconciliation on a war-weary world. The theme had both a public and a private aspect as H. D. wove into her poem a series of personal reconciliations with people from her past. Getting in touch with the female divine was not, therefore, an academic exercise but had relevance for H. D.'s identity as a woman and an artist. She recognized the importance to her creative development of her Moravian upbringing with its emphasis on faith as a direct illumination from God but, like many female modernists, felt the need to reconstruct her religious inheritance in a more empowering way. Her invocation of female deities was part of her drive to explore new aesthetic and spiritual values.

Nature, myth, and nation

In "The Magician" (1933), H. D. speaks in the voice of a disciple of Christ who places his trust, not in the crucifixion, but in the nature images that recur in the parables. Nature as a channel to the divine was another means for women writers in the modernist era to bypass religious orthodoxy and experience the divine directly. It was also a theme that lent itself to making political points.

In Sylvia Townsend Warner's novel *Lolly Willowes, or the Loving Huntsman* (1926), Lolly finds that the Christian God has become too implicated in the masculinist thinking of her society to be of use to her as a single woman whose life is assumed to center around service to others. Reversing the myths that sustain the patriarchy, Lolly reasons that Satan, the loving hunts-man of the title, must be on the side of spinsters, since his opposite number, God, so clearly is not. Lolly leaves city life, which is aligned with masculinity and mechanization, and finds freedom in the countryside, under the protec-tion of a gentle and feminized Satan. In contrast with her nephew's possessive and controlling attitude toward the countryside, Lolly learns to live in har-mony with nature and Warner anticipates later ecofeminist writing in sug-gesting a link between the exploitation of the environment and the exploitation of women. But *Lolly Willowes* is also very much of its time. Margaret Murray's recently published study, *The Witch-Cult in Western Europe* (1921), had argued that witchcraft represented the remnants of a pagan religion and Warner's strategy for defending the spinster, arguably code here for the lesbian, is to connect her with a coven of witches.

The preservation of the English countryside regarded as embodying central spiritual and national values became a concern in the inter-war period.[14] In Mary Butts's novels, *Armed with Madness* (1928) and *The Death of Felicity Taverner* (1932), conservation of the English countryside is a major theme in writing that privileges nature, females, Englishness, the primitive, and the sacred.[15] Her heroines, Scylla and the eponymous Felicity, are earth mother goddesses identified with nature and England's pre-industrial past, as well as thoroughly modern women exploring their sexuality. In *Armed with Madness*, Butts draws on her reading of Harrison's *Themis* (1912), James Frazer's *The Golden Bough* (1890–1915), and Jessie Weston's *From Ritual to Romance* (1920) for her modernist rewriting of the Grail legend, feminized through the figure of Scylla. In her diary Butts noted that she and T. S. Eliot were working in parallel on the Grail legend, but that whereas Eliot employed Frazer's pessimistic imagery of sterility and social disorder, she was drawing on Weston's association of the Grail with fertility, rebirth, and the female body.[16] The quest takes place in the countryside where a group of five men and Scylla seek refuge from an urban industrialized society dominated by material values they regard as diseased. Though there are forays into this urban wasteland, the emphasis of the novel is on spiritual renewal and healing through the twin forces of nature and the female after the devastations of the First World War. Grail imagery is developed through Scylla ("a living cup") and Picus, the lance. The novel ends inconclusively – Boris's appearance may or may not herald a new beginning after Clarence's insane assault on Scylla – but what counts for Butts is not resolution but the quest itself, which has awakened the characters' awareness of the sacred, holding out the hope that it may still have a place in modern life.

Scylla and Picus reappear in *Felicity Taverner*, an ecological allegory in which Scylla and her brother battle against Nick Kralin's desire to develop their cousin Felicity's home and the surrounding countryside in a move seen to threaten both the land and Englishness itself. It is not irrelevant that Kralin is a Bolshevik Jew. Just as Clarence, the black homosexual, is removed at the end of *Armed with Madness*, so the threat posed by the alien Kralin is resolved by his ritual murder by the White Russian exile, Boris, in order to preserve both Felicity's reputation and her land. In her celebration of Englishness and the English countryside Butts, like Woolf in *Between the Acts*, was influenced by Harrison's *Ancient Art and Ritual* (1913), defining ritual as a collective experience aimed at the public good, thereby providing a bridge between art and religion.[17] Unlike *Between the Acts*, which celebrates the English landscape while remaining ambivalent, even in the face of war, about English nationalism, Butts's novels are heavily redolent of the xenophobia, racism, and antisemitism characteristic of modernism in some of its guises, attitudes from which Woolf herself was not always exempt.[18]

In her novels, Butts combines Hellenic myth with legends of the Grail to align women with nature and position them as saviors of the land and of England. The theme had its roots in her early childhood: her memoir, *The Crystal Cabinet* (1937), reveals the formative influence of her upbringing in the Dorset countryside, describing the moment when she first became conscious of the sacred in nature. This, together with a later mystical experience on Badbury Rings, was to be a defining moment, akin to Woolf's "moments of being," providing the central motivation for Butts's work in which she connects the visible and the invisible and seeks to give meaning to a world she believed had lost its spirituality. Like Rose Macaulay, Butts found refuge at the end of her life in Anglo-Catholicism and with hindsight the wise vicar in *Armed with Madness*, who recommends healing through adherence to religious ritual, becomes a significant figure.

The researches of Augusta Gregory into the world of Irish folklore and fairy tale were marked, as much as Butts's work, by resistance to an urban, industrialized age and by a wish to reclaim an ancient world-view. Gregory published two collections of Irish saga and romance and six books of folk material and translations, of which her most significant was *Visions and Beliefs in the West of Ireland* (1920). Her work was inspired by a combination of the nationalist impulse behind the Irish Literary Revival, the Romantic embrace of the irrational and the mysterious as sources of creative inspiration, and faith in nature as a sacred force and in the innate spirituality of the Irish peasant. Her researches led her to uncover stories of subversive women like Biddy Early, a healer whose powers challenged those of the male priests and doctors.

Gregory's plays have been read as feminist rewritings of Irish myth. *Kathleen Ni Houlihan*, first produced in 1902 and written with W. B. Yeats to commemorate the 1798 Rising, draws on seventeenth- and eighteenth-century *aisling* poetry and nineteenth-century revolutionary ballads like *Shan Van Vocht* to personify Ireland as a woman who inspires Irishmen to fight for her. The play likens Irishmen's sacrifice to Christ's and Irish nationalists interpreted it as reclaiming a feminized Ireland from the colonizers' discourse. The power of the play to rekindle revolutionary romantic nationalism was enhanced by Maud Gonne playing the part of the queen. This coupling of the Irish nation and Irish womanhood was to prove problematic for Irish women in the newly established Irish state and later writers like Eavan Boland criticized the use of women as passive embodiments of Mother Ireland. Nevertheless, there is an element of female empowerment in Gregory's plays: *Grania* (1910) transforms Grania from a helpless victim of fate into a strong woman who negotiates the terms of her return to her community and demands the transformation of its masculinist power structures.

The occult and the supernatural

Interest in the paranormal, intense around the turn of the century, increased again after the end of the First World War when there was a boom in spiritualism and séances as bereaved relatives sought contact with their war dead, and interest continued throughout the inter-war period.[19] In her youth, Mary Butts explored the world of black magic and the occult, spending time in 1921 at Aleister Crowley's "Abbey of Thelema" in Sicily. In Butts' first novel, *Ashe of Rings* (1925), Vanna, like Scylla and Felicity, represents the potential for healing in a war-weary world. Her white magic introduces a fairy-tale element into the novel, but fairy tale moves into occult in the figure of Judy, whose black witchcraft contrasts with Vanna's healing powers. Like Townsend Warner and Margaret Murray, Butts places witchcraft in the context of everyday life where witches are ancient priestesses practising pre-Christian religion in the service of Satan. But unlike the Satan of *Lolly Willowes*, Butts's Satan is actively evil. May Sinclair admired *Ashe of Rings* and the two writers met occasionally. In her diary, Butts paid tribute to Sinclair's ghost stories for abandoning Gothic trappings in favour of delving into the supernatural and the subconscious.[20] This was something Butts herself attempted in stories such as "With and Without Buttons," "Mappa Mundi," and "From Altar to Chimney-Piece" (*Last Stories* [1938]) where the dangers of tampering with magic without appreciating its sacred associations are evident.

If the Gothic tales of Hoffmann and Poe anticipated modernism by exploring such themes as the fragility of the self and the dissolution of rational boundaries and moral certainties, ghost stories at the turn of the century, most notably Henry James's *The Turn of the Screw* (1898), had begun to explore psychical states.[21] In the modernist era, the genre was given further impetus to shed its Gothic trappings by Freud's argument in "The Uncanny" (1919) that the strange is intertwined with the homely. Both Woolf and Sinclair were influenced by Henry James's shift to psychical ghost stories and their exploration of supernatural themes was part of their interest in states of mind where rational boundaries are dissolved. Woolf's fascination with what survives after death is evident in stories and sketches like "A Haunted House," "The Fascination of the Pool," "The Widow and the Parrot: A True Story," and "The Shooting Party." The survival after death of the disembodied human consciousness is posited by Clarissa in *Mrs. Dalloway* and by the narrator in the "Time Passes" section of *To the Lighthouse*, after which the spirit of Mrs. Ramsay returns to help Lily complete her painting. In Woolf, the exploration of the supernatural was propelled not so much by belief as by a wish to extend the boundaries of realism and explore hitherto uncharted mental states.

May Sinclair's interest in the occult was linked to her reading in psychoanalysis, both representing an effort to explore what she called in *A Defence of Idealism* "the haunted world below our working consciousness."[22] Her involvement with psychoanalysis led her to join the Society for Psychical Research in 1914, but her interest in the supernatural continued and during the 1920s she attended séances in an effort to get in touch with her dead brother. Her short stories, published in 1923 under the Freudian title *Uncanny Stories* highlight this intermingling of psychoanalysis and the occult. In "The Intercessor," the ghost-child, Effie, may be interpreted as the return of the repressed, a reminder of sexuality and mortality that Effie's family has tried to suppress, while in "The Token," Donald only ceases to be haunted when he overcomes the suppression of his emotions. "The Finding of the Absolute" mingles the occult with Einstein's theories of space and time and Sinclair's reading of Kant and Hegel, to give a more optimistic view of the after-life than "Where Their Fire is not Quenched," in which the adulterers are doomed to repeat their empty affair for all eternity. Sinclair uses the ghost story to probe gender constraints in "The Nature of the Evidence," where a haunting is connected to a husband's reliance on stereotypes about female sexuality. In "The Flaw in the Crystal" Agatha's healing powers, like Mary Olivier's moments of ecstasy, give her the authority to bypass her society's gender constraints. Discovering that sexual love compromises her powers she sacrifices it, as good mediums were supposed to, in order to preserve her visionary life.[23]

The number of short stories by female modernists devoted to the occult is striking and supports the view of some critics that the story is essentially a liminal form, suited to exploring dreams, visions, hauntings, and the unconscious.[24] Elizabeth Bowen, for instance, seems to have found the form suited to the supernatural, writing only one novel of a haunting (*A World of Love*) but many fine ghost stories that capture the edginess and fragmented consciousness of the modernist era. In "The Back Drawing Room" (1926), a conversation that begins with a group of sophisticates discussing psychology and the after-life in an English drawing room evolves into an Irish ghost story that contains a rebuke to the English for their abandonment of the Anglo-Irish. In stories like "The Demon Lover" (1941) and "The Mysterious Kôr" (1944), Bowen uses the ghost theme to convey the eeriness and dislocations of life during the Blitz. For all these writers, Butts, Woolf, Sinclair, and Bowen, the realist mode was insufficient to represent the subconscious states revealed, not only by recent investigations into psychoanalysis and the paranormal, but by their own experience of modern life.

It is apparent that many female modernists drew on their spiritual experiences to challenge received notions of gender and sexuality and explore political questions of national identity, social progress, and scientific development. The female becomes aligned in many of their works with spiritual regeneration and resistance to an increasingly urbanized, technological, and individualistic society. They participated in the modernist engagement with matriarchal prehistory and primitivism, influenced in this by Freud and Jane Harrison, but siding rather with the latter in how they evaluated these primitive societies: inverting Freud's hierarchy of the primitive and the civilized, female modernists suggest that civilization's healing will come through the feminized primitive. At the same time, writers like Butts, Sinclair, and Woolf kept up to date with recent scientific discoveries, showing particular interest in their implications for a more sophisticated exploration of the subconscious: "How does the mind move to Einstein's physics? What is the correspondence?" Butts asked in her diary.[25] It was a question Woolf herself might have posed.

A remarkable number of female modernists recorded the mystical experiences that underpinned their careers as artists: H. D.'s "writing on the wall," Sinclair's "ecstasies," Butts's mystic initiation at Badbury Rings, Woolf's childhood "moments of being." For Butts, as for many of these writers, art was her way of approaching the spiritual. "I do not mean to be sidetracked into mysticism," she commented, after her stay with Crowley, "I'd sooner be a Villon than AE."[26] Art provided an oblique approach to the spiritual, liberating many female modernists from conventional thinking about religion and giving them confidence in their own artistic and spiritual resources.

NOTES

1. See John Stevenson, *British Society 1914–45* (Harmondsworth: Penguin, 1984), pp. 356–72.

2. For the Macaulay-Johnson correspondence, see Rose Macaulay, *Letters to a Friend 1950–52* (London: Fontana, 1968).

3. Maren Tova Linett, *Modernism, Feminism and Jewishness* (Cambridge: Cambridge University Press, 2007), pp. 70–9.

4. John Rosenberg, *Dorothy Richardson: The Genius they Forgot* (London: Duckworth, 1973), p. 48.

5. Claire Harman, *Sylvia Townsend Warner: A Biography* (1989; London: Minerva, 1991), p. 249.

6. See, for example, Suzette Henke, "*Mrs Dalloway*: The Communion of Saints," in *New Feminist Essays on Virginia Woolf*, ed. Jane Marcus (Lincoln: University of Nebraska Press, 1981), pp. 125–49; and Douglas Howard, "*Mrs Dalloway*: Virginia Woolf's Redemptive Cycle," *Literature and Theology* 12.2 (1998), 149–58.

7. Suzanne Raitt, "'The Girl Beside Me': Vita Sackville-West and the Mystics," in *Vita and Virginia: The Work and Friendship of Vita Sackville-West and Virginia Woolf* (Oxford: Clarendon Press, 1993), pp. 117–45.

8. Jane Marcus, "The Niece of a Nun: Virginia Woolf, Caroline Stephen, and the Cloistered Imagination," in *Virginia Woolf and the Languages of Patriarchy* (Bloomington: Indiana University Press, 1987), pp. 115–35.

9. Julie Kane, "Varieties of Mystical Experience in the Writings of Virginia Woolf," *Twentieth Century Literature* 41.4 (1995), 328–49.

10. Virginia Woolf, *A Writer's Diary*, ed. Leonard Woolf (London: Granada, 1981), p. 137.

11. Rebecca Neff, "'New Mysticism' in the Writings of May Sinclair and T. S. Eliot," *Twentieth Century Literature* 26.1 (1980), 82–108.

12. See Barbara Guest, *Herself Defined: The Poet H. D. and Her World* (London: Collins, 1985).

13. H. D., *Trilogy* (Manchester: Carcanet, 1973), p. 29.

14. See Jane Garrity, *Step-Daughters of England: British Women Modernists and the National Imaginary* (Manchester: Manchester University Press, 2003).

15. For further exploration, see Roslyn Reso Foy, *Ritual, Myth and Mysticism in the Work of Mary Butts: Between Feminism and Modernism* (Fayetteville: University of Arkansas Press, 2002).

16. Mary Butts, *The Journals of Mary Butts*, ed. Nathalie Blondel (New Haven and London: Yale University Press, 2002), pp. 263–4.

17. For Harrison's influence on Woolf, see Sandra D. Shattuck, "The Stage of Scholarship: Crossing the Bridge from Harrison to Woolf," in *Virginia Woolf and Bloomsbury: A Centenary Celebration*, ed. Jane Marcus (New York: Macmillan, 1987), pp. 278–98.

18. See Linett, *Modernism, Feminism, and Jewishness*, pp. 88–97.

19. See Jenny Hazelgrove, *Spiritualism and British Society Between the Wars* (Manchester: Manchester University Press, 2000).

20. Butts, *The Journals*, p. 269.

21. David Seed, "'Psychical' Cases: Transformations of the Supernatural in Virginia Woolf and May Sinclair," in *Gothic Modernisms*, ed. Andrew Smith and Jeff Wallace (London and New York: Palgrave, 2001), pp. 44–61.

22. May Sinclair, *A Defence of Idealism* (New York: Macmillan, 1917), p. 8.

23. For the purity required of mediums, see Hazelgrove, *Spiritualism and British Society*, pp. 86–8.
24. Charles May, ed., *The New Short Story Theories* (Ohio: Ohio University Press, 1994), p. 133.
25. Butts, *The Journals*, p. 218.
26. *Ibid.*, p. 189.

GUIDE TO FURTHER READING

Chapter 1 Transforming the novel

Bennett, A. and N. Royle. *Elizabeth Bowen and the Dissolution of the Novel: Still Lives.* New York: St. Martin's Press, 1994.

DeKoven, Marianne. *Rich and Strange: Gender, History, Modernism.* Princeton: Princeton University Press, 1991.

DeSalvo, L. A. *Virginia Woolf: The Impact of Childhood Sexual Abuse on her Life and Work.* Boston: Beacon, 1989.

DuPlessis, Rachel Blau. *Writing Beyond the Ending: Strategies of Twentieth Century Women Writers.* Bloomington: Indiana University Press, 1985.

Ellmann, Maud. *Elizabeth Bowen: The Shadow across the Page.* Edinburgh: Edinburgh University Press, 2003.

Hanson, Clare, ed. *The Critical Writings of Katherine Mansfield.* Basingstoke: Macmillan, 1987.

Marcus, Jane. "A Wilderness of One's Own: Feminist Fantasy Novels of the Twenties – Rebecca West and Sylvia Townsend-Warner." *Women Writers and the City.* Ed. S. M. Squier. Knoxville: University of Tennessee Press, 1984. 134–60.

Palowski, M., ed. *Virginia Woolf and Fascism: Resisting the Dictators' Seduction.* Basingstoke: Palgrave, 2001.

Radford, Jean. *Dorothy Richardson.* Hemel Hempstead: Harvester, 1991.

Scott, Bonnie Kime, ed. *The Gender of Modernism: A Critical Anthology.* Bloomington: Indiana University Press, 1990.

Gender in Modernism: New Geographies, Complex Intersections. Urbana: University of Illinois Press, 2007.

Shiach, Morag, ed. *The Cambridge Companion to the Modernist Novel.* Cambridge: Cambridge University Press, 2007.

Starr, M., ed. "May Sinclair." *The Future of the Novel: Famous Authors and Their Methods: A Series of Interviews with Renowned Authors.* Boston: Small, Maynard, 1921. 87–9.

Chapter 2 Modernist women poets and the problem of form

Albright, Daniel. "Modernist Poetic Form." *The Cambridge Companion to Twentieth-Century English Poetry.* Ed. Neil Corcoran. Cambridge: Cambridge University Press, 2007. 24–41.

Beasley, Rebecca. *Theorists of Modernist Poetry: T. S. Eliot, T. E. Hulme, and Ezra Pound*. London: Routledge, 2007.

Benstock, Shari. *Women of the Left Bank*. Austin: University of Texas Press, 1986.

Brooker, Peter and Simon Perril. "Modernist Poetry and Its Precursors." *A Companion to Twentieth-Century Poetry*. Ed. Neil Roberts. Oxford: Blackwell, 2001. 21–36.

Bush, Ronald. "Modernist Poetry and Poetics." *The Cambridge History of Twentieth-Century English Literature*. Ed. Laura Marcus and Peter Nicholls. Cambridge: Cambridge University Press, 2004. 232–50.

Clark, Suzanne. *Sentimental Modernism: Women Writers and the Revolution of the Word*. Bloomington: University of Indiana Press, 1991.

Davis, Alex and Lee Jenkins, eds. *The Cambridge Companion to Modernist Poetry*. New York: Cambridge University Press, 2007.

DeKoven, Marianne. *Rich and Strange: Gender, History, Modernism*. Princeton: Princeton University Press, 1991.

Dickie, Margaret and Thomas Travisano, eds. *Gendered Modernisms: American Women Poets and Their Readers*. Philadelphia: University of Pennsylvania Press, 1996.

Gilbert, Sandra M. and Susan Gubar. *No Man's Land: The Place of the Woman Writer in the Twentieth Century*. 3 vols. New Haven: Yale University Press, 1989.

Hanscombe, Gillian E. and Virginia L. Smyers. *Writing For Their Lives: The Modernist Women 1910–1940*. Boston, MA: Northeastern University Press, 1988.

Harrison, Elizabeth and Shirley Peterson, eds. *Unmanning Modernism: Gendered Re-readings*. Knoxville, TN: University of Tennessee Press, 1997.

Irvine, Dean J. *Editing Modernity: Women and Little Magazine Cultures in Canada 1916–1956*. Toronto: University of Toronto Press, 2008.

Kenner, Hugh. *The Pound Era*. Berkeley: University of California Press, 1971.

Longenbach, James. "Modern Poetry." *The Cambridge Companion to Modernism*. Ed. Michael Levenson. Cambridge: Cambridge University Press, 1999. 100–29.

Nicholls, Peter. *Modernisms: A Literary Guide*. London and New York: Routledge, 1995.

Rado, Lisa. *Modernism, Gender, Culture: A Cultural Studies Approach*. New York: Garland, 1997.

Rado, Lisa, ed. *Rereading Modernism: New Directions in Feminist Criticism*. New York: Garland, 1994.

Scott, Bonnie Kime, ed. *The Gender of Modernism*. Bloomington: Indiana University Press, 1990.

Gender in Modernism: New Geographies, Complex Intersections. Chicago: University of Chicago Press, 2007.

Trehearne, Brian. *The Montreal Forties: Modernist Poetry in Transition*. Toronto: University of Toronto Press, 1999.

Witemeyer, Hugh. "Modernism and the Transatlantic Connection." *A Companion to TwentiethCentury Poetry*. Ed. Neil Roberts. Oxford: Blackwell, 2001. 7–20.

Chapter 3 Women's modernism and performance

Archer-Straw, Petrine. *Negrophilia: Avant-Garde Paris and Black Culture in the 1920s*. New York: Thames and Hudson, 2000.

Barlow, Judith, ed. *Plays by American Women: 1900–1930*. New York: Applause, 1981.

Black, Cheryl. *The Women of Provincetown, 1915–1922*. Tuscaloosa: University of Alabama Press, 2002.

Borshuk, Michael. "An Intelligence of the Body: Disruptive Parody through Dance in the Early Performances of Josephine Baker." *EmBODYing Liberation: The Black Body in American Dance*. Ed. Dorothea Fischer-Hornung and Alison D. Goeller. Münster, Germany: LIT, 2001. 41–57.

Broe, Mary Lynn, ed. *Silence and Power: A Reevaluation of Djuna Barnes*. Carbondale: Southern Illinois University Press, 1991.

Cima, Gay Gibson. *Performing Women: Female Characters, Male Playwrights, and the Modern Stage*. Ithaca, NY: Cornell University Press, 1993.

Duncan, Isadora. *My Life*. New York: Liveright, 1927.

The Art of the Dance. Ed. Sheldon Cheney. New York: Theatre Arts, 1928.

Isadora Speaks. Ed. Franklin Rosemont. San Francisco: City Lights Books, 1981.

Farfan, Penny. *Women, Modernism, and Performance*. Cambridge: Cambridge University Press, 2004.

Farfan, Penny and Katherine E. Kelly. "Staging Modernism: Introduction." *South Central Review* 25.1 (Spring 2008): 1–11.

Fletcher, Winona L. "From Genteel Poet to Revolutionary Playwright: Georgia Douglas Johnson." *Theatre Annual* (1985): 41–64.

Gardner, Vivien and Susan Rutherford, eds. *The New Woman and Her Sisters: Feminism and Theatre 1850–1914*. Ann Arbor: University of Michigan Press, 1992.

Green, Barbara. "Spectacular Confessions: 'How It Feels to Be Forcibly Fed.'" *Review of Contemporary Fiction* 13.3 (Fall 1993): 70–88.

Herring, Phillip. *Djuna: The Life and Work of Djuna Barnes*. New York: Viking, 1995.

Hill, Errol G. and James V. Hatch. *A History of African American Theatre*. Cambridge: Cambridge University Press, 2003.

Kelly, Katherine E., ed. *Modern Drama by Women 1880s–1930s: An International Anthology*. London: Routledge, 1996.

Kuenzli, Rudolf E. "Baroness Elsa von Freytag-Loringhoven and New York Dada." *Women in Dada: Essays on Sex, Gender, and Identity*. Ed. Naomi Sawelson-Gorse. Cambridge, MA: MIT Press, 1998. 442–75.

Marcus, Jane. "Some Sources for *Between the Acts*." *Virginia Woolf Miscellany* 6 (Winter 1977): 1–3.

Murphy, Brenda. *The Provincetown Players and the Culture of Modernity*. Cambridge: Cambridge University Press, 2005.

Perkins, Kathy A. and Judith L. Stephens, eds. *Strange Fruit: Plays on Lynching by American Women*. Bloomington: Indiana University Press, 1998.

Reilly, Eliza Jane. "Elsa von Freytag-Loringhoven." *Women's Art Journal* 18.1 (1997): 26–33.

Reiss, Robert. "'My Baroness': Elsa von Freytag-Loringhoven." *Dada/Surrealism* 14 (1985): 81–101.

Rose, Phyllis. *Jazz Cleopatra: Josephine Baker in Her Time*. New York: Doubleday, 1989.

Scott, Bonnie Kime, ed. *The Gender of Modernism: A Critical Anthology*. Bloomington: Indiana University Press, 1990.

Gender in Modernism: New Geographies, Complex Intersections. Urbana: University of Illinois Press, 2007.

Spender, Dale and Carole Hayman, ed. *How the Vote Was Won and Other Suffragette Plays*. London: Methuen, 1985.

Stein, Gertrude. *Selected Writings of Gertrude Stein*. Ed. Carl Van Vechten. New York: Vintage, 1990.

Last Operas and Plays. Ed. Carl Van Vechten. Baltimore: Johns Hopkins University Press, 1995.

Stowell, Sheila. *A Stage of Their Own: Feminist Playwrights of the Suffrage Era*. Ann arbor: University of Michigan Press, 1992.

Woolf, Virginia. *Between the Acts*. San Diego: Harcourt Brace Jovanovich, 1941.

"The Memoirs of Sarah Bernhardt." *Books and Portraits: Some Further Selections from the Literary and Biographical Writings of Virginia Woolf*. Ed. Mary Lyon. London: Hogarth, 1977. 201–7.

Chapter 4 *Magazines, presses, and salons in women's modernism*

Anderson, Margaret. *My Thirty Years' War*. 1930. New York: Horizon Press, 1969.

Barney, Natalie Clifford. *Adventures of the Mind*. Trans. John Spalding Gatton. New York: New York University Press, 1992.

Bornstein, George. *Material Modernism: The Politics of the Page*. Cambridge: Cambridge University Press, 2001.

Carby, Hazel V. *Reconstructing Womanhood: The Emergence of the Afro-American Woman Novelist*. New York: Oxford University Press, 1987.

Crunden, Robert M. *American Salons: Encounters with European Modernism 1885–1917*. New York: Oxford University Press, 1993.

Darroch, Sandra Jobson. *Ottoline: The Life of Lady Ottoline Morrell*. New York: Coward, McCann, and Geoghegan, 1975.

Fitch, Noel Riley. *Sylvia Beach and the Lost Generation: A History of Literary Paris in the Twenties and Thirties*. New York: Norton, 1983.

Ford, Hugh. *Published in Paris: American and British Writers, Printers, and Publishers in Paris, 1920–1939*. New York: Macmillan, 1975.

Habermas, Jürgen. *The Structural Transformation of the Public Sphere*. 1962. Trans. Thomas Burger. Cambridge, MA: MIT Press, 1989.

Hanscombe, Gillian and Virginia L. Smyers. *Writing for Their Lives: The Modernist Women 1910–1940*. London: Women's Press, 1987.

Hull, Gloria T. *Color, Sex, and Poetry: Three Women Writers of the Harlem Renaissance*. Bloomington: Indiana University Press, 1987.

Johnson, Abby Arthur and Ronald Maberry Johnson. *Propaganda and Aesthetics: The Literary Politics of African-American Magazines in the Twentieth Century*. Amherst: University of Massachusetts Press, 1991.

Lee, Hermione. *Virginia Woolf*. London: Chatto & Windus, 1996.

Lewis, David Levering. *When Harlem Was in Vogue*. New York: Vintage, 1982.

Lidderdale, Jane and Mary Nicholson. *Dear Miss Weaver: Harriet Shaw Weaver 1876–1961*. New York: Viking, 1970.

Marek, Jayne E. *Women Editing Modernism: "Little" Magazines and Literary History*. Lexington: University Press of Kentucky, 1995.

Mellow, James R. *Charmed Circle: Gertrude Stein and Company.* New York: Praeger, 1974.

Miller, Cristanne. *Cultures of Modernism: Marianne Moore, Mina Loy, and Else Lasker-Schüler.* Ann Arbor: University of Michigan Press, 1995.

Rainey, Lawrence. *Institutions of Modernism: Literary Elites and Public Culture.* New Haven: Yale University Press, 1998.

Rodriguez, Suzanne. *Wild Heart: A Life. Natalie Clifford Barney's Journey from Victorian America to Belle Epoque Paris.* New York: HarperCollins, 2002.

Rudnick, Lois Palken. *Mabel Dodge Luhan: New Woman, New Worlds.* Albuquerque: University of New Mexico Press, 1984.

Scott, Bonnie Kime, ed. *The Gender of Modernism: A Critical Anthology.* Bloomington: Indiana University Press, 1990.

Gender in Modernism: New Geographies, Complex Intersections. Urbana: University of Illinois Press, 2007.

Sylvander, Carolyn Wedin. *Jessie Redmon Fauset, Black American Writer.* Albany, NY: Whitston, 1981.

West, Dorothy. *Where the Wild Grape Grows.* Amherst: University of Massachusetts Press, 2004.

Willis, J. H., Jr. *Leonard and Virginia Woolf as Publishers: The Hogarth Press, 1917–41.* Charlottesville: University Press of Virginia, 1992.

Wolff, Geoffrey. *Black Sun: The Brief Transit and Violent Eclipse of Harry Crosby.* New York: Vintage, 1985.

Chapter 5 Gender in women's modernism

Abraham, Julie. *Are Girls Necessary?: Lesbian Writing and Modern Histories.* New York: Routledge, 1995.

Adickes, Sandra. *To Be Young Was Very Heaven: Women in New York Before the First World War.* New York: Macmillan, 2000.

Ardis, Ann L. *New Women, New Novels: Feminism and Early Modernism.* New Brunswick, NJ: Rutgers University Press, 1991.

Benstock, Shari. *Women of the Left Bank: Paris, 1900–1940.* Austin: University of Texas Press, 1987.

Bland, Lucy. *Banishing the Beast: Feminism, Sex and Morality.* London: Tauris, 2002.

Boone, Joseph Allen. *Libidinal Currents: Sexuality and the Shaping of Modernism.* Chicago: University of Chicago Press, 1998.

Butler, Judith. *Bodies That Matter.* New York: Routledge, 1993.

Castle, Terry. *The Apparitional Lesbian: Female Homosexuality and Modern Culture.* New York: Columbia University Press, 1995.

DeKoven, Marianne. *Rich and Strange: Gender, History, Modernism.* Princeton, NJ: Princeton University Press, 1991.

Delap, Lucy. *The Feminist Avant-Garde: Transatlantic Encounters of the Early Twentieth Century.* Cambridge: Cambridge University Press, 2007.

Doan, Laura. *Fashioning Sapphism: The Origins of a Modern English Lesbian Culture.* New York: Columbia University Press, 2001.

Faderman, Lillian. *Surpassing the Love of Men: Romantic Friendship and Love Between Women from the Renaissance to the Present.* New York: William Morrow, 1981.

Felski, Rita. *The Gender of Modernity*. Cambridge, MA: Harvard University Press, 1995.

Gambrell, Alice. *Women Intellectuals, Modernism, and Difference: Transatlantic Culture, 1919–1945*. Cambridge: Cambridge University Press, 1997.

Garrity, Jane and Laura Doan, eds. *Sapphic Modernities: Sexuality, Women and National Culture*. New York: Palgrave Macmillan, 2006.

Gilbert, Sandra M. and Susan Gubar. *No Man's Land: The Place of the Woman Writer in the Twentieth Century*, 3 vols. New Haven: Yale University Press, 1988.

Hackett, Robin. *Sapphic Primitivism: Productions of Race, Class, and Sexuality in Key Works of Modern Fiction*. New Brunswick, NJ: Rutgers University Press, 2004.

Jagose, Annamarie. *Inconsequence: Lesbian Representation and the Logic of Sexual Sequence*. Ithaca, NY: Cornell University Press, 2002.

Johnston, Georgia. *The Formation of 20th-Century Queer Autobiography: Reading Vita Sackville-West, Virginia Woolf, Hilda Doolittle, and Gertrude Stein*. New York: Palgrave Macmillan, 2007.

Kent, Kathryn R. *Making Girls into Women: American Women's Writing and the Rise of Lesbian Identity*. Durham, NC: Duke University Press, 2002.

Rado, Lisa. *Modernism, Gender, and Culture: A Cultural Studies Approach*. New York: Routledge, 1997.

Schwarz, Judith. *Radical Feminists of Heterodoxy: Greenwich Village, 1912–1940*. Norwich, VT: New Victoria Publishers, 1986.

Scott, Bonnie Kime, ed. *Gender in Modernism: New Geographies, Complex Intersections*. Urbana: University of Illinois Press, 2007.

Sedgwick, Eve Kosofsky. *Tendencies*. Durham, NC: Duke University Press, 1993.

Smith, Patricia Juliana. *Lesbian Panic: Homoeroticism in Modern British Women's Fictions*. New York: Columbia University Press, 1997.

Chapter 6 Black women's modernist literature

Bennett, Michael and Vanessa D. Dickerson, eds. *Recovering the Black Female Body: Self-Representations by African American Women*. New Brunswick, NJ: Rutgers University Press, 2001.

Brooks, Daphne A. *Bodies in Dissent: Spectacular Performances of Race and Freedom, 1850–1910*. Durham, NC: Duke University Press, 2006.

Davis, Thadious M. *Nella Larsen, Novelist of the Harlem Renaissance*. Baton Rouge: Louisiana State University Press, 1994.

DeJongh, James. *Vicious Modernism: Black Harlem and the Literary Imagination*. Cambridge: Cambridge University Press, 1990.

duCille, Ann. *The Coupling Convention: Sex, Text, and Tradition in Black Women's Fiction*. New York: Oxford University Press, 1993.

hooks, bell. *Yearning: Race, Gender, and Cultural Politics*. Boston, MA: South End Press, 1990.

Hull, Gloria T. *Color, Sex and Poetry: Three Women Writers of the Harlem Renaissance*. Bloomington: Indiana University Press, 1987.

Lamothe, Daphne. *Inventing the New Negro: Narrative, Culture, and Ethnography*. Philadelphia: University of Pennsylvania Press, 2008.

McDowell, Deborah E. *"The Changing Same": Black Women's Literature, Criticism, and Theory*. Bloomington: Indiana University Press, 1995.

Nadell, Martha Jane. *Enter the New Negro: Images of Race in American Culture.* Cambridge, MA: Harvard University Press, 2004.

Pavlić, Edward M. *Crossroads Modernism: Descent and Emergence in African-American Literary Culture.* Minneapolis: University of Minnesota Press, 2002.

Plant, Deborah G. *Every Tub Must Sit on Its Own Bottom: The Philosophy and Politics of Zora Neale Hurston.* Urbana: University of Illinois Press, 1995.

Quashie, Kevin Everod. *Black Women, Identity, and Cultural Theory.* New Brunswick, NJ: Rutgers University Press, 2004.

Sherrard-Johnson, Cherene. *Portraits of the New Negro Woman: Visual and Literary Culture in the Harlem Renaissance.* New Brunswick, NJ: Rutgers University Press, 2007.

Smith, Valerie. *Not Just Race, Not Just Gender: Black Feminist Readings.* New York: Routledge, 1998.

Spillers, Hortense J. *Black, White, and in Color: Essays on American Literature and Culture.* Chicago: University of Chicago Press, 2003.

Stephens, Judith L., ed. *The Plays of Georgia Douglas Johnson: From the New Negro Renaissance to the Civil Rights Movement.* Urbana: University of Illinois Press, 2006.

Tate, Claudia. *Psychoanalysis and Black Novels: Desire and the Protocols of Race.* New York: Oxford University Press, 1998.

Wall, Cheryl A. *Women of the Harlem Renaissance.* Bloomington: Indiana University Press, 1995.

Wallace, Michele. *Dark Designs and Visual Culture.* Durham, NC: Duke University Press, 2004.

Wallace-Sanders, Kimberly, ed. *Skin Deep, Spirit Strong: The Black Female Body in American Culture.* Ann Arbor: University of Michigan Press, 2002.

Chapter 7 Race and ethnicity in white women's modernist literature

Begam, Richard and Michael Valdez Moses. *Modernism and Colonialism: British and Irish Literature, 1899–1939.* Durham, NC: Duke University Press, 2007.

Benstock, Shari. *Women of the Left Bank: Paris, 1900–1940.* London: Virago, 1987.

Cheyette, Bryan, ed. *Between "Race" and Culture: Representations of "the Jew" in English and American Literature.* Stanford: Stanford University Press, 1996.

Cheyette, Bryan and Laura Marcus, eds. *Modernity, Culture and "the Jew."* Cambridge: Polity, 1998.

Childs, Peter. *Modernism and the Post-Colonial.* London: Continuum, 2007.

DuPlessis, Rachel Blau. *Genders, Races, and Religious Cultures in Modern American Poetry, 1908–1934.* Cambridge: Cambridge University Press, 2001.

Esty, Jed. *A Shrinking Island: Modernism and National Culture in England,* Princeton, NJ: Princeton University Press, 2004.

Fanon, Frantz. *Black Skin, White Masks.* Intro. H. K. Bhabha. London: Pluto, 1986.

Garrity, Jane. *Step-Daughters of England: British Women Modernists and the National Imaginary.* Manchester: Manchester University Press, 2003.

Konzett, Delia Caparoso. *Ethnic Modernisms: Anzia Yezierska, Zora Neale Hurston, Jean Rhys, and the Aesthetics of Dislocation.* New York and Basingstoke: Palgrave Macmillan, 2002.

Linett, Maren. *Modernism, Feminism and Jewishness.* Cambridge: Cambridge University Press, 2007.

Marcus, Jane. *Hearts of Darkness: White Women Write Race*. New Brunswick, NJ: Rutgers University Press, 2004.

Miller, Cristanne. "Tongues 'Loosened in the Melting Pot': The Poets of *Others* and the Lower East Side." *Modernism/Modernity* 14 (2007): 455–76.

Miller, Eugene E. "Richard Wright and Gertrude Stein." *Black American Literature Forum* 18 (1982): 107–12.

Morrison, Toni. *Playing in the Dark: Whiteness and the Literary Imagination*. Cambridge, MA: Harvard University Press, 1992.

North, Michael. *The Dialect of Modernism: Race, Language, and Twentieth-Century Literature*. New York and Oxford: Oxford University Press, 1994.

Parry, Benita. *Postcolonial Studies: A Materialist Critique*. London: Routledge, 2004.

Phillips, Kathy J. *Virginia Woolf Against Empire*. Knoxville: University of Tennessee Press, 1994.

Raiskin, Judith. *Snow on the Cane Fields: Women's Writing and Creole Subjectivity*. Minneapolis: University of Minnesota Press, 1996.

Said, Edward. *Culture and Imperialism*. London: Chatto and Windus, 1993.

Wachman, Gay. *Lesbian Empire: Radical Crosswriting in the Twenties*. New Brunswick, NJ: Rutgers University Press, 2001.

Ware, Vron. *Beyond the Pale: White Women, Racism and History*. London and New York: Verso (New Left Books), 1992.

Wright, Patrick. *On Living in an Old Country: The National Past in Contemporary Britain*. London: Verso, 1985.

Young, Robert J. C. *Colonial Desire: Hybridity in Theory, Culture and Race*. London and New York: Routledge, 1995.

Chapter 8 Geomodernism, postcoloniality, and women's writing

Blackburn, R. *The Overthrow of Colonial Slavery, 1776–1848*. London and New York: Verso, 1988.

Boehmer, E. *Empire, the National, and the Postcolonial, 1890–1920: Resistance in Interaction*. Oxford: Oxford University Press, 2002.

Braithwaite, E. K. *Roots*. Ann Arbor: University of Michigan Press, 1993.

Brantlinger, P. *Rule of Darkness: British Literature and Imperialism 1830–1914*. Ithaca, NY: Cornell University Press, 1988.

Clarkson, T. "The True State of the Case, Respecting the Insurrection at St. Domingo." Reprinted in *Slave Revolution in the Caribbean, 1789–1804: A Brief History with Documents*. Ed. L. Dubois and J. D. Garrigus. New York: St. Martin's Press, 2006. 113–15.

Doyle, L. and L. Winkiel. *Geomodernisms: Race, Modernism, Modernity*. Bloomington: Indiana University Press, 2005.

Eby, C. D. *Road to Armageddon: The Martial Spirit in English Popular Literature, 1870–1914*. Durham, NC: Duke University Press, 1987.

Fanon, F. *The Wretched of the Earth*. Trans. Constance Farrington. 1961; Harmondsworth: Penguin, 1986.

Gikandi, S. *Maps of Englishness: Writing Identity in the Culture of Colonialism*. New York: Columbia University Press, 1996.

Gillies, M., H. Sword, and S. Yao, eds. *Pacific Rim Modernisms*. Toronto: University of Toronto Press, 2009.

Linebaugh, P. and M. Rediker. *The Many-headed Hydra: Sailors, Slaves, Commoners, and the Hidden History of the Revolutionary Atlantic* Boston, MA: Beacon, 2000.

Maldonado-Torres, N. "On the Coloniality of Being: Contributions to the Development of a Concept." *Cultural Studies* 21.2/3 (March/May 2007): 240–70.

Maingot, A. P. "Haiti and the Terrified Consciousness of the Caribbean." *Ethnicity in the Caribbean*. Ed. Gert Ootindie. London: Macmillan, 1996. 53–80.

Morrow, John H., Jr. *The Great War: An Imperial History*. London and New York: Vintage, 2004.

Ramazani, J. *The Hybrid Muse: Postcolonial Poetry in English*. Chicago: University of Chicago Press, 2001.

Said, Edward. *Culture and Imperialism*. New York: Vintage, 1994.

Tuck, P. J. N. *Warfare, Expansion, and Resistance*. London: Routledge, 2002.

Woolf, Virginia. "The Narrow Bridge of Art." *Collected Essays*. Vol. ii. New York: Harcourt Brace Jovanovich, 1967. 218–29.

Chapter 9 Women modernists and visual culture

Benjamin, W. "A Short History of Photography." *Screen* 13:1 (1972): 5–26.

Colette. *Colette at the Movies: Criticism and Screenplays*. Ed. A. Virmaux and O. Virmaux, trans. S. W. R. Smith. New York: Frederick Ungar, 1980.

Dick, S., ed. *The Complete Shorter Fiction of Virginia Woolf*. San Diego: Harcourt Brace, 1989.

Donald, J., A. Friedberg, and Marcus, L., eds. *Close Up 1927–1933: Cinema and Modernism*. London: Cassell, 1998.

Gillespie, D. F. *The Sisters' Arts: the Writing and Painting of Virginia Woolf and Vanessa Bell*. New York: Syracuse University Press, 1988.

Humm, M. *Modernist Women and Visual Cultures: Virginia Woolf, Vanessa Bell, Photography and Cinema*. Edinburgh: Edinburgh University Press, 2002.

Snapshots of Bloomsbury. London: Tate Publishing, 2006.

Lee, Hermione. *Virginia Woolf*. London: Chatto and Windus, 1996.

Stein, Gertrude. *Writings and Lectures 1911–1945*. Ed. P. Meyerowitz. London: Peter Owen, 1967.

Woolf, Virginia. "The Narrow Bridge of Art." *Granite and Rainbow: Essays by Virginia Woolf*. Ed. Leonard Woolf. London: Hogarth Press, 1958.

"Portraits." *The Complete Shorter Fiction of Virginia Woolf*. Ed. S. Dick. San Diego: Harcourt Brace, 1989.

"The Cinema." *The Essays of Virginia Woolf*. Vol. iv, *1925–1928*. Ed. A. McNeillie. London: Hogarth Press, 1994.

Chapter 10 Modernism and trauma

American Psychiatric Association. *Diagnostic and Statistical Manual of Mental Health Disorders*. 4th rev. edn. Washington, DC: American Psychiatric Association, 1994.

Booth, Allyson. *Postcards from the Trenches: Negotiating the Space between Modernism and the First World War*. New York: Oxford University Press, 1996.

Caruth, Cathy. *Unclaimed Experience: Trauma, Narrative, and History*. Baltimore: Johns Hopkins University Press, 1995.

Caruth, Cathy, ed. *Trauma: Explorations in Memory*. Baltimore: Johns Hopkins University Press, 1995.

Douglass, Ana and Thomas A. Vogler. *Witness and Memory: The Discourse of Trauma*. New York: Routledge, 2003.

Henke, Suzette A. *Shattered Subjects: Trauma and Testimony in Women's Life-Writing*. New York: St. Martin's Press, 1998; rev. edn. New York: Palgrave, 2000.

Herman, Judith Lewis. *Trauma and Recovery*. New York: Harper Collins, 1992.

Leys, Ruth. *Trauma: A Genealogy*. Chicago: University of Chicago Press, 2000.

Scott, Bonnie Kime, ed. *Gender in Modernism: New Geographies, Complex Intersections*. Urbana: University of Illinois Press, 2007.

Showalter, Elaine. *The Female Malady: Women, Madness, and English Culture, 1830–1980*. New York: Viking Penguin, 1987.

Tal, Kali. *Worlds of Hurt: Reading Literatures of Trauma*. Cambridge: Cambridge University Press, 1996.

Van der Kolk, Bessel A., Alexander C. McFarlane, and Lars Weisaeth, eds. *Traumatic Stress: The Effects of Overwhelming Experience on Mind, Body, and Society*. New York: Guilford Press, 2007.

Chapter 11 *Political activism and women's modernism*

Billington-Greig, Teresa. *The Militant Suffrage Movement: Emancipation in a Hurry*. London: Franklin Palmer, 1911.

Cockin, Katharine, Glenda Norquay, and Sowon S. Park, eds. *Women's Suffrage Literature*. 6 vols. London: Routledge, 2007.

Crawford, Elizabeth. *The Women's Suffrage Movement: A Reference Guide 1866–1928*. London: Routledge, 1999.

Eagleton, Terry. *The Ideology of the Aesthetic*. London: Basil Blackwell, 1990.

Friedman, Ellen G. and Miriam Fuchs, eds. *Breaking the Sequence*. Princeton, NJ: Princeton University Press, 1989.

Harrison, Brian. *Separate Spheres*. London: Croom Helm, 1978.

Huyssen, Andreas. *After the Great Divide*. Bloomington: Indiana University Press, 1986.

Kaplan, Joel K. and Sheila Stowell. *Theatre and Fashion: Oscar Wilde to the Suffragettes*. Cambridge: Cambridge University Press, 1994.

Levenson, Michael, ed. *The Cambridge Companion to Modernism*. Cambridge: Cambridge University Press, 1999.

Nelson, Carolyn Christensen, ed. *Literature of the Women's Suffrage Campaign in England*. Ontario: Broadview Press, 2004.

Pugh, Martin. *Women and the Women's Movement in Britain, 1914–1959*. London: Macmillan, 1992.

Richardson, Mary. *Laugh a Defiance*. London: Weidenfeld & Nicolson, 1953.

Rhondda, Viscountess, Margaret Haig Thomas. *This Was My World*. London: Macmillan, 1933.

Taylor, Ronald, ed. *Aesthetics and Politics*. London: Verso, 1977.

Willett, John. *The New Sobriety 1917–1933: Art and Politics in the Weimar Period.* London: Thames and Hudson, 1978.

Chapter 12 Religion and the occult in women's modernism

Foy, Roslyn Reso. *Ritual, Myth and Mysticism in the Work of Mary Butts: Between Feminism and Modernism.* Fayetteville: University of Arkansas Press, 2002.

Garrity, Jane. *Step-Daughters of England: British Women Modernists and the National Imaginary.* Manchester: Manchester University Press, 2003.

Guest, Barbara. *Herself Defined: The Poet H. D. and Her World.* London: Collins, 1985.

Hazelgrove, Jenny. *Spiritualism and British Society Between the Wars.* Manchester: Manchester University Press, 2000.

Linett, Maren Tova. *Modernism, Feminism and Jewishness.* Cambridge: Cambridge University Press, 2007.

Raitt, Suzanne. "'The Girl Beside Me': Vita Sackville-West and the Mystics." *Vita and Virginia: The Work and Friendship of Vita Sackville-West and Virginia Woolf.* Oxford: Clarendon Press, 1993. 117–45.

Seed, David. "'Psychical' Cases: Transformations of the Supernatural in Virginia Woolf and May Sinclair." *Gothic Modernisms.* Ed. Andrew Smith and Jeff Wallace. London and New York: Palgrave, 2001. 44–61.

Cambridge Companions to ...

AUTHORS

TOPICS